Haiti

Haiti
Dangerous Crossroads

edited by
Deidre McFadyen and Pierre LaRamée
with Mark Fried and Fred Rosen
from the North American Congress on Latin America
(NACLA)

South End Press   Boston, MA

The photographs in the text are from the traveling exhibit "Haiti: Dangerous Crossroads," directed by Catherine Orenstein. The exhibit began under the sponsorship of the North American Congress on Latin America (NACLA), with the generous assistance of Ken Taranto Photo Gallery, Baboo Color Labs, and Fuji Photo Film U.S.A. The exhibit, which is updated with each new location, documents a decade of human tragedy and bravery in Haiti's ongoing struggle for democracy. It is designed to provide an alternative to the often inadequate or distorted North American news coverage of Haiti, in a format that is easily accessible and understandable to all.
Cover painting by Franceska Schifrin: "The Yellow Silence of Morning Light." Oil on canvas 50" x 34".
Cover design by Jane Cook.
Text design by South End Press.

CIP Data
    Haiti : dangerous crossroads / edited by North American Congress on Latin America.
       p. cm.
  ISBN 0-89608-505-8 (pbk. : alk. Paper), — ISBN 0-89608-506-6
      1. Haiti—Politics and government—1986- 2. United States—Relations—Haiti. 3. Haiti—Relations—United States. 4. Haiti-Economic conditions. 5. Human rights—Haiti—History. I. North American Congress on Latin America.
F1928.2.H285 1995
303.48'27294073—dc20   95-9783
                                                  CIP

South End Press, 116 Saint Botolph Street, Boston, MA 02115

03 02 00 99 98 97 96 95   1 2 3 4 5 6 7 8

TABLE OF CONTENTS

INTRODUCTION

THE EDITORS

Not so long ago, most everyone on the Left agreed that U.S. intervention in the internal affairs of another country should be opposed *a priori*. The case of Haiti shattered that consensus. In the topsy-turvy world of post-Cold War politics, U.S. troops landed on Haiti's shores in September 1994 to remove a right-wing military dictatorship and restore a popularly elected leftist priest to power. What did this intervention mean? Did such an action merit our cautious support?

The issue divided the Lavalas alliance that voted Father Jean-Bertrand Aristide into presidential office, and it divided the U.S. Left. At one end of the spectrum were those who opposed intervention in Haiti in any form, whether by U.S. troops or UN and Organization of American States (OAS) human rights monitors. They recalled recent U.S. interventions in Latin America, as well as the last time the U.S. Marines landed on Haitian shores in 1915 and hunkered down for a nineteen-year occupation. On the other end were those who thought only the United States had the clout, not to mention a moral responsibility, to restore Aristide to office.

A related debate concerned whether the answer to Haiti's crisis lay in the diplomatic suites of Washington or in the Haitian streets and mountains. Many in the Haitian popular movement and some sectors of the U.S. Left believed that only armed struggle or other forms of popular mobilization within Haiti could break the back of military domination. Others placed their faith in negotiations and a transition to democracy under U.S. tutelage.

Easy answers to the Haitian crisis have proven elusive. Haitian—and Latin American—history has taught us not to expect the United States to ride in on a white horse and altruistically save the day for democracy. Indeed, the United States has rarely aided a government with a progressive agenda at odds with U.S. business interests. Even the *New York Times* has reported on U.S. support for Haiti's corrupt military rulers over the years. Confusing matters further, U.S. policymakers seemed at war with themselves during Aristide's years in exile. On the one hand, the United States said it supported the Haitian president's return and was a driving force in negotiations to end military rule. Yet, on the other hand, the U.S. government systematically subverted Aristide and appeared to favor Lieutenant General Raoul Cédras, who headed the September 1991 coup, and his cronies.

In many respects, Haiti is a paradigm of the new potentials and liabilities of U.S. foreign policy in the 1990s. Without the Soviet Union as a countervailing superpower, and therefore without anticommunist dogma to neatly divide the world into friends and enemies, the United States has had to readjust its ideological compass. While there is substantial continuity within planning circles concerning the definition of the national interest, U.S. policymakers now debate where significant U.S. interests lie, and how far the scope of U.S. military power should reach. Even where there is consensus, new geopolitical strategies, diplomatic tactics and political-ideological rationales have been brought into play. The crisis in Haiti has forced U.S. policymakers to directly confront these issues.

The conservative media tend to depict Haiti as a hopeless quagmire into which the United States has blindly waded. Anxiously awaiting the pull-out of U.S. troops in late March 1995, they are primed to explode with righteous wrath if a single U.S. soldier's life is lost in what one writer has coined "the immaculate invasion." By contrast, those in the liberal press typically applaud the Clinton Adminstration for doing its duty to "restore democracy" in Haiti. This school of thought empathizes, however, with an occupying force that does not want to take on difficult tasks—such as disarming the paramilitary *attachés*—that might endanger the lives of U.S. soldiers.

Despite their obvious differences, conservatives and liberals share one premise: they consider the United States to be an unalloyed force for good in Haiti. *Haiti: Dangerous Crossroads*—the first book to analyze Haiti after the U.S. intervention—questions that central assumption by detailing the role the United States played in *creating* the crisis it is now trying to resolve. To counter the mainstream media's characteristic historical amnesia, this volume places current events within the wider context of twentieth-century Haitian history. Starting with the nineteenth-century War of Independence, through the Duvalier dynasty, the election of Aristide, the coup, and the current intervention, this volume traces the Haitian majority's tireless efforts to bring about democracy—and the equally tireless efforts of those determined to squash it.

The North American Congress on Latin America (NACLA) was founded in 1966 to investigate the underlying dynamics of U.S.-Latin American relations and to encourage a more humane and democratic U.S. inter-American policy. The bimonthly *NACLA Report on the Americas*, in which the majority of these essays first appeared, is the most widely read English-language magazine on Latin America and the Caribbean. *Haiti: Dangerous Crossroads* is divided into four sections. Part I, "Haitian History to the 1990 Coup," consists of a detailed chronological account of events in Haiti, focusing particularly on the years after the fall of Jean-Claude Duvalier in February 1986. Part II, "The United States' Haiti Policy," analyzes the United States' ambivalent, at times contradictory, Haiti policy since the September 1991 coup. Part III, "Haitian Development and U.S. Economic Policy," focuses on the U.S. economic agenda in Haiti—a frequently misunderstood and neglected factor driving U.S. policy. Part IV, "Resistance and Human Rights," examines Haiti's post-1986 human rights record, the birth of the country's popular movement, and the efforts of Haitians and the Left in the United States to support democracy in Haiti. The book's concluding essay, by Paul Farmer, makes the case for why Haiti's fate should matter to all of us concerned with social justice in the hemisphere.

Haiti's dilemma reveals the strengths and limitations of a nascent constitutional democracy in a society rent by class war. The popular movement in Haiti likens its efforts to sweep away the old order to *dechoukaj*, a Creole word meaning "uprooting." Yet, as the movement has discovered, the roots of oppression run deep. They are grounded in Haiti's centuries-old "semi-feudal" class structure, the militarization of a divided society and a long-standing U.S. policy to avert profound structural change by supporting—at times overtly, at times covertly—the country's military and its business elite.

The planners and perpetrators of the 1991 coup were clearly Haiti's old-guard elite: the oligarchic families and their allies in the brass, who were terrified not so much of Aristide's policies, which by and large were quite moderate, but of the masses of poor to whom Aristide and his Lavalas movement gave voice and vote. While there is no "smoking gun" to prove that the United States was behind the coup, suspicions of U.S. involvement range from a deliberate turning of a blind eye to active encouragement and abetting of Aristide's ouster.

Haiti's old-time politicians were banking on a series of legalistic machinations to make the coup appear to be a constitutional effort to defend democracy. Key to this strategy was their attempt to smear Aristide by pointing to his alleged disregard for parliament's role in government, especially by highlighting statements in which he appeared to tolerate the "necklacing" of political opponents.

U.S. Ambassador Alvin Adams lent a hand to this process of discrediting Aristide, despite the official U.S. stance in favor of his return. In the weeks after the coup, Adams worked tirelessly to steer journalists and visiting OAS delegations toward Aristide's conservative critics—politicians who garnered minimal support at the polls. Adams was what Latin Americans call an *"embajador de choque"*—a "shock-troop" ambassador—who began his career with the U.S. Agency for International Development (AID) in Vietnam and, before going to Haiti, had climbed to the number two spot in the State Department's counter-terrorism office. Schooled in the old pro-consul style, he never hesitated to meddle in Haiti's internal affairs.

As Aristide languished in exile and the coup regime consolidated its grip on power, the debate about Haiti began to center on the role of the United States and the international community in restoring democracy. U.S. policy under President Bill Clinton, carried over from the Bush Administration, clearly consisted of cultivating a "stable political center"; maintaining access to a cheap labor pool for U.S.-owned off-shore assembly plants; "professionalizing" the police and military to reduce human rights abuses while still controlling the popular movement; and—most of all—preventing, at all costs, a massive exodus of Haitian refugees to south Florida.

The failed Governors Island Accord of June 1993 had been tailor-made to meet these objectives. Clinton's pledge to restore Aristide to office would have been honored, but Aristide would have served out his term with little power to carry out his original program. The Haitian military and police would have been left largely intact; and the Lavalas movement, already weakened by repression, would have been progressively marginalized by massive U.S. funding for right-wing organizations and political parties.

Throughout the negotiating process, the U.S. government forced Aristide into deeper and deeper compromises—essentially eviscerating his power—while demanding little from the military. By the end of 1993, U.S. displeasure with Aristide's "intransigence" became more overt, to the point of speculation at the time that the United States might simply opt to "dump" him, lift the embargo and accept the status quo. Despite the blockade—the key prong of U.S. policy on Haiti—contraband flowed across the Dominican-

Haitian border and the elite that stood behind the coup still did its shopping in Miami.

The U.S. response to the coup—the inhumane refugee policy, a leaky embargo, a sustained CIA campaign to paint Aristide as demagogic and mentally unstable, and increasingly cool relations with Aristide—laid bare the U.S. government's contempt for democratic and legal processes. By early 1994, Haitian democracy seemed to have been grievously betrayed.

In early May 1994, however, the Clinton Administration seemed to make a dramatic policy shift. To begin with, Lawrence Pezzullo, Clinton's point man on Haiti, was replaced as special envoy by William Gray III, a former ranking member of the Congressional Black Caucus with no previous foreign-service experience. Whereas senior policy advisors had argued earlier that the embargo against the military regime in Haiti was "stronger even than that against Cuba," Clinton was now proposing to give the blockade real teeth by including the previously exempt U.S.-owned assembly plants, sealing Haiti's border with the Dominican Republic and freezing the assets of Haitian military leaders. The same advisors had also claimed that the in-country asylum review process was safe and effective. Clinton was now proposing to allow offshore hearings to ensure due process for applicants. Furthermore, only three months prior to the policy shift, the very idea of using military intervention to restore democracy to Haiti had been categorically dismissed. Now, in what appeared to be the most substantive shift, military intervention—albeit as "a last resort"—was openly proposed.

These developments notwithstanding, it gradually became apparent that both U.S. policy and the way it was being implemented remained constant. The administration sent Gray to ask Dominican President Joaquín Balaguer for his cooperation in closing the border. Balaguer promised to cooperate in exchange for U.S. promises to disregard massive fraud in his recent reelection. Despite Balaguer's pledge, however, the border was not effectively sealed. Further limiting the effectiveness of the new embargo, only the assets of the top officers in the Haitian military were frozen. Even though direct financial transactions and commercial flights between Haiti and the United States were banned, these moves were at best irritants to wealthy Haitians who could still access their funds—already transferred abroad—via third countries.

A closer look at the change in U.S. policy toward Haitian refugees was even more disheartening. Asylum hearings for Haitian refugees were now permitted outside of Haiti, but only on board a special ship anchored off Kingston, Jamaica, and at a beach site on the Turks and Caicos Islands. Refugees not screened for a full hearing in the United States were still being summarily repatriated, and the percentage of asylum claims accepted remained the same. Worse yet, the infamous refugee camp at the Guantánamo Bay naval base in Cuba was reopened and thousands of Haitians were interned for the duration.

If the policy shift on Haiti turned out to be little more than a public-relations stunt, why did it happen at all? In spite of mounting human rights violations, pressure for some sort of change became irresistible only when Aristide finally went on the offensive, branding the Clinton policy racist. TransAfrica Executive Director Randall Robinson's highly publicized fast in protest against the refugee policy, coupled with growing Congressional pressure, particularly from the Black Caucus, also required a response.

In the end, the fly in the ointment was the intransigence not, as alleged, of Aristide, but of the U.S.-trained and funded Haitian military. Only after Clinton had set the wheels in motion to launch an all-out military invasion of the country did the military agree to a sweetheart deal devised at the eleventh hour by special envoys Jimmy Carter, Lieutenant General Colin Powell and Senator Sam Nunn.

Despite appearances and rhetoric to the contrary, the invasion was not intended primarily to "end human rights abuses and restore democracy." Although it did stem the blood-letting, the main purpose of the military action was to get the original U.S. policy back on track. Because of its unpopularity, a "surgical" intervention might not have paid Clinton, as it had Ronald Reagan and George Bush, the political dividends of an easy military victory. However, the "permissive entry" of U.S. forces, in cooperation with the Haitian military, seemed the ideal solution.

Is Haiti's weak democracy—backed up for the time being by U.S. guns—capable of disarming a brutal oligarchy and its hired guns? As of March 1, 1995—five months into the U.S. occupation—all bets are off. Indisputably, human rights violations have significantly decreased since U.S. troops arrived on the scene. Using the presence of U.S. troops to shield him from reprisal, Aristide has also dismissed all of the highest-ranking officers in the military.

Yet these positive developments may have a lifespan no longer than the duration of the U.S. and UN forces' sojourn on the island. While U.S. officials have recanted their earlier statements that the paramilitary Front for the Advancement and Progress of Haiti (FRAPH) is a legitimate opposition party, the U.S. occupying force has been slow to disarm these thugs. As of late December 1994, only 19,065 weapons had been recovered. According to international estimates, some 200,000 guns may still remain in the possession of the country's paramilitary squads.

Equally disconcerting is the slowness of judicial reform. Little has been done to revamp Haiti's obsolete and corrupt court system. To date, the government has not pressed charges against anyone involved in the most prominent political assassination cases. By early December, the multinational forces were holding only 22 Haitians nationwide, even though it is estimated that between 200 and 300 suspects had been apprehended and handed over to them by Haitian crowds.

Although Aristide has promised to bring "poverty with dignity" to his people, the neoliberal agenda of AID, the World Bank and the International Monetary Fund is nonetheless rolling full steam ahead. At the end of February 1995, the government disclosed the first contingent of public enterprises—including the national cement company, flour mill and electrical company—that are slated to be put on the auction block.

For the time being, the U.S. occupying force has the support of the majority of Haitians. Yet even that good will is starting to fray around the edges. When Carter and his sidekicks Powell and Nunn returned to the island in late February to pave the way for parliamentary elections scheduled for June 1995, the public mood had perceptibly soured. The former president was greeted not by an official delegation, but by graffiti scrawled on the walls of Port-au-Prince that said "Carter Go Home" and "Carter, the fake democrat."

Aristide's dramatic election as president under the banner of Haiti's popular movement and his subsequent overthrow by the military a scant seven months later occurred in 1991, the 200th anniversary of the Boukman slave uprising that launched the Haitian revolution. During the subsequent four years, few have paused to reflect on our debt to Haiti's valiant past.

What C.L.R. James called the Haitian revolution's "revenges of poverty and oppression" put fear in the hearts of the planters of the U.S. South and convinced England and the United States to end the slave trade. The revolution forced Napoleon to unload Louisiana for a song. And Haitian revolutionary leader Alexandre Pétion's material support was essential to the ultimate success of Simón Bolívar's quest for independence from the Spanish Crown in South America. But Haitians paid dearly for the lesson that they taught the world from 1791 to 1804. France exacted $150 million in reparations; a U.S. embargo lasted over half a century; and Haitians did not themselves experience democracy until Aristide's foreshortened administration.

The Haitian crisis has its roots in colonial times, came of age in the era of gun boat diplomacy, and exemplified Cold War policy. Its *dénouement* today is paradigmatic of the "new world order." The United States' so-called immaculate invasion was touted as Bill Clinton's first foreign policy success. How successful it will ultimately prove for the majority of Haitians, however, remains in serious doubt.

Sugar cane hands. *Photo by Les Stone, 1993.*

Part I

Haitian History to the 1990 Coup

UP BY THE ROOTS

Haitian History Through 1987

GREG CHAMBERLAIN

After a spectacular war of independence, which jolted the world's European masters two centuries ago, Haitians kept their guns and a sturdy tradition of confronting their rulers. Yet disputes were mostly petty, personal or based on color, and produced merely defiance rather than revolution.[1]

Most people retreated to tiny plots of land in remote valleys and *mornes* (mountains), their Voodoo religion partially insulating them against poverty and injustice.[2] The countryside was pitted against the power and officials of the towns—simply called *l'état*—and against "the Republic of Port-au-Prince," as the capital was nicknamed. Only rarely did a major class-based mass movement appear, such as the one which formed around Jean-Jacques Acaau in Grande Anse (1843-1845) or around President Sylvain Salnave (1867-1869) before an alliance of the ruling mulatto minority and black *cacos* (rebels) pushed him out.[3]

When U.S. Marines arrived in July 1915 to begin a nineteen-year occupation—officially to "restore order" after President Guillaume Vilbrun Sam was lynched—Haitians again rose up to defend the rights whose initial proclamation had made their country a beacon of liberty to Spain's Latin American empire.[4] At least 3,000 Haitians died fighting the occupiers between 1918 and 1920. The *caco* leader Charlemagne Péralte was shot dead in his camp in October 1919 by a U.S. Marine disguised as a Black who had been led there by a Haitian mercenary.[5] The North Americans lashed his half-naked body to a door. The resulting Christ-like image has been a powerful symbol of Haitian national identity and resistance ever since.

After the fall of President Elie Lescot in 1946, a brief opening saw the first organization of trade unions and left-wing groups in Haitian history and the full expression of the nationalist intellectual movement that the occupation had spawned. The new Black bourgeoisie had advanced under the occupation, ensuring the election of the populist Black Dumarsais Estimé as president; but the bourgeoisie was not yet strong enough to break the power of the mulattos, whom the North Americans had promoted.[6]

The old order, however, was breaking up. By 1957, the name of Black demagogue Daniel Fignolé was on the lips of Port-au-Prince slumdwellers. Fignolé—who became education minister at the age of thirty three during the promising first months of Estimé's rule in 1946—founded trade unions and the first modern political party to escape control of the capital's aristocracy and touch ordinary Haitians.

But Fignolé's party, the anti-communist and *noiriste* (Black nationalist) Worker and Peasant Movement (MOP), was swept away as the system once more closed in. After only nineteen days as provisional president in 1957, the man who terrified the mulattos when he walked before the famous *rouleau compresseur* (steamroller)—comprised of his followers as they ground their way through the streets destroying everything in their path—was on a plane to New York and exile. Three days later, troops and police massacred hundreds of demonstrators in the capital's solidly Fignolist slums in a bid to root out this populist cancer.[7]

The army that overthrew Fignolé arranged the election in September 1957 of François "Papa Doc" Duvalier, an apparently retiring former Fignolist involved in the nationalism of the 1930s and 1940s. Twenty-nine years later, six weeks after the Duvaliers fled Haiti, a dying Fignolé returned to Port-au-Prince to reclaim his political domain. A presidential limousine met him at the airport.

But Fignolé's following had dwindled to polite respect for a revered old man of 73, who had once dared to make speeches in Creole, the national language, instead of the official French understood by only 10% of Haitians. Five months later, he was dead.

The efficiency of the Duvaliers' repression, and the country's high population density, gave dissidents little cover, blocking any classic mass movement for a quarter of a century. Instead, in July 1958 the Duvaliers founded their own mass movement, the Tontons Macoutes, from 1962 officially dubbed, more grandly, the National Security Volunteers (VSN). Created a few days after a serious attempt to oust Duvalier and with the aim of neutralizing the army, the VSN was recruited overwhelmingly from the poor, Black and illiterate in a calculated exploitation of poverty. But, like the *cacos* and the earlier *piquets*, the force included some Black landowners and even, in the last years of the dictatorship, some mulattos.

Despite its rapid degeneration into brutality and murder, the Duvaliers' militia—which their ideologues described as a "people-army duality"—was a genuine elevation of the poor Black majority for the first time in Haiti's tortured history. This sociological shift, engineered by François Duvalier to protect his own power, was challenged in May 1980 when Duvalier's son and successor, Jean-Claude ("Baby Doc"), married into the mulatto aristocracy that Papa Doc had tried to destroy.

The Macoutes came to despise the young Duvalier as a traitor, and their brooding hostility exacerbated existing divisions, contributing to the dictatorship's collapse. The Macoutes' champion, sharp-tongued Interior and Defense Minister Roger Lafontant, was ousted just five months before the end, after three years as the country's *de facto* ruler.

Some of the VSN's grassroots links were revealed after the Duvaliers fled, when the murderous rage directed at the Macoutes also touched hundreds of Voodoo priests, or *houngans*, who often doubled as VSN chieftains.[8] Scores were killed. Those who hunted them down were sometimes led by youthful zealots egged on by Christians, mainly Protestant pastors but some Catholics, many of them white and foreign.[9] Voodoo followers, however, as key actors of everyday rural life, began working with the young left-led popular movements planning a new Haiti.

The origins of these post-Duvalier mass movements are to be found in the mid-1970s—in the expansion of communications, a certain liberalization of the dictatorship after Papa Doc's death and the awakening of a divided and corrupted Roman Catholic Church. Before 1976, only a few miles of roads outside the capital were paved. By 1980, most major towns had been linked by modern highways, giving farmers easier access to the markets of Port-au-Prince. An efficient telephone system was established at the same time.

Perhaps the most important foundation of the modern mass movements, given 80% national illiteracy, was the flowering of the country's radio stations. The younger Duvalier's regime, offering a new official ideology of "Jean-Claudism"—which it defined as "Duvalierism reconsidered, corrected and broadened"—set up the first official radio (1977) and government television (1979) stations. These were matched and overtaken, however, by stations such as Jean Dominique's Radio Haiti Inter, which broadcast from the countryside the complaints of ordinary Haitians about the Duvaliers' misrule. It also pioneered the extensive use of Creole in the media. Anchor Compère Filo, later to be exiled by the Duvaliers, became one of the country's most popular figures.

The elite—both mulatto and Black—snobbishly clung to the written media in French, ignoring dissidence in the form of Creole political satire. The capital's theaters were packed for months before the regime realized the danger and cracked down. But the seeds of revolt had been planted.[10] Despite the dictatorship, the enormous town-country gap began to narrow. Prospects for national unity improved and with it the chance of successful resistance. For some time, even the new government radio, starring

Compère Plume, who later became a left-wing activist, gave vent to peasant complaints.

The Catholic Church—powerful despite competition from Voodoo and from hundreds of foreign Protestant missionaries, mostly conservative Americans—was also stirring.[11] The archbishop of Port-au-Prince, François Wolf Ligondé, named to the post by Duvalier in 1966 as the first Black Haitian-born bishop, was politely ignored by the rest of the hierarchy and by an increasingly radical rank and file.

In 1977, the bishop of Gonaïves, Emmanuel Constant, produced—in Creole—the country's first handbook of human rights. When liberalization ended abruptly in November 1980 with mass arrests, the deportation of twenty three leading dissidents and the silencing of the media, the Church was the only institution left with any built-in immunity to State power and became a natural umbrella for all dissent.

On the one hand was the Church's Radyo Solèy, which took over from the closed Haiti Inter as a voice of the powerless. Founded in May 1978 and managed by U.S. and Belgian priests, its network of provincial reporters chronicled the regime's abuses and united the country as rarely, if ever, before. On the other hand was the *Ti Legliz* (Little Church) movement of village groups for discussion, prayer and self-help.[12] Churches were the only place that political gatherings could be held with impunity.

In May 1984, the first major street protests against the Duvalier regime in nearly twenty-five years erupted when hungry slumdwellers looted CARE food warehouses in Gonaïves and Cap-Haïtien and attacked a prison and police station. A half-dozen people were killed. By early 1985, Catholic activists were sponsoring demonstrations against hunger and in favor of "social justice" and democracy. In September, the dismissal of Lafontant—at U.S. urging—proved to be the catalyst for the decisive move against the Duvaliers. His fall came soon after a campaign by Radio Soleil against the regime's plan to legalize political parties on its own strict terms.

Protests erupted anew, centered again on Gonaïves, as cassettes circulated of a revolutionary sermon by Father Yvan Pollefeyt, one of three expelled Belgian priests. Peasants in the Arti-bonite Valley, where a mass mobilization had halted construction of a dam, mounted a makeshift radio network.[13] The Duvaliers' repression was no longer efficient.

After the shooting of four schoolchildren in a demonstration in Gonaïves on the fifth anniversary of the November 28, 1980 crackdown, the regime's authority outside the capital evaporated. Radyo Solèy's reporting of protests helped the movement to spread. The government shut the radio down but, open or closed, it provoked demonstrations. When Duvalier reopened the station against the advice of his senior ministers in late December, the U.S. Reagan Administration began seriously planning for post-Duvalierism.

Demonstrations continued almost daily through January, but government warnings that communists were involved, aimed at the United States, drew no public reaction from Washington. It was clear, however, that the longer the revolt went on, the more radical influences and anti-U.S. sentiment would grow. Washington had to act, organizing a night escape of the Duvaliers into exile in France on February 7, 1986. "It was that or an American invasion," Rosny Desroches, the post-Duvalier government's education minister, told reporters.

The country now expected or hoped for revolution. But Haiti's elite—except for some who had made too many headlines or too many enemies—was safe. The U.S.-approved junta that took over, the National Government Council (CNG), contained key figures of the old regime, who arranged the exile or protection of many former colleagues.

The Church hierarchy, despite its insistence that it was "non-political," flew to the defense of the CNG to denounce the "communist" danger—in effect its own radical priests. Radio Soleil softened its broadcasts.[14] Some recalled the frequent visits by the Papal Nuncio to the U.S. Embassy as the Duvalier regime crumbled. "The Church hierarchy has no interest in real change," said trade-union leader Yves Richard. "After all, the Church is the second biggest landowner in the country."[15]

The way seemed clear for the grassroots to confront the CNG regime directly. The dictatorship had left a broad distrust of all civilian politicians and of "the Republic of Port-au-Prince." Leading Duvalier opponents within Haiti, despite the courage of those such as the populist Christian Democrat Sylvio Claude, were seen as inadequate. Other political figures were slow to return from exile and, when they did, found themselves relatively unknown.

Catholic activists, led by men like Jean-Bertrand Aristide, the charismatic parish priest of the La Saline slum in Port-au-Prince, and others estranged from the Church hierarchy, encouraged the activity of neighborhood committees of all kinds. A movement to beautify the capital, which later spread to provincial towns, saw volunteers sweeping streets and decorating walls and even road surfaces with colorful religious, nationalist and political illustrations.[16]

Because of the CNG's initial reluctance to crack down on the population, and its restoration of basic freedoms, especially in the press, street demonstrations managed to force the removal of major Duvalierists still in power and the arrest and token trial of others. Most spectacular was the "people's arrest" of the dictatorship's most hated secret police chief, Luc Désyr, three weeks after the Duvaliers left. A mob of thousands rushed the six miles from the capital to the airport when a counter clerk tipped off a radio station about Désyr's imminent departure. He was tried and sentenced to death.

Dechoukaj—"uprooting"—ruled the land as Haitians administered a people's justice, looting the villas of the rich, lynching Tontons Macoutes and staging strikes and sit-down protests to drive Duvalierists out of their jobs and into hiding. The Macoutes' new national headquarters was turned into a school; some cabinet ministers handed back their salaries; communist historian Roger Gaillard was named head of the university; the Cité Simone slum, named for Duvalier's mother, was renamed after the Church's Radyo Solèy; and women marched to demand their rights for the first time in Haitian history.

But by the first anniversary of the Duvaliers' fall, pressure for change was blunted by the distraction of campaigning presidential candidates for the November 1987 elections, such as the popular but lightweight Louis Dejoie II and industrialist Thomas Desulmé—both old-style operators unlikely to challenge seriously the bankrupt political system.

Despite its sharp criticism that the CNG regime's early promise had been betrayed and that the situation "continued to deteriorate economically, politically and socially," the Conference of Catholic Bishops kept at arm's length the "liberationists"—better represented in the more vocal Conference of Priests. Despite the bishops' calls for land reform and "deep-rooted change," the hope of some that the Church might sponsor "a party of the masses" faded.

According to Claudette Werleigh, the activist secretary general of the Catholic welfare agency Caritas, conservative Protestant pastors were also redoubling their efforts in the *mornes*. "The hierarchy has lost a lot of credibility with young people," she admitted. "The Church now has to share with the new grassroots organizations the space it once monopolized."[17]

The countryside continued to seethe; old resentments toward the capital resurfaced. The Duvaliers had been driven out, after all, by a provincial revolt. Port-au-Prince had been calm, with only a few minor incidents, right to the end. Now some felt politicians in the capital were trying to take over again as usual.

Thousands of peasants joined a tax boycott, protesting the lack of government services, and government-appointed local officials *(chefs de section)* were rejected in many places. Haiti Inter and Radio Soleil publicized the new peasant organizations and their angry demands for justice and action. In the town of Hinche, enraged roadworkers lynched a government engineer who shot at them when they demanded to be paid. Violence was common in the northern plain and the Artibonite Valley as peasants tried to repossess land taken from them under the Duvalier dictatorship.[18] After serious flooding in Les Cayes in June 1986, peasants refused food relief, demanding instead jobs, land, tools and housing.

Minor Tontons Macoutes went on trial in many towns and were sentenced to death for murders committed as long as twenty years earlier. The rural revolt drew tacit encouragement from workers in the Church's ambitious national literacy campaign, *Misyon Alfa*, although some literacy workers were attacked as "communists" by villagers. The long-planned campaign, launched with fanfare and government blessing a month after the Duvaliers left, aimed to eradicate illiteracy in five years.

W hen the CNG organized the election in October 1986, of a constituent assembly to start a transition to formal democracy, less than 5% of the electorate turned out. But assembly members—many of them young technicians, lawyers or returnees with few political ties—surprised Haitians in four months of often tumultuous public sessions by producing a daringly liberal Constitution promising rights most Haitians have never known. The new Constitution curbed the power of the president, devolved authority to the provinces and banned leading Duvalierists from public life. Voters endorsed it almost unanimously (99.8%, though with a turnout of under 50%) in a referendum in March 1987 that foreign and local observers agreed had been honest.

The far Left—grouped in the small Popular Assembly coalition around the controversial New York-based Ben Dupuy and his smartly produced and widely-read weekly *Haïti Progrès*—opposed the Constitution as a ruling-class trick.[19] The leftist Democratic Unity Confederation (KID), urging abstention, called it "a pretty flower with no fragrance, fine-sounding promises...aimed at putting the people to sleep."

Former Duvalier minister and 1987 presidential candidate Hubert de Ronceray complained that the Constitution would make the president "a puppet in the hands of parliament," and warned that proposed provincial councils would "institutionalize civil war." It was unworkable, he said, voicing the fears of not a few, including one foreign diplomat who speculated that "people like the Constitution because it embodies the spirit of the revolution. It's a useful healing document. It may not be a useful operating document."[20]

But the feeling of most Haitians was that it was far better than nothing and something worth fighting for. The Church hierarchy, in an intervention that perhaps clinched approval, said the Constitution "seems a good guarantee of freedom...despite gaps and contradictions."

In this atmosphere of hope, a group of center-left intellectuals organized a five-day National Congress of Haitian Democratic Movements in the capital in January 1987 to try to coordinate the broad will for meaningful change and a clear break with the "old politics." The organizers of the meeting claimed to have rallied more than 300 organizations, mostly peasant-based, making it the largest gathering of its kind in Haitian history. The 1,000 participants spanned a wide political spectrum, which included Catholic progressives. Many of the meeting's demands found their way into the new Constitution. "We've done the work the political parties should have done," declared one prominent congress figure. Congress leaders also set up the Committee of 57, which directed the protests in the summer of 1987.

Dupuy and his supporters rejected the congress as "a club of opportunists and pseudo-democrats."[21] It was also boycotted by Yves Richard, head of the largest and most left-wing of the country's three main labor federations, the Independent Haitian Workers' Organization (CATH). Richard was not followed, however, by CATH's largest constituent and the country's most powerful union, the Port-au-Prince drivers' union.

Richard, a self-educated man of humble origins, denounced the congress as "just a seminar manipulated by a small group of intellectuals from the bourgeoisie—people from Port-au-Prince who said they represented the peasantry."[22] Agreeing with him was Claude René, the young coordinator of the capital's neighborhood committees, which had organized bookmobiles, a cinema and a literacy program of their own. "We have to avoid false democrats, those who pretend they are friends of the people," he said. "We've waited two centuries for true democracy. We have to prepare the structures and not act in a hurry."[23]

But the congress, which set up a standing body, Konakom, to push for a "democratic, nationalist state," impressed most Haitians with its representativeness and its calls for purging the "Macoutist remnants" of the Duvalier regime, decreasing dependency on foreign countries, declaring Creole an official language and bolstering respect for Voodoo, the national religion. Among congress participants was a new organization, Children of the Haitian Tradition (Zantray), which helped successfully petition the constituent assembly to abolish a 1935 anti-Voodoo law. Zantray head Hérard Simon was once a Tonton Macoute leader in Gonaïves.

Three weeks after the popular congress, an alarmed government organized its own smaller gathering of rural delegates in the capital, at which CNF head General Namphy insisted that the peasantry was "in power" for the first time in Haitian history and must make decisions. He praised the rural councils (CASEC) that the government had set up in 1986 as "the most important action for democracy" since the Duvaliers' fall.

Another peasant congress, backed by Catholic activists and Konakom at Papaye, near Hinche, in late March 1987, called for an end to the import of pigs and smuggled rice and sugar which it said was destroying the national economy.

S choolteacher Victor Benoît, the leading figure in Konakom, said the Left's participation in the 1987 elections would depend on whether the independent electoral council was allowed real control of the scheduled local, legislative and presidential polls. "Our first task is to expand democracy's territory here," he said. "People are mobilized. We also have a favorable international situation right now." He denied Richard's charge of intellectual vanguardism. "Ben Dupuy and the maximalists want to immediately install a revolutionary people's democracy. That just isn't possible. We have neither a progressive military nor an armed people. We have to have a pluralist regime first. But I wouldn't favor a one-party state anyway."

Benoît denied charges that the January congress fudged criticism of the United States. "The state here is domesticated by the United States. But we have to take U.S. power in the region into account. We can't afford irresponsible sorties. It's not all black and white. Let's remember, for example, that U.S. music is tremendously influential in Cuba, yet Cuba remains a socialist society."[24]

The immense economic weight of the United States however, was an obstacle to building meaningful democracy in Haiti at that juncture. Apart from the economic and psychological ties created by the some $125 million that Haitians received annually from relatives working in the United States, total U.S. investment in Haiti was around $130 million and more than half of Haiti's trade was with the United States. Perhaps a quarter of a million people depended on the earnings of some 50,000 workers at 140 light assembly plants, primarily U.S. owned, that had been built around the capital over the past twenty years and had become the economy's most dynamic sector. Most of the U.S. plant owners considered any hint of unionism as grounds for instant dismissal.[25]

Unionization would likely have made these firms leave for countries where labor was even cheaper than Haiti's $3.20 official daily minimum wage. Yves Richard—whose father, a mechanic, was murdered after trying to unionize one of the country's main coffee trading houses—was optimistic, however. He said CATH had some 176,000 members in 172 unions, 126 of them among the peasantry. Sensing that union demands, which had already led to strikes, might become a major threat to the economy and public order, General Namphy appealed to employers in April 1987 not to "close your minds" to the "legitimate demands" of workers.

The U.S. government, with its familiar interest in dividing the labor movement, gave strong financial backing to the conservative Federation of Unionized Workers (FOS), through the National Endowment for Democracy (NED) and the CIA-linked American Institute for Free Labor Development (AIFLD), known for its destabilizing work over the past quarter-century in Guyana, El Salvador and Grenada. Not surprisingly, FOS was given a good write-up in U.S. Embassy literature, which said Washington and the CNG favored the growth of "apolitical, responsible unions."

But if trade unions could be contained by overwhelming economic and political forces, other factors were less easily tamed. The "legalization" of Creole gave confidence and thus power to ordinary Haitians. The Constitution now had to be written in Creole as well as French. "Creole has become the political language," said dismissed liberal Justice Minister François Latortue with approval. "It is enabling the masses to participate and a stronger national identity to emerge."[26] Official recognition of Creole was a subversion that Haiti's elite could not easily combat.

The establishment was more successful in fighting the Moscow-aligned Unified Party of Haitian Communists (PUCH), the oldest of the country's major political parties. Despite its serious organizational work, the attraction of a clear ideology and the popularity of its shrewd leader, René Théodore, the party met tough opposition from the Protestant and Catholic churches, which managed to spread a visceral anti-communism throughout the country.[27]

Until the summer of 1987, Théodore backed the CNG as the best hope for the moment, opposed general strike calls as foolish or premature and urged approval of the new Constitution—all positions with which Washington would concur. "We have to concentrate on building up a body of laws," he said.

Théodore, a forty-seven year old math and physics teacher, publicly defended Voodoo as a part of the national culture. "Marxists hold that religion is a protest against intolerable living conditions," he said. "There's been a lot of curiosity about us and a lot of respectful debate," he added.[28] But threats restricted his campaigning.

Papa Doc had made communism a capital crime in April 1969 and a few weeks later his police murdered sixteen of the party's twenty-one-strong central committee and five of its six-member politburo. The lone politburo survivor was Théodore, party leader since October 1978, who claimed that more than 1,000 PUCH members died under the Duvalier dictatorship. In a supreme irony—with the media silenced by a state of siege in the week before Duvalier's departure—most Haitians received their news of the final crisis of the Duvalier regime by tuning into PUCH broadcasts beamed from nearby Havana.

CATH leader Richard dismissed the PUCH, however. "Communist parties don't make revolution in the Third World," he said. Neither Théodore nor the country's other major leftist leader, social democrat Serge Gilles of the Haitian Revolutionary Progressive Nationalist Party (PANPRA), ran for president in the November 1987 elections.

I t was the old order, not the new forces, however, which provoked the crisis of the summer of 1987. The former Duvalierists and ex-Tontons Macoutes in the army, government service and among the wealthy reasserted themselves. When Duvalierists tried to form a political party in October 1986, they were forced to retreat after huge public protests. In January 1987, however, they engineered the firing of the government's four most liberal ministers. French courts boosted their morale by refusing to expel the exiled Duvaliers or help the Haitian government's bid to recover part of the family's estimated $500 million ill-gotten fortune.

The Duvalierists and army leaders took fright at the new Constitution's removal of the military's traditional supervision over elections. But the CNG's double violation of the Constitution in late June only a few weeks after it took effect—overriding the independent electoral council (CEP) and dissolving CATH—only succeeded in producing the most impressive general strike since the Duvaliers fled.

As the opposition closed ranks, the army, along with presumed Duvalierist civilian gunmen, gunned down more than thirty people. Remaining confidence in the CNG evaporated. Namphy's public geniality, personal modesty and official use of Creole—a significant factor in the relative calm of post-Duvalierism—no longer cut any ice.

Lacking sufficiently strong or united leadership, however, the opposition had difficulty sustaining a general strike.[29] Namphy fulminated against "extremists," "agitators" and "anarchists," and his colleagues claimed to see Cuba's hand behind the protests. But the opposition succeeded in forcing the withdrawal of the repressive decrees. The CNG survived by default. Electoral preparations resumed under the restored CEP, but prospects for a free election remained poor.

The army—still united despite an opposition call to the rank and file for a revolt against corrupt senior officers "with bank accounts and villas abroad"—was reorganized in mid-July to enable special tactical units to be based in the provinces and to increase the number of generals from two to nine.

Yet the military violence against the vigorous media, a partial ban on demonstrations in the capital, the attempted eviction of the revolutionary Father Aristide from his parish and Duvalierist-linked atrocities in Jean-Rabel and elsewhere, including the assassination of center-left presidential candidate Louis-Eugène Athis, temporarily set back the opposition. Interest in elections was tepid so long as the CNG stayed in charge.

"There are more urgent problems here than having elections," said Father Jacques Mésidor, influential head of the militant local Salesian order.[30] "Haitians are poorer now than under the Duvaliers," said Konakom leader Benoît.[31]

The U.S. government, which had escaped serious public blame after its long backing of the Duvaliers, took a fall in the 1987 crisis and came to be perceived and hated by many as the CNG's last crutch. U.S. support for the CNG was double-edged: aid would be cut if there was any "radical change" in the junta's composition but also if the CNG "perverted" the election timetable. The sight of the army's new U.S.-supplied riot gear and tear gas revived the powerful anti-American sentiments in Haitian society, especially since the trigger-happy troops had just been trained by a U.S. military mission in what U.S. officials said were "humane ways to control civil disorders."

The murdered Charlemagne Péralte, whose face now appeared on coins, became a public hero for the first time since the U.S. occupation. U.S. flags were burned and walls daubed with anti-U.S. slogans. "Haitians' pride is hurt when they see how dependent they are on us," one U.S. diplomat insisted. "Our policy is to reduce this dependence."[32] Father Mésidor accused the United States of conniving to discourage the poor from winning power.

The Catholic progressives remained in the vanguard of the movement against neo-Duvalierism and were led by Bishop Willy Romélus of Jérémie, whose tough statements, highly critical of the United States, had been the backbone of the July 1987 demonstrations. But the Conference of Bishops, under the control of the Church's *de facto* head, Bishop François Gayot of Cap-Haïtien, also strongly condemned the army repression and spoke of possible civil war, though its tone was more conciliatory.

Meanwhile, the presidential candidates for the upcoming 1987 elections liked to theorize. University professor Leslie Manigat warned that all classes, particularly the elite, had a debilitating "welfare mentality" that had to be eradicated. The masses had "a kind of virginity which makes it easier to educate them for democracy" than the ruling class, he said.[33]

Conservative ex-Finance Minister Marc Bazin cautioned that if a democratic foundation was not laid now, the extremes of communism or Duvalierism would take over.[34] Former minister Desroches, a non-candidate despite some public support, warned that if the next president was not backed by a political party, he would be "obliged by the people to become a dictator." And if there was no serious economic and social change, he predicted, Duvalierism could return.[35]

But the presidential candidates, said Serge Gilles, didn't realize that things had changed. "They arrive in the provinces in a fine car, with a suit and their Port-au-Prince airs, but the peasants don't care about that. They want to know about water, their land, when there'll be a doctor coming, what's going to be done about the rats which destroy a sixth of the crops in the Artibonite. The politicians aren't used to talking about immediate problems—they prefer long-term issues," said Gilles. "They're easier to talk about."[36]

The war between the unarmed poor majority and the armed rich in the Caribbean's most tragic country had not yet begun in earnest. Despite intelligence, energy and often goodwill on both sides, bad political habits, inexperience, the ruthless pressure of poverty and the perpetual shadow of a selfish neighbor to the North worked against resolving the acute national crisis.

"February 1986 was just the tip of the iceberg," said Georges Werleigh, a government economist. "If people are given the same old pill, it won't work."[37]

2

THE ABORTED 1987 ELECTIONS

GREG CHAMBERLAIN

❝We've failed this time round. We've made too many mistakes. Democracy is very difficult," said former Haitian Education Minister Rosny Desroches.

"It isn't easy. We won't have the answer tomorrow," said Evans Paul, a leader of the radical Democratic Unity Confederation (KID).

The two men, of different social classes and political inclinations, were surveying the desolate political scene in Haiti after the army and its Duvalierist allies destroyed the country's first free elections in thirty years in an orgy of violence and killings in November 1987.

General Henri Namphy, brushing aside U.S. and other international charges that his soldiers were directly involved in the bloodshed, called a new vote for January 1988 with the aim of installing a president who would watch over the interests of the army and its allies. At the same time, Namphy's National Government Council (CNG) launched a ferocious propaganda campaign to convince Haitians that a spotless, patriotic army had saved them in the nick of time from both the "communists" and the "Catholic Church."

But what there is of the Left in Haiti, including the tiny Communist Party, had hardly been discussing armed struggle, much less using it. The election had been shaping up to be a contest between moderate opponents. The fragile center-left National Front for Concerted Action, which grew out of the broad Committee of 57 coalition that had led the unsuccessful anti-regime protests in the summer of 1987, had chosen Gerard Gourgue as its presidential candidate. In the context of Haiti's enormous wealth, color and class divides, the Front was hampered by its mainly middle-class leadership. There was also hostility within the Front itself toward Gourgue. Some leaders saw him as an old-fashioned right-winger who kept himself apart from the previous summer's protests but who had been chosen to appease Washington.

The Left's constituency was undermined by the rise of two populist presidential candidates, Louis Dejoie and Sylvio Claude, from opposite ends of the social spectrum. Dejoie, a cheery millionaire mulatto, aroused little enthusiasm among his own class but successfully struck a chord with the poor. His colorful speeches contrasted with the drier, less comprehensible talk of Gourgue and Marc Bazin, briefly finance minister under the Duvaliers, who was still the U.S. favorite in the elections.

Claude, a fiery Baptist preacher with the card of never having yielded to the Duvaliers, may well have won the most votes in the three hours of balloting on November 29. He was dismissed, yet feared, by the intelligentsia and foreigners for his erratic positions, religious fervor and incoherent "Caritatism," based on his own notion of Christian charity. But this mystique and his charisma as the "Martyr," as his election posters called him, drew Haiti's poor to him. His movement recalled the eastern Caribbean populism of the 1950s and 1960s, particularly of Grenada's Eric Gairy.

Parts of the Left had remained aloof and skeptical about elections. "We won't solve the country's problems by voting," said Father Jean-Bertrand Aristide, the unofficial leader of the *Ti Legliz*, the radical wing of the Catholic Church in Haiti. "The candidates can't bring change. Like anywhere else in Latin America, elections are in the hands of the oligarchy who use them to undermine popular demands."

The U.S. government had provided the bulk of the independent electoral council's $7 million budget. The rest came from Venezuela, Canada and France. Namphy didn't contribute a penny. Through understandable over-enthusiasm and veiled anti-Duvalierist statements ("we must banish forever the sound of gunfire and the groan of torture, the distress of the hungry, and the stink of the slums"), the electoral council made itself an easy prey for Namphy, who never forgot the humiliation of his failed attempt to crush the council during the July 1987 unrest.

Namphy did not give the slightest consideration to the council's desperate pleas for protection from the Duvalierist thugs who threatened its members with death, burned down its offices and stopped ballots from getting to the provinces.

A few weeks before the November election, Namphy violated the spirit of the new national Constitution by naming himself armed forces chief for the next three years. "Military values at the service of the nation," proclaimed the State television in a long-shot public relations effort. The vigilance brigades that had sprung up all over the country to ensure that the November 29 poll would take place were outlawed a few days before election day as well.

The elections came to a bloody end, including the schoolyard massacre of sixteen queuing voters in Port-au-Prince. To justify the election's cancellation, Namphy told the Paris daily *Libération* that "foreigners" had financed and supported the independent council in its "plot" to ensure a leftist victory by stuffing ballot boxes. Army commander General Carl Michel Nicolas said the army had stopped the violence "in time" and that there had been danger of a communist takeover.

The army's complicity in the killing was, however, witnessed by scores of foreign and local journalists. The United States accused Colonel Jean-Claude Paul—the commander of the country's main military unit, the Dessalines Battalion, and the army's suspected top drug smuggler—of organizing much of the election-day violence. The United States suspended all except humanitarian aid to Haiti.

The Church, which was at the forefront of the fight against the Duvaliers, condemned the carnage. Namphy lashed out at the clergy in response. "The Catholic Church has controlled education here for the past 100 years but it has left Haitians illiterate," he snapped. "I'm a Catholic, but I don't have any respect for the priests."

The National Front for Concerted Action joined the three other major parties, all center-right, led by Louis Dejoie, Marc Bazin, and Sylvio Claude, in announcing a boycott of the new military-sponsored elections, hastily scheduled for January 17.

Despite armed attacks and some temporary shutdowns after the November vote, critics of the army still had a mighty weapon in the vigorously free radio and press. Yet the opposition as a whole was still divided and inexperienced, and failed to mobilize effective resistance to Namphy. Opposition figures, many in partial hiding, were under heavy pressure to lay low. Some had their passports confiscated.

A two-day general strike called by the opposition in December was barely followed, as a result of a mixture of fear, extreme poverty, the proximity of Christmas and the spoiling tactics by the far left group around the New York-based editor and activist Ben Dupuy.

"The political class here is so backward. It's incapable of marshaling the potential for resistance," said economist Jean-Jacques Honorat. "But then people want to vote for a messiah. They seem to think their misery will end at once. It's depressing. And none of the candidates in November seriously discussed any of the issues."

But Evans Paul of KID, who stands somewhere between the National Front and Dupuy on the political spectrum, said the election failure had at least weeded out the false democrats. Like most others, he dreamt of divisions emerging within the armed forces. He also suggested that the Left would have to rethink its policy of non-violence. "We can't leave the ground to the Macoutes," he said.

Haitians meanwhile came up with a name for this third stage in their battle to stamp out Duvalierism. The fight began with *dechoukaj* (uprooting) as soon as the Duvaliers fell. In the summer of 1987, the cry had been *"rache manyok, bay nou te blan"* (pull up your roots and clear off). After the massacre, it became *balewouze*, which means "sweep them out and wash the place down."

Namphy faced strong international condemnation over the cancellation of the election. The United States suspended two-thirds of its aid. U.S. diplomats in Port-au-Prince said the United States had gambled on Namphy's honesty about elections and had lost. France and the European Economic Community cut back their aid as well.

Some Haitians were convinced, however, that Washington had wanted the November elections to be cancelled (albeit without the bloodshed) to avert a victory by Gourgue or Claude. In a visit to Haiti in December, a group of Caribbean leaders headed by Jamaican Edward Seaga, a major U.S. ally, reflected Washington's attitude by trying to steer Namphy toward the center. The opposition, however, firmly rejected a U.S. proposal that they agree on a single candidate and drop their boycott of the January vote.

Namphy received his only comfort when he telephoned Panamanian ruler Manuel Noriega, an earlier target of a U.S. aid cut. The two men commiserated on the phone about the "foreign misinformation campaigns" and "domestic destabilization" they had to tolerate.

For January 17, 1988, Namphy took no chances. He named his own electoral council and gave it a long list of orders, despite a constitutional ban on doing so. The new electoral law abolished voting secrecy and voter registration. Candidates also had to print and distribute their own ballot papers. A maximum two-year jail term for advocating abstention, a clause held over from the earlier election law, took on special significance because of the broad threatened boycott.

In a conciliatory gesture to Washington, the Duvalierists— twelve of whose presidential candidates were banned under the

Constitution by the old council, thus unleashing a wave of killings—were also barred from running in the January poll. But they
remained otherwise untouched and could hope for a comfortable
existence under Namphy's wing.

In anticipation of the election, the garden of the villa of the
Duvalierists' official leader, former army chief General Claude
Raymond, in Port-au-Prince's chic hillside suburb of Debussy, was
filled round the clock with armed men. It was from this garden that
many of the commandos had been seen to emerge on November
29 to violently disrupt the elections.

Namphy seemed to be threatening more of the same when he
told *Libération*, "believe me, the day the army really intervenes, then
there'll be complete silence."

"When the people are ready to fight," riposted Evans Paul,
"everyone will find a weapon."

3

AN INTERREGNUM

Haitian History from 1987 to 1990

GREG CHAMBERLAIN

As Haiti's political class struggled to understand the failure of the country's first try at free elections, in November 1987, several politicians with little popular support declined to join the condemnation of the Duvalierists and the army for destroying the elections. Army leader General Henri Namphy had announced new elections for January 1988 and, with a virtually total boycott in prospect, these politicians saw an easy back door to the presidency.

The most prominent of these politicians was Leslie Manigat, a shrewd fifty-seven-year-old university professor who had spent much of his life teaching abroad after the dictator François "Papa Doc" Duvalier forced him into exile in 1963. His blunt assertion that the army was "an inescapable fact of life" outraged many, but he knew he had to tame the army if he was to have any real power. A deal with the army leaders saw him declared the winner of the January election against a dozen virtual unknowns. The turnout was estimated at little more than 5%.

Manigat tried to govern honestly, despite the democratic sector's refusal to work with him and his failure to win resumption of much foreign aid. He was the first modern Haitian leader with any real knowledge of the outside world. His way was blocked by the army, however, at every turn. Military appointees clogged government ministries and army-linked Duvalierist death squads roamed the streets. The Right forced the closure of the Church's "subversive" mass literacy campaign, *Misyon Alfa*. The army opposed Manigat's attempts to end their smuggling rackets, but so did ordinary Haitians who liked the cheap rice and other contraband from the United States and the Dominican Republic. Demonstrations in the coastal town of St. Marc in May sounded the alarm.

Manigat then took on the army leadership. He had made a strategic alliance with Colonel Jean-Claude Paul, the Dessalines Battalion commander, whom the United States was trying to extradite as the Haitian kingpin of the cocaine traffic from Colombia (via Haiti) to the United States. When Namphy, as army chief, ordered Paul transferred, Manigat put Namphy under house arrest, an action which was cheered by many officers who saw their commander as incompetent. But a second round of changes angered them. On June 19, Namphy was brought by junior officers to the palace where he gave a drunken televised speech announcing he had taken over again. Manigat was packed off into exile. "Only the army can bring democracy and human rights to Haiti," Namphy said.

With Namphy back in power, the Duvalierist barons returned in force. The death squads stepped up their killings. On September 11, 1988, about fifty thugs sent by the Duvalierist Mayor of Port-au-Prince Colonel Franck Romain burst into St. Jean Bosco Church, on the edge of the capital's La Saline slum, where a packed congregation was listening to a fiery sermon by the popular "liberationist" priest Father Jean-Bertrand Aristide. They shot or hacked to pieces a dozen or so parishioners and then burned the church down. Aristide escaped.

A week later, disgusted young soldiers chased Namphy out of the palace but could not agree on who should replace him. Eventually they appealed to the army's shrewdest power broker,

Colonel Prosper Avril, who had long managed the Duvaliers' stolen millions and had close ties with U.S. officials. He took over, but by then an extraordinary grassroots rebellion was underway in the army. The rank and file—the "little soldiers"—overturned the entire army leadership, arresting officers and delivering them in handcuffs to army headquarters. A group of left-wing soldiers announced themselves.

The canny Avril promised democracy and accepted one of the rebels, twenty-seven-year-old Sargent Joseph Hébreux, as "co-president." Avril began lengthy consultations with the democratic sector, including the Left, ostensibly to establish a national democratic consensus. He seemed sincere. Political prisoners were freed and some Duvalierists were pursued. Washington said it was pleased. Avril sacked Colonel Paul, the drug king, who conveniently died—apparently poisoned—a few weeks later. Paul's demise bolstered Avril's shaky position; he also hoped it would open the way for resumption of U.S. aid.

Soon afterwards, Avril made an about-face. He briefly jailed fifteen radicals at the center of the "little soldiers" movement for plotting a coup. Within a few months, the army had returned to normal. Many commanders were restored and the "little soldiers" and their demands, which included democracy, were sidelined.

At the same time, the conservative Church hierarchy was moving against Aristide, who had denounced Avril as "a big-time criminal" and the Church leaders as "imperialists in cassocks." In December 1988, Aristide was expelled from the Salesian Order for "inciting violence and class struggle," and retreated to run his orphanage in the capital.

The Haitian political class and Washington were growing disillusioned with Avril, who in turn said he was disappointed in the politicians and that elections were far off. Avril, however, continued to talk of democracy, partly revived the suspended Constitution and was rewarded with a small amount of U.S. aid.

Avril's attempts to walk a tightrope between the army, the democrats and the Duvalierists collapsed when, in April 1989, two of the army's three main units, the Leopards Corps and the Dessalines Battalion, rose against him. The issue was pay but also, in the case of their commanders, U.S. attempts to stamp out their drug-smuggling rackets. Avril also saw the hand of exiled Duvalierist leader Roger Lafontant behind the rebellion. After a week of shooting and confusion, Avril came out on top, applauded by the United States, and the plotters fled abroad. But he was a prisoner of the junior officers who saved him.

The army continued to sink into gangsterism and the country into Duvalierist lawlessness. Avril tried new diversions, such as naming the country's first woman cabinet minister. The Church's pioneering Radyo Solèy was purged of all progressive journalists in August. The regime also half-heartedly applied an International Monetary Fund-demanded austerity plan in the hope of getting loans.

The democratic sector grew bolder, however, and political parties on the Right and Left formed tentative alliances. Avril announced a drawn-out timetable in October for free elections in 1990 and again called for resumption of foreign aid.

But Avril's credibility was soon destroyed by a series of army killings and brutalities, including the torture of three leftist leaders, among them Evans Paul, head of KID. Even the Church denounced the violence. An energetic new U.S. ambassador, Alvin Adams, publicly demanded democratic reforms. Faced with demonstrations and a possible new army revolt, Avril panicked and imposed a state of siege in January 1990 to "protect democracy against terrorism and civil war," only to cancel it after ten days at U.S. insistence. Politicians were beaten and deported.

With the blessing of Washington, the opposition united against Avril to isolate him and call for his departure. The accidental killing of a schoolgirl by soldiers set off new protests and sealed Avril's fate. The democrats, led by left-wing priest Father Antoine Adrien, declared themselves ready to take power. Ambassador Adams forced Avril to flee abroad on March 12, 1990 by threatening to freeze his U.S. bank accounts.

The democrats' new council of state, chaired by Dr. Louis Roy, sought a provisional president from the Supreme Court, as the Constitution demanded. Only one judge, Ertha Pascal-Trouillot, was willing. Her mandate was to share power with the council and organize the free elections that Avril had promised. The liberal new army commander, General Hérard Abraham, agreed to cooperate, but had little real power.

The head of the human rights league and Claudette Werleigh, a leading grassroots activist, were named ministers. But relations soon soured between the president and the council of state. Duvalierist violence increased, with the complicity of the army. A member of the council of state was assassinated. With Washington backing the powerless president, now reviled by the democratic sector, Haiti stumbled toward a vote on December 16.

The United States paid most of the $12 million cost of the election, which was supervised by the United Nations. Aristide had scorned suggestions that he run for president. Elections were a trick by the elite (the "bourgeoisie") and the United States, he said. Under the banner of the National Front for Change and Democracy (FNCD), the Left chose a respected but uncharismatic teacher, Victor Benoît as its candidate. Evans Paul had Benoît dumped in favor of Aristide, who announced at the last minute that he was running "to stop the Duvalierists" from taking power "as a matter of historical necessity." Lafontant's candidacy was then banned by the electoral council on a technicality. Despite Aristide's immense popularity, the FNCD failed to put up enough parliamentary candidates. So while Aristide won the presidential election by a landslide of 67.5% of the vote, he could only construct the most fragile parliamentary majority.

The United States bit its tongue and said it could work with Aristide, whose "stability" and fitness to rule it privately doubted. They had banked on victory for Marc Bazin, an urbane and aristocratic former World Bank official and finance minister. Bazin received only 14% of the vote.

4

THE LAVALAS ALLIANCE PROPELS ARISTIDE TO POWER

KIM IVES

E ssentially, the movement that formed around President Aristide's candidacy represented an alliance of Haiti's traditional merchant bourgeoisie with an array of grassroots worker, peasant and student organizations, commonly referred to as the popular movement.

Since 1986, the traditional bourgeoisie was represented politically by the "democratic sector," so called because of its focus on the mainstays of bourgeois democracy—a Constitution and elections—while eschewing revolutionary tactics, sharp confrontation with Duvalierist and U.S. power and radical economic change.[1] Democracy was, for the bourgeoisie, a means to overcome the Duvalierist grip on state power while channeling the revolutionary anger of the Haitian slumdwellers and peasantry. In this sense, the traditional bourgeoisie has been fighting a war on three fronts.

First, the traditional bourgeoisie sought to hold down and harness the popular uprisings of the Haitian masses who were

41

demanding radical economic and political change. Since 1986, the Haitian masses had generally followed this bourgeoisie's political lead—most notably in campaigns for the March 1987 Constitution, the November 1987 elections and the March 1990 appointment of President Ertha Pascal-Trouillot. But by late 1990, the Haitian people were looking for alternatives.

On the second front, the traditional bourgeoisie had a symbiotic rivalry for political power with the land-owning oligarchy, called *gwandon*, going back almost two centuries. The *gwandon* exploit their parceled land-holdings by means of sharecroppers with whom they have feudal relations of production, collecting rent in the form of crops. The traditional bourgeoisie would then sell that agricultural product on the world market. Historically, whoever controlled power in Port-au-Prince took the lion's share of the profit stolen from the Haitian peasant. Trying to protect the oldest and most entrenched semi-feudal economy in the Western hemisphere against the incursions of foreign capital, the Haitian oligarchy is arch-reactionary, opposed to all social, economic or political reforms, even those advanced by the United States. It is represented on the political spectrum by the Duvalierists—whose armed expression is the league of thugs called the Tontons Macoutes—and the "hard line" in the army.

Finally, the traditional bourgeoisie, which imports foreign manufactured goods and exports agricultural products, is also fighting for its economic survival against the onslaught of foreign capital, which seeks to "modernize" and "Puerto Ricanize" the Haitian economy by introducing direct foreign investment, thereby cutting out the middleman. Foreign capital, primarily North American, works with a rival sector of the Haitian bourgeoisie, called the "technocrats." This sector is essentially a managerial class tied to the assembly industries and agribusinesses. Its political orientation matches that of North American businessmen and the U.S. State Department. Their political *chef de fil* was Marc Bazin.

Haiti's political turmoil since 1986—which has involved eleven governments and three coups—is basically a map of the struggle between these four key sectors: the technocratic bourgeoisie, the traditional bourgeoisie, the feudal oligarchy and the popular movement.

In October 1990, as national presidential elections neared, the democratic sector faced a very grim political scenario. The oligarchy's candidate, Roger Lafontant, former head of the Tontons Macoutes, was rallying Duvalierists and holding mass demonstrations in downtown Port-au-Prince. The army refused to act on warrants for his arrest, and the Duvalierists were clamoring to be included in the 1990 elections, from which they were constitutionally barred.

The principal challenge to Lafontant was from former World Bank official Marc Bazin, whose rich, polished and oiled electoral machine—financed by the United States primarily through the National Endowment for Democracy (NED)—was picking up speed. Bazin was the favorite contender of the U.S. and multilateral lending agencies to loosen the grip of Haiti's Duvalierist landed oligarchy on state power and finances. The corruption, incompetence and backwardness of the Duvalierist bureaucrats hindered the investment of foreign multinational corporations in agribusiness, mining and light manufacturing. The U.S. Embassy had a dream ticket in a dream situation, in which Lafontant could be the "straw man" for Bazin to confront in the elections.

The democratic sector, meanwhile, was in disarray. Under the banner of the National Front for Change and Democracy (FNCD), it fielded a lackluster candidate, Professor Victor Benoît, in whom the masses were completely uninterested. Faced with flagging political fortunes, the traditional bourgeoisie turned to Father Jean-Bertrand Aristide, who was identified with the popular movement and symbolized the Haitian masses' aspirations. Up to that point Aristide had rejected the idea of elections—especially U.S.-sponsored elections—until there were structural reforms in Haitian society.

Aristide also had close contacts with the traditional bourgeoisie. A few rich Haitian merchants had underwritten his education and travels as a young priest, as well as his orphanage, Lafanmi Selavi. Entreated by the bourgeoisie to run and seeing that the result of a Bazin-Lafontant contest would be a U.S.-Duvalierist compromise similar to Jean-Claude Duvalier's regime, he took the gamble of entering the race. Benoît was unceremoniously dumped, and Aristide became the presidential candidate of the FNCD.

This combination of the people's candidate running under the bourgeoisie's banner unleashed the electoral outpouring that became known as *Lavalas*. The word means the "flood" and is a biblical image which had been evoked by popular organizations since 1986 to convey the purifying and sweeping nature of the popular uprising that would rid the country of the twin evils of Duvalierist terror and foreign domination.

The essence of Aristide's promise was democracy and nationalism. He was the living embodiment of anti-Duvalierism, having survived several assassination attempts from the Tontons Macoutes. He vowed to bring about land redistribution and an end to the Duvalierist favoritism, corruption and violence that had so traumatized the Haitian people since François "Papa Doc" Duvalier's rule began in 1957. In contrast, both the technocrats and the democratic sector had often proposed "reconciling" with the Duvalierists and reuniting the "Haitian family."

Aristide also embodied anti-imperialism. "We would rather die standing up, than live on our knees," he often repeated during his sermons as a fire-brand priest at Saint Jean Bosco Church in the Port-au-Prince slum of La Saline. He was a staunch opponent of the U.S. neoliberal prescriptions for Haiti, which sought to 1) privatize State-run enterprises like the telephone company, flour mill and cement factory, 2) reduce taxes, duties and wages to suit foreign investors, 3) cut social spending and ensure regular debt payments to foreign banks and 4) foster an export-oriented economy, thereby increasing Haiti's already great dependence on foreign food and capital.

Aristide's program called for supporting Haiti's faltering national industries, revitalizing Haitian agriculture and increasing self-sufficiency through land reform, stanching the hemorrhage of contraband imports through regional ports, raising the minimum wage and overhauling the government bureaucracy. Such a program was revolutionary in Haiti.

Aristide's entry into the presidential race only sixty days before the polling allowed him to outwit election strategists at the U.S. Embassy, who did not expect his candidacy. The result was perhaps the greatest malfunction of U.S. election engineering carried out since the early 1980s throughout Latin America. Despite the money Bazin distributed throughout the country in an attempt to buy votes and the $36 million spent on his campaign, thousands of Haitians poured into the streets during Aristide's gigantic campaign rallies chanting *"Li pa lajan, non, se volontè, wi"* (I'm not here for money, it's of my free will).

Aristide's electoral victory—with 67.5% of the vote—was one of the most joyous episodes in Haitian history. The popular will triumphed—momentarily—with little violence or repression. Aristide dubbed his inauguration "Haiti's Second Independence."

Aristide Electoral Poster on the Cross (Pleine-du-Nord). *Photo by Catherine Orenstein, 1993.*

5

ARISTIDE

Man of the People

J.P. SLAVIN

Nowhere was Aristide's popularity and skill as an orator more evident than when he opened the gates of the white-washed National Palace in Port-au-Prince for events that had the aura of a rock concert or a fundamentalist revival meeting.

One such occasion, a celebration marking International Women's Day on March 8, 1991, started hours before the president's mid-day speech. Thousands of peasant women wearing plastic sandals, baggy dresses and brightly colored headscarfs swarmed past the palace's iron gates to gather on the manicured lawn of the forbiddingly elegant presidential mansion, a relic of the nineteen-year-long U.S. occupation that many Haitians fear and despise as a symbol of the ruthless Duvalier dictatorships.

Jammed together on this lawn nearly the size of two football fields, the crowd sang songs and joked while they waited for Aristide, the first liberation theologian ever to lead a nation, to speak from the palace's front steps. Some carried signs saying "Aristide will not be toppled like Allende"; others used the occasion to roam the grounds selling cups of water and cheap imported trinkets.

As the afternoon heated up, hundreds pushed and shoved their way to the front and a sultry pandemonium ensued. The heat near the palace steps was suffocating; at least ten people passed out from exposure. Streams of letters to the president—filled with praise for Aristide and requests for jobs and medicine—were passed around and, when a mail sack was sent out, dozens lunged for it, a fight erupted and the bag was torn to bits.

When the president reached the microphone, the audience surged forward, nearly engulfing him. Despite three assassination attempts against him, including a 1988 machete and pistol attack on his Port-au-Prince parish that left thirteen dead, Aristide seemed unfazed by the surrounding chaos. He folded his hands, looked at the ground and silently gathered his thoughts.

The sleepy-eyed Aristide is a wisp of a man. He stands about 5'5" and weighs about 135 pounds. His forearms are so thin that during an interview in 1990, his watchband kept sliding off his wrist and would hang near the palm of his hand. In small groups, he speaks in a quiet, soft voice and appears unassuming but when he addresses an audience—from a pulpit or wearing the presidential sash—he becomes a very big man.

To calm the crowd that afternoon, a presidential aide began to sing the national anthem, something the Roman Catholic priest-turned-president had often done to end his fiery sermons. The throng, many of whom consider Aristide a prophet, joined in. At the anthem's conclusion, the crowd moved back and the president began to speak.

For twenty minutes, Aristide spoke with a calm elegance. Then he led the chants Haitians first heard at his church and later, after his 1988 expulsion from the Salesian Order for preaching political evangelism, on the radio where he continued to speak as Haiti's militant social conscience.

"Are some people still under the table?" he asked the crowd.

"Yes," they cheered.

"Are some people sitting at the table?"

"Yes!"

"Would you like all of us to sit at the table like brothers and sisters? Would you like to sit at the table? As days go by, we will succeed in sitting around the table."

Aristide concluded by chanting along with his audience: "Alone we are weak. Together we are strong. Together, together, we are *lavalas*." Lavalas, a Creole word, is the name of Aristide's political organization and is another metaphor: when heavy rains fall in the mountains, *lavalas* is the flow that becomes a river and washes filth into the sea, leaving the country clean.

6

HAITI'S "SECOND INDEPENDENCE"

Aristide's Seven Months in Office

GREG CHAMBERLAIN

Father Jean-Bertrand Aristide's election as president gave most Haitians a rare and exhilarating sense of participation in their savagely divided country's political life. It aroused great fear, however, among the hugely wealthy mulatto and Arab elite that Aristide had roundly denounced from the pulpit for so long. He would have to calm these fears to govern effectively.

A desperate and deeply religious people had elected Aristide more as a messiah than a democrat, in elections guaranteed by the international community. The required return on this U.S. and United Nations political investment was that Aristide work with the immature and dysfunctional Haitian political class he so despised. All the country's major institutions were ill-disposed toward him: the army, because they feared for the privileges and power they had built since the Duvalier family dictatorship collapsed in 1986; the Catholic Church, because Aristide had denounced its bishops as heartless enemies of the people; parliament, because of Aristide's fragile majority; and the traditional political parties, because he scorned their emptiness.

Despite soothing words, reconciliation did not seem to be Aristide's first concern on the day he was sworn in as president. He served a writ to outgoing President Ertha Pascal-Trouillot, dismissed six generals and gave their successors only provisional appointments, a source of great resentment. As he did this, Aristide talked, more in hope than conviction, of a "marriage between the army and the people." For the moment, he had the good luck to have the moderate General Hérard Abraham, who had yielded power to civilians a year earlier, at the head of the army.

Aristide's humorous and conversational inaugural speech in Creole alarmed the elite because it spoke to the poor. Even more shocking in the elite's eyes, scores of beggars and poor people were invited onto the palace lawns for a symbolic feast at which Aristide—priest-like—hugged and personally fed some of them. Hundreds of ordinary soldiers had an unprecedented day at the palace too. Later, women and Voodoo priests were given audiences. The Catholic Church called a truce and joined the political honeymoon.

Aristide named a cabinet composed more of personal friends than of political figures or technocrats, though he did appoint three women. For prime minister he chose the pliant figure of René Préval, to get around the inconvenience that the position constitutionally had more power than the president. Though he was aiming to change an entire system, a task which demanded an exceptional team, Aristide rose to the challenge with ministers of only average ability and experience. Furthermore, half of the twelve ministers, as well as several of his key advisors, were drawn from the bourgeoisie—Haiti's mulatto upper class. This disturbed some of his grassroots supporters.

In selecting his cabinet, Aristide passed over members of the traditional political parties. There was no place in the cabinet for the new National Front for Change and Democracy (FNCD), the party whose leader, Evans Paul, the recently elected mayor of the capital, had masterminded Aristide's election campaign. Nor did Aristide choose anyone from the social democratic Konakom or PANPRA parties, which had also backed him. "You cannot drink the soup of democracy with a fork of division," Aristide enigmatically admonished as he set up his own organization, Lavalas, to make more direct contact with the people. The seeds of resentment were thus sown among the traditional politicians. Several months later, private bitterness against Aristide among these groups had become alarming, though it was dressed up as exasperation with his sluggish administration.

Right at the start, Préval made a carefully phrased appeal to the rich to share their wealth or run the risk of social explosion. He set out government aims of mass literacy, reforms in health, agriculture, and justice, including probes into political violence, separation of the police from the army (as constitutionally required), decentralization, respect for private property and the obligatory fight against corruption.

Aristide himself began his term by warning against the traditional clean sweep of outgoing civil servants, land seizures and the "necklacing" (*Père Lebrun*) of Tontons Macoutes by supporters exasperated at a virtually non-existent system of formal justice. At regular intervals, he urged the rich to change their ways and mocked them as "pocketbook patriots." The people "may snore today, but they can snarl tomorrow," he warned.

Despite this, Aristide's relations with the elite were cautiously friendly, though its members defied orders to cut prices and were furious at proposals to almost double the minimum wage to $3.20 a day. The private sector wanted peace, preferably on its own terms, so that it could continue making money. One rich family even donated thousands of pots of paint for Aristide supporters to paint dazzling murals all over the capital to celebrate his inauguration as president.

Aristide had little interest in or knowledge of economics, but he no longer seemed to believe that capitalism was the "mortal sin" he had once dubbed it or that the United States was "the devil." One of his major successes was to persuade international lenders, already well-disposed toward him for wanting to create democracy and effective government, to pledge nearly $450 million in aid. By the time of the coup two months later, few concrete projects had been presented by the Haitians to enable the money to be released.

Ever the parish priest Aristide was also trying to raise millions in fund-raising marathons abroad. A bank for street traders was announced. Cheap rice was imported.

But Aristide did not manage to roll back hunger in the countryside, while thousands of jobs continued to drain away in the "offshore" assembly sector. A contract with a Canadian firm to end the serious electricity failures blocking economic revival was bungled, though supply later improved sharply. A $1 million check from Taiwan was made out to Aristide's orphanage instead of to the government. Canadian aid appeared to have been spent on the president's house.

Aristide's impulsive style of governing also caused problems. He often made snap decisions on the basis of advice from people other than his official advisors. Several ministers quit in frustration.

Aristide had little respect for a fractious parliament that tried to reduce his powers. The two chambers contained many incompetent, inexperienced and corrupt members. Nearly two-thirds of parliament had been elected in runoffs on a turnout of no more than 15% of voters, but the international community had recognized them as democratically chosen. Aristide ignored parliament's rejection of his summary appointment of a new chief justice, accusing legislators of sabotage, and snubbed them in other ways, though he later apologized.

Much of Aristide's time was taken up by the issue of some 50,000 Haitian immigrants forced out of the neighboring Dominican Republic after revived accusations of slavery in its sugar canefields. Some saw the expulsions as a plot to destabilize Aristide's government.

A ristide was infuriated by the past impunity enjoyed by killers and other criminals. "While we're waiting for bread in our bellies, we can share the bread of justice," he said, as numerous thugs were jailed and some tried. Anti-government plots were also unearthed and plotters arrested. Even ex-president Pascal-Trouillot spent a night in prison. When a crowd brandishing tires intimidated the judges at Lafontant's trial into passing an illegal life sentence, Aristide indicated his approval. Two weeks later, on

August 13, he pointedly failed to condemn a tire-waving mob that frightened parliament into adjourning a session called to censure Préval and later burned down an anti-government trade union headquarters and the offices of his old ally, the FNCD. Nevertheless, the thousands of tire necklacings claimed by his enemies to have taken place under his rule were a fiction. Only a few dozen occurred.

Aristide's two most urgent tasks were to stamp out urban gangsterism and to regain control of the countryside, which the feudal neo-Duvalierist sheriffs (*chefs de section*) had long held in their thrall. With the army's help, the streets of the capital were soon safe again at night. Shrinking before the numbers and confidence of Aristide's supporters, most *chefs de section* deferred to the new communal councils (CASEC).

An equally urgent task was to defang the armed forces by separating them from the police and creating a civilian-controlled constabulary. This was a tougher nut to crack. By June, the "marriage" vaunted by Aristide had already soured. Five youths were shot dead by police, and fingers pointed at police chief Colonel Pierre Chérubin. In July, after a scandal about the private sale of military equipment, army chief Abraham was sacked and replaced by Lieutenant General Raoul Cédras, who seemed a good choice as he had been in charge of the army's contribution to the successful elections seven months earlier. But still Aristide made an effort to reign in the army, meeting rank-and-file soldiers, quelling three revolts against unpopular commanders and naming retired officers to his government. He earmarked $6 million to improve soldiers' working conditions.

A bill to separate the police and the army was sent to parliament, but was not acted on. Aristide also wanted to trim the armed forces budget, a move that was naturally resisted. At the same time, the government was training—with the help of Swiss, American and French experts—a small personal guard of several dozen civilians to stand between Aristide and the army. Rumor transformed the new force into a thousands-strong new Tontons Macoutes militia that would replace the army itself. Also, one ambitious officer, Major Michel François, became convinced that Aristide wanted to destroy him one way or another. It was François who was to lead the coup against him.

At first, relations were warm with the U.S. Embassy and its ambassador, Alvin Adams, for whom the U.S.-sponsored free elections that produced the Aristide presidency were the pinnacle of his career (his previous post had been ambassador to tiny Djibouti). Later, Adams was less enthusiastic. After the coup—which the Americans must have seen coming and done nothing to stop—the Embassy distributed anti-Aristide documents produced by his enemies. But a CIA-sponsored coup, predictably a favorite explanation of many Haitians and foreign friends, makes no sense and only the shakiest evidence has so far been presented to support this theory. Aristide was not remotely a threat to U.S. interests in Haiti or elsewhere.

Aristide knew a coup was afoot two weeks before he was overthrown but could not stop it. When he returned from a triumphant appearance at the UN in New York, where he said democracy had "finally triumphed" in Haiti, he found his fate virtually sealed. Three days later, the bourgeoisie had reportedly slipped Michel François and his men a few thousand dollars, the deed was done and the people's hero was bundled out of the country.

The elite's fear of Aristide and his failure to eschew radical politics completely were largely responsible for his overthrow after only seven months in power. The elite had the money, the education, the foreign friends and the arms to defeat the new slave rebellion they feared Aristide might foment against the 200-year-old feudal system they administered. Aristide only had fair-weather foreign allies and the power of numbers. In the end, the low level of organization among the unlettered masses who supported democracy was no match for the elite's arsenal.

Aristide's record in office was a meager one. He achieved little because of inexperience, lack of resources, lack of time and the power of his enemies. But, for all his faults, he had cheered and begun to empower most Haitians and had made a brave start on reducing corruption, collecting more tax revenue, cleaning up state agencies and institutions, cutting prices, introducing democratic norms and creating international respect for Haiti. It would be enough for now, Aristide said, to move the country from "misery to a dignified poverty."

7

THE ELITE'S REVENGE

The Military Coup of 1991

J.P. SLAVIN

For many Haitians, the presidency of Father Jean-Bertrand Aristide marked a joyous new beginning, a "second independence." The first occurred on New Year's Day, 1804, when Haiti separated from France. The second ended on September 30, 1991, less than eight months after it began, when the country's traditional power brokers—the military and business elite—afraid that Haiti's first legitimately elected leader was beyond their control, moved quickly, efficiently and brutally to bring him down.

The day of the coup, the military moved to shut down private radio stations and take over broadcasts of the two state-owned stations. "For the first time, the military controlled information," said former planning minister Renaud Bernadin, now in hiding in Port-au-Prince. "All alternative sources of information were eliminated." Later, an army communiqué ordered the press not to report anything that "would incite the population."

The army was vicious in establishing control. "They attacked...for the purpose of terrorizing people," said Bernadin. "The people who suffered the most are from the areas where Aristide has his base of support." Gunmen riding in unmarked cars enforced a 6 p.m. to 6 a.m. curfew. Soldiers showed no mercy when firing into crowds. As many as 500 people may have been killed by the Haitian army in the first few weeks after the coup. The popular rebellion in defense of Aristide never got off the ground.

The first test of the breadth of Aristide's support had come in January 1991, a month before his inauguration, when Jean-Claude Duvalier's former Interior Minister Roger Lafontant, along with twenty-one accomplices, seized control of the National Palace and declared himself provisional president. In less than an hour, thousands of Aristide supporters, alerted by conch-shell horn blasts and the clanging of machetes on iron gates, streamed into the streets. They built barricades of flaming tires, engulfing Port-au-Prince in a thundercloud of black smoke. Scores of homes and offices of alleged coup sympathizers or suspected Aristide enemies were destroyed and more than 100 people were killed. When the smoke cleared, Lafontant was in handcuffs. His coup lasted only ten hours.

The violent reaction of Aristide's backers to the attempted takeover did not go unnoticed by the organizers of the September coup. Indeed, it aroused fears among Haiti's political, economic and military establishment that Aristide and his supporters would use any means necessary to advance his social agenda and safeguard his presidency.

Aristide's populist rhetoric and planned reforms further dismayed powerful sectors in Haitian society. "This is a political revolution, but it's not a social revolution," Aristide said in July 1990. "Now we are trying to achieve a social revolution. If we don't do that, the political revolution will not go anywhere."

Relying on his enormous popular support as protection from reprisals, Aristide attempted to ease the 7,000-member army out of politics. In his February 7 inaugural speech, the president retired six of the seven officers who made up the army's general staff. In their stead, he promoted officers who were viewed as either nonpolitical or pro-Aristide. On July 2, Aristide retired Haiti's top officer, General Hérard Abraham, replacing him with General

Raoul Cédras, the man who would later lead the successful coup
against him.

Realizing that his attempted reforms might prompt the military to try to assassinate him, Aristide created a small independent
guard, the Presidential Security Force (SSP), trained by advisors
from the United States, France and Switzerland. The exact size of
the SSP is unknown, but estimates range from 30 to 300. Furious
army officers likened the SSP to Duvalier's ferocious Tontons
Macoutes, an untrained private militia, which some have numbered at 300,000, that was loyal only to the president and effectively
blocked the army from the political arena. "We had a presidential
militia in 1957," said a Haitian colonel, referring to the Macoutes.
"It started with ten people. Then it became fifteen. Then it became
100, then 1,000, then 10,000, then 300,000... The army cannot tolerate something like that again."

Aristide also alienated members of Haiti's 108-seat parliament. Using the broad constitutional powers granted the president
to clean up government in the first six months of his term, Aristide
gave scant deference to the "advise and consent" role of the legislative branch. "The executive has shown no willingness to search
for a solution," said centrist parliamentarian Guy Bauduy before
the coup, commenting on Aristide's attitude toward the legislature.
"Relations are not as harmonious as they should be."

Bernadin argues that Aristide's fierce commitment to social
change led him to deliberately separate himself and the executive
branch from politicians in the legislature who had little popular
support. "Political parties here cannot be compared with political
parties in the United States," he said. "Every so-called professional
politician in Haiti creates a political party on paper, but has nothing
at the grassroots. These politicians make decisions without consult-
ing the people. They distribute jobs and money to their clients."

Aristide's decision not to appoint political party leaders as
cabinet ministers, Bernadin added, was a deliberate attempt to
"rupture" Haiti from its corrupt political class.

Not only did Aristide fail to cooperate with the legislature,
his critics accused him of condoning vigilante violence and *Père
Lebrun*, the Creole phrase for "necklacing," or killing someone by

placing a burning tire around the victim's head. They cite as evidence Aristide's September 27 speech in which he called on the poor to defend their rights, and referred to "a beautiful tool" they might use against the Duvalierists.

"Whenever you feel the heat of unemployment," Aristide said, "whenever the heat of the pavement gets to you, whenever you feel revolt inside you, turn your eyes in the direction of those with the means (money). Ask them why not. What are they waiting for? For the sea to dry up?"

The speech rattled the country's elite, stirring alarm that Aristide was leading the country to "a dictatorship of the proletariat," using presidential sermons to preach death to political enemies. Aristide used threatening language, Bernadin said, because he had learned of an imminent assassination plot against him and wanted to warn the conspirators that the general population would seek violent vengeance if his government was toppled. Other Aristide defenders claim that his words were misinterpreted, that he was speaking metaphorically. But even if he intended to advocate the use of *Père Lebrun*, they argue, his stance reflected his commitment to social justice, which he considered more important than any "law."

In the first week following the coup, it seemed that military intervention to restore Aristide to power was being considered. The Bush Administration rushed U.S. Marines to its Guantánamo naval base in Cuba. Secretary of State James Baker called the junta "illegal" and said the new regime was "without aid, without friends, and without a future." The Organization of American States (OAS) and the United States imposed sanctions and a trade embargo. But, as the days passed, direct intervention seemed less and less likely, derailed by a carefully orchestrated attempt to portray Aristide as a dictator in the making.

When a thirty-member OAS delegation arrived in Haiti on October 4, 1991 to negotiate the return of Aristide, the diplomats met only once with four Aristide cabinet ministers. The majority of the OAS meetings were held with Aristide's political enemies who complained pointedly about Aristide's human rights record. U.S. Ambassador Alvin Adams had given huddled with political opposition leaders before they made their presentation to the OAS delegation. Adams had given Aristide strong public support before the coup. While he was probably not involved in its planning, the career foreign service officer (who got his start as an area development officer for AID in Vietnam, 1968-1969) appeared to seize the diplomatic moment to try to rein Aristide in and turn him into a president "he could control," in the words of one Aristide supporter.

Aristide's ouster deflated Haiti. "With Aristide, we never felt hungry, even when we were starving," summed up one resident of a Port-au-Prince shantytown. "Now we feel hungry after we've eaten, because we've lost him."

"As a prophet, I wanted to be a sign in the eyes of Haitians," Aristide said before the coup. "Then I realized I had to follow them." Aristide paid a high price for trying to serve the will of his people.

Haitian immigrants living in New York protest U.S. policy toward Haiti. *Photo by Frederick Philipps, 1991.*

Part II

The United States' Haiti Policy

8

THE UNMAKING OF A PRESIDENT

KIM IVES

On the afternoon of October 2, 1991, two days after the September 30 *coup d'état* against Haitian President Jean-Bertrand Aristide, the Organization of American States (OAS) held an extraordinary emergency session at its headquarters in Washington, DC. The immense marble "Hall of the Americas," normally serene with its dignified flags and soaring pillars, was crammed with dignitaries, diplomats and journalists straining to see the podium where the ousted president and a long succession of Latin American ministers spoke. The air was electric with television lights, camera flashes and official outrage. The distinct strains of bull horns and choruses from the hundreds of Haitians demonstrating their support for President Aristide outside the building added to the excitement within.

A hush fell over the hall when it was addressed by U.S. Secretary of State James Baker. The slightest nuance in the U.S. position would be more weighty than the combined bombast of the OAS' other thirty-three member nations. "This junta is illegal," Baker solemnly declared. "Until President Aristide's government is restored, this junta will be treated as a pariah, without friends, without support and without a future. This coup must not and will not succeed." The hall responded with thunderous applause. "It is imperative," he went on, "that we agree for the sake of Haitian democracy, and the cause of democracy throughout the hemisphere, to act collectively to defend the legitimate government of President Aristide."

"We want to see President Aristide returned to power," President Bush echoed two days later after a twenty-minute discussion and a photo-op with Aristide at the White House. In those early hours of the coup, to the surprise of many, the U.S. government seemed to unequivocally champion the return to power of the anti-imperialist liberation theologian. The coup's days seemed numbered.

However, over the weekend of October 5-6, the focus of U.S. government reproach shifted 180 degrees from the *coup d'état* to President Aristide's human rights record. The slow strangulation of Haiti's first democratically elected president and his nationalist program had begun.

Most likely, Baker and Bush forcefully supported Aristide's return in that first week after the coup so as not to challenge the shock and indignation of Haitians and other Latin Americans against so brazen and illegal an ouster. But, in concert with the press, the U.S. government soon began tempering its call. "It is the rule of democracy that we support," White House press secretary Marlin Fitzwater announced on October 7. "We don't know [if Aristide will return to power] in the sense that the government in his country is changing and considering any number of different possibilities." Fitzwater stressed that during President Aristide's nearly eight months in office—from a triumphant inauguration on February 7, 1991 to the start of the coup on September 29—he had relied on "mob rule," a theme that was bleated in dutiful unison throughout the mainstream media. "Returning President Aristide to Haiti is going to be difficult for reasons to which he himself has greatly contributed," asserted an October 6 *Washington Post* editorial. "The president is a hero to the desperate people who live in the slums of Port-au-Prince.... He has organized them into an instrument of real terror.... He has left the country deeply polarized between his followers and the substantial numbers of people who have reason to fear them."[1]

The October 7 *New York Times* explained the dumbfounding rash of nationwide press reports attacking the beleaguered Haitian president: "American officials are beginning to quietly disclose a thick notebook detailing accounts of human rights abuses that took place during Father Aristide's rule" and that "jeopardized his moral authority and popularity." This "thick notebook" of abuses was compiled by Jean-Jacques Honorat, whose human rights outfit, CHADEL, was a recipient of National Endowment for Democracy (NED) funding to the tune of about $40,000 a year.[2] Within a week, Honorat was appointed by the military-controlled parliament to be the first post-coup prime minister.

Despite the State Department-driven media campaign targeting Aristide's human rights record—which, Aristide correctly asserted, contained not a single case of government-endorsed or government-encouraged vigilante violence—international support and Haitian community mobilization remained very strong. On October 2, OAS ministers met late into the night drafting and adopting a resolution to embargo and diplomatically isolate the renegade regime. On October 11, over 100,000 Haitians marched six miles from central Brooklyn to a rally in downtown Manhattan, all but shutting down the Wall Street area. The multitude then marched through rain another four miles uptown to the United Nations, where the 166 members of the General Assembly were unanimously voting for a resolution that bolstered the OAS embargo and branded as "illegal" the junta of coup leader Lieutenant General Raoul Cédras and his confederates. The document also dismissed as illegal any puppet government that the military might set up.

Not until November 5, almost a month later, did President Bush order U.S. compliance with the trade and oil embargo recommended by the UN and OAS resolutions. The embargo, however, was tough only on paper. The U.S. government never enforced it against the coup-makers. The restrictions were jauntily breached by exporters and importers not only from Europe, but from the

United States and Latin America as well. In Port-au-Prince, rich families who had helped finance the coup made fortunes selling goods at inflated cost in the pseudo-black market. Oil tankers from Europe soon replaced those from Venezuela and Mexico. The rocky dirt route from Jimani on the Dominican border to Port-au-Prince became so traveled by trucks carrying fuel, arms and other merchandise from the Dominican Republic that the coup-makers resurfaced it in smooth blacktop, making it far and away Haiti's best road.

As the months passed, the completely porous embargo became a symbol of the U.S. government's contempt for Aristide's return. But Aristide clung to the embargo, mainly because he was unprepared or unwilling to choose either of his other two alternatives: U.S. military intervention or popular revolution. After the coup, the mass movement behind President Aristide gradually split into two distinct currents adhering to Aristide's diametrically opposed choices. Aristide, perhaps unwillingly, chose the path of calling for military intervention.

By forging a coalition between the popular movement and the traditional bourgeoisie, Aristide soundly defeated the U.S.-backed candidate in the 1990 presidential elections. But, rather than judging his electoral victory as a fluke, Aristide tried to universalize the tactic into a political strategy of trying to beat the system at its own game. The question is whether or not the U.S. government lured Aristide into a new, hopelessly rigged game by letting him think he could win again. In the high-stakes match, Aristide saw his strength and resources whittled down by time and compromise. The essence of the U.S. strategy was to drive Aristide to surrender to Duvalierism and imperialism by striking a deal with the coup leaders and inviting foreign military intervention.

Aristide's circle of advisors and diplomats, particularly after the coup, were almost all drawn from the democratic sector of the traditional bourgeoisie. With time, Aristide even turned toward the more conservative and "pragmatic" of this group, who better understood and conformed to the U.S. optic. The traditional bourgeoisie, rather than calling on the Haitian masses to defend their nascent revolution after the coup, sought to compromise with the ruling powers in Haiti and the United States.

The democratic sector ridiculed the popular sector's revolutionary goals as utopian and unrealistic. Its representatives said a non-violent settlement could be negotiated using the influence of North American and European powers. Even though the United States had been wary of, if not obsessed with, Aristide the liberation theologian, the Lavalas bourgeoisie thought it could sell Aristide the statesman to the United States as the man who could make Haiti safe for investment. "The United States is best served by a democratic and stable Haiti which is able to pursue economic and social development for its entire population," said Haitian Foreign Minister Claudette Werleigh, then with the Washington Office on Haiti, before Congress in July 1993. "The Haitian people are aware of the great power of the United States in the world. We ask you to use that power to pressure for the restoration of our constitutional government."[3] Flowing from this logic, the recourse to foreign military intervention always lurked—unspoken and denied—just below the surface of the bourgeoisie's agenda.

From the very start of the coup, the U.S. press also raised the "option" of U.S. intervention. On October 3, the *New York Times'* Thomas Friedman complained that the OAS had not gone far enough in its October 2 emergency session. "The question of intervention has bedeviled and paralyzed the organization for the 40 years of its existence," Friedman wrote, apparently unaware of OAS participation in the 1965 invasion of the Dominican Republic and its acquiescence to numerous unilateral U.S. forays from the Bay of Pigs in 1962 to Grenada in 1983 to Panama in 1989. On October 6, the *Washington Post* opined that the only way to guarantee Aristide's "respect for human rights and for a kind of democracy that goes beyond mob rule" was to send "a peacekeeping force sponsored by the OAS" to provide "a lot of Haitians...assurance that Mr. Aristide is not going to turn his mob on them."

Meanwhile, the Bush Administration quickly sought to force Aristide to bargain with the coup leaders. Aristide initially refused to make any deals with Cédras, saying the general and other coup leaders had no alternative but to go into exile or face justice upon his return. Although on the defensive about his human rights record, Aristide remained confident in his ability to play the loopholes in the U.S. agenda, as he had with the 1990 elections. The key contradiction he perceived was that the United States had to support his return and oppose the coup or else give a green light to generals throughout Latin America to start a new era of *coup d'états* against civilian regimes that were still servicing U.S. interests. Underestimating the chasm between the U.S. government's official rhetoric and its true intent, Aristide took his first step down the slippery slope of negotiations.

On October 4-5, 1991, an OAS delegation was dispatched to Port-au-Prince, supposedly to convince Cédras that resistance was futile and to give up power. Instead, the U.S. Embassy set up a tribunal condemning Aristide. "The United States was ignoring supporters of the elected government," according to French Ambassador Raphael Dufour, who was barred from the OAS meetings by U.S. Ambassador Alvin Adams. The OAS delegation, said Dufour, only "met with a solid line of politicians and businessmen who have been opposed to Aristide.... I'm not certain the delegation got all the points of view and the view of the Haitian people. The Haitian people are dying under the bullets of the military. Those are the ones who haven't been heard from."[4]

The delegation returned to Washington on October 6 to chastise Aristide for his political behavior and to advise negotiations with Haitian parliamentarians. Aristide could have referred the delegation to the OAS resolution made in its own October 2 session, and to a similar resolution approved on October 11 by the UN, rejecting all dealings with confederates of the coup. But Aristide instead assumed a defensive posture, hoping to counteract the media message that he was a political bully.

The parliamentary delegation Aristide met with in Cartagena, Colombia in November 1991 was almost exclusively made up of coup supporters. Also in attendance, though uninvited, was U.S. Ambassador Adams. The parliamentarians were looking to buy time for the coup to consolidate its grip over a resentful and resistant population. They also hoped to negotiate a lifting of the embargo.

The parliamentarians, with U.S. support, presented an agreement to lift the embargo in exchange for more negotiations, but the document acknowledged neither Aristide's presidency nor mentioned his return to Haiti. Aristide had walked into a trap. He refused to sign the document and denounced the "bad faith" of the parliamentarians. They, in turn, along with Adams, branded him as "intransigent," a term that would become familiar to negotiation followers in the months ahead. After offering an olive branch, Aristide was now accused of blocking resolution of the crisis. He had given the pro-coup parliamentarians the moral legitimacy to continue their diplomatic sabotage when he might have been better off shunning them for their treason.

In November and December 1991, U.S. Ambassador Adams and OAS special envoy Augusto Ramirez Ocampo, a Colombian diplomat, increased their dealings with the pro-coup parliamentarians. However, once again, the concessions being formulated were to come from Aristide.

The office of prime minister became the key bargaining chip in the negotiations. It is Haiti's most powerful executive post under the 1987 Constitution, the president being only the formal head of state with the power to make appointments and nominations. Reeling under the U.S. media and government assault on his administration, Aristide almost immediately sacrificed his popular prime minister, René Préval. This was a giant and crippling concession.

After rejecting Aristide's proposals for compromise candidates, Adams and Ocampo gave Aristide an ultimatum to accept either Marc Bazin or Communist Party head René Théodore for prime minister, branding his reluctance to do so "intransigence." Citing anonymous "diplomats," the December 28 *New York Times* described what would happen if Aristide did not comply: "Failing an agreement,…new elections are likely to be held and eventually, the consensus around the hemispheric embargo imposed on Haiti for the last three months will dissipate." Already several tankers had docked in Haiti, giving the putschists ample reserves of oil.

"This is not diplomacy, but just strong-arm tactics," said Paul Dejean, a close Aristide advisor who heads a human rights group in Haiti. "It is the dictatorship of big powers which think they can impose any solution they want."[5]

On January 8, 1992, Aristide buckled under the pressure and nominated René Théodore for prime minister. Despite his communist credentials, Théodore had long since forsaken any revolutionary principles. Théodore had been a fierce opponent of Aristide and others in the popular sector both before and after the December 1990 election. The moderate Miami-based weekly *Haïti en Marche* described him as the "Théodore bomb," who was part of a "plan carefully conceived on the banks of the Potomac and at Langley."[6] In Théodore, the United States had the perfect combination of a nominal leftist and an Aristide opponent.

"The majority of the people do not want Théodore as prime minister, and their opinion is also mine," said Willy Romélus, the progressive archbishop of Jérémie, in a December 23 radio broadcast. Numerous statements emanating from the popular sector warned that Aristide was being outflanked and driven into unjustifiable compromises.

The apprehensions of the popular sector of the Lavalas movement were supported by the revelations of a document that was leaked in October at the U.S. Embassy by a Haitian security guard who was assassinated by soldiers at his home a few days later. The U.S. Embassy never protested the murder. The document was reportedly written by an anonymous counselor in the U.S. Embassy at the request of army chief Lieutenant General Raoul Cédras, Senate leader Dejean Bélizaire and Jean-Jacques Honorat, the first *de facto* prime minister after the coup. It outlined a strategy for undermining Aristide's reinstatement. "The United States would agree to recognize a new prime minister and unblock the Haitian government assets in the United States," the document said. "If Aristide comes back, it could not be earlier than a few months from now...and only so that he can be sent back, destitute, into exile shortly thereafter... The Prime Minister will become the real power in the government." The document also notes that "what is needed presently is a broad, sustained, and very discrete approach from the U.S. policymakers and the media which will counteract and nullify the propaganda of the Lavalas organization." Within a few months, the recommendations outlined in the secret document would become painfully obvious as the broad strategy of the Bush Administration.

Even though the United States tried to smoothly phase in Théodore as prime minister, unruliness from the Duvalierists threatened U.S. plans. On January 25, Duvalierist thugs attacked a meeting being held by Théodore, executing his bodyguard. The oligarchy did not want Aristide's return under any conditions, and Théodore's nomination seemed to be a step in that direction.

The attack almost scuttled the process. Adams was recalled to Washington and, once again, the United States began blustering. "Some type of military action might be necessary," warned Howard French in a January 29 article in the *New York Times*. French cited an anonymous U.S. diplomat who predicted that "ultimately the wrath of God will fall," referring to U.S. military action, which could range "from a special-forces type of operation aimed at quickly arresting several officers to a full-scale occupation of the country."

The toughness, however, remained talk. In deeds, the Bush Administration was largely lifting the three-month-old trade embargo against the *de facto* regime. The Treasury Department began to allow shipping by assembly industries with plants in Haiti. On February 4, State Department spokesperson Margaret Tutweiler tried to sell the measure as a "fine-tuning" of the embargo, arguing that "the sanctions on the assembly sector largely affect innocent Haitians only and have no serious impact on those behind the coup."

"The State Department's decision was prompted by complaints from American companies that relied on Haiti as a source of cheap labor to produce apparel and electronics items," explained the February 7 *Washington Post*. Foreign investors' associations like the Washington-based Caribbean Latin American Action (CLAA) and former Assistant Secretary of State Elliott Abrams lobbied hard behind the scenes. "The Defense Department,…convinced the exodus of boat people was largely economic, [was] quickly receptive to CLAA's arguments," the article reported. "The White House also was receptive, especially the office of Vice President Dan Quayle, who heads the Council on Competitiveness."

After Aristide's reluctant acceptance of Théodore for prime minister, the United States began pushing hard for a meeting in Washington. The result was the February 23 signing in Washington of the "Protocol of Accord," the first major agreement to emerge from negotiations on the future of Haiti. The document was greeted with satisfaction from the U.S. State Department, horror from the popular sector and contempt from the Duvalierists.

The key elements of the accord were: 1) an amnesty for the army and other authors of the coup; 2) respect of parliamentary legislation ratified after the coup, which included Cédras' appointment as head of the army through 1994; and 3) the lifting of the embargo "immediately after the ratification of the prime minister and the inauguration of the government of national consensus." Although it acknowledged Aristide's presidential title, the accord fixed no date for the return of President Aristide.

This ambiguity was, of course, the element on which coup partisans sought to play. Théodore had said in early February 1992 that he supported Aristide's "political return" to Haiti, but that his "physical return, that is something else." He projected it would be more than one year before Aristide could return to Haiti. Pro-coup Senator Serge Joseph affirmed that it "was not at all a question of President Aristide's return as some have said."[7] Even detached observers said that Aristide had given away a lot for nothing in return.

But within days, the Washington Protocol was defunct. President Aristide interpreted the accord differently than the U.S. State Department and even many of his own advisors. He asserted that there would be no amnesty for Cédras, since "common criminals" were excluded from the amnesty.

The U.S. government and mainstream press cried foul, saying that Aristide was backing out of the accord. In a New York-area radio broadcast on March 1, Aristide urged members of the Haitian community in the United States not to succumb to the "disinformation machine," which characterized him as reneging on the agreement, urging them to "maintain your mobilization and resistance, without which we could not apply pressure at all."

Meanwhile, in Haiti, the Duvalierists were taking no chances. In parliament, hard-line deputies and senators brandished revolvers and started fist fights during the sessions leading up to the final non-ratification of the Washington accord. Even parliamentarians who had signed the document disowned it, saying, like Senator Eddy Dupiton, that it was just a "proposal." In addition, the Duvalierist-recaptured Supreme Court ruled the agreement to be unconstitutional.

The Duvalierists, having effectively torpedoed the Washington Protocol, went on the offensive. They calculated, with good reason, that Washington was not really enthusiastic about Aristide's return and that they should offer an alternative. This was the origin of the "tripartite meeting" in late May and early June among *de facto* Prime Minister Jean-Jacques Honorat and President Joseph Nerette, pro-coup parliamentarians and the army. The result was the putschists' Villa d'Accueil accord, which called for "a government of consensus," a euphemism for a power-sharing arrangement between the Lavalas coalition and hard-line Duvalierists.

The person the putschists chose to head this remodeled civilian front government was someone they were sure the United States could not resist: Marc Bazin. Bazin was ratified as the new *de facto* prime minister on June 10. The putschists hoped that Bazin would be able to have the embargo lifted and encourage the United States to make Aristide strike a deal with the "government of consensus."

Bazin's ratification as prime minister marked the end of the first phase of the *coup d'état*. The dirty work of terror and consolidation had been completed. Now it was time to try to sell it to the international community.

Until this time, the conflict between the two currents in Lavalas—bourgeois and popular—remained mostly friction, the former calling for negotiations and the latter for mobilization. Aristide sought to balance the two strategies, saying, with some justice, that they were symbiotic. However, Aristide, surrounded mostly by advisors from the democratic sector, leaned more toward the bourgeoisie's scheme. He remained basically on the defensive, always trying to seem as reasonable and inoffensive to the U.S. government as possible. He thus sank ever deeper into a swamp of bargaining and concessions, leaving the people waiting for resolution from talks and never taking the offensive in the streets and mountains.

The logic of reconciliation led inevitably to direct negotiations between Aristide and Cédras. This is the path the bourgeoisie counseled and that the popular sector opposed. This was the beginning of the real division in Lavalas.

After the Villa d'Accueil accord, the Lavalas bourgeoisie formulated its riposte. Forty-five of the current's key representatives went to Miami for a meeting in June 1992. The Miami meeting responded to the Duvalierists' "government of consensus" with a "government of national concord." According to a document issued at the meeting's opening, Lavalas sought "to put in place a real government of concord...integrating the political parties, the diverse organized sectors of civil society and all the institutions likely to aid in the national renaissance." The group appointed a ten-member "Presidential Commission," a non-official negotiating body, headed by Father Antoine Adrien, which was to be set up in Haiti to search for avenues for negotiations and democratic openings.

The whole project was shrouded in ambiguity. The Lavalas "concord" seemed almost identical to the Duvalierists' "consensus," which democratic rhetoric did nothing to elucidate. The Presidential Commission had all the trappings of representing Aristide, yet it was distinct from the government *per se* and Aristide called it an independent initiative. All this double talk was simply meant to appease the popular organizations, which were alarmed that one of the principles of the December 16 coalition—"*makout pa ladann*" (Macoutes are disqualified)—was being betrayed. The popular sector—as well as Aristide up to that point—opposed direct negotiations with either Bazin or with Cédras, since this would confer legitimacy on them and constitute recognition of the coup. Any negotiations with the putschists, the popular sector argued, could only result in a power-sharing deal, and even that deal the coup-makers would double-cross.[8]

But direct negotiations with Bazin—and eventually Cédras—seemed to be exactly what the Lavalas bourgeoisie had in mind when it formed the Presidential Commission. When asked in July if he endorsed negotiations between Aristide and Cédras, Father Adrien responded: "Why not? Why not? We have seen more surprising things than that."[9] Thus, on September 1, 1992, a meeting was arranged between Adrien and Marc Bazin's "foreign minister" François Benoît at OAS headquarters in Washington, DC.

At the meeting, Father Adrien in essence asked for the *de facto* Bazin government to prove its good faith by putting an end to the fierce repression still raging in Haiti in order to open up a "democratic space." The overseers of this project would be a force of "international observers." The first incarnation of this effort was the OAS/DEMOC mission, which was to consist of hundreds of foreigners flooding the country to stay the hand of Macoute violence, according to the thinking in the bourgeois Lavalas circles. In the view of the popular organizations, the OAS/DEMOC observers could provide the excuse for foreign military intervention if any of them were attacked or killed. In any case, the deployment of the OAS observer force during the autumn of 1992 never exceeded more than twenty individuals, who essentially remained ensconced in the luxurious Hotel Montana in the cool heights of the wealthy Port-au-Prince suburb of Petionville.

The ineffectiveness of the OAS observers increased calls by the Lavalas bourgeoisie for a more forceful international role. Since the OAS has no enforcement arm, UN Ambassador Fritz Longchamps began pressing for direct intervention from the UN Security Council. "If the UN General Assembly judges that the violations of human rights are continuing despite the different initiatives of the UN and that the only way to guarantee and preserve these rights is a 'peace-keeping force,' it will consult the Haitian government...and it can then ask the Security Council to deploy this 'peace-keeping force' so as to stop [the putschists] from assassinating the Haitian people," Longchamps told a Haitian press conference in late November.[10]

The popular sector remained completely opposed to all forms of foreign military intervention into Haiti, whether under the banner of the UN or the United States. Furthermore, it was pointed out—primarily in the pages of *Haïti Progrès*—that the UN charter explicitly forbids the intervention of the Security Council in the internal affairs of member states.

As the observer mission and negotiations foundered in the autumn of 1992, Lavalas diplomats figured that the U.S. government's thinly cloaked subversion of Aristide's return was mainly Republican in nature and began to look for salvation in the election of Democrat Bill Clinton as president. Already the advisors constantly talking to Aristide included such Democratic Party heavyweights as Congressman Charles Rangel (D-NY), former El Salvador Ambassador Robert White and former Congressman Michael Barnes. Hundreds of Clinton/Gore campaign placards dotted the September 30, 1992 rallies of thousands of Haitians in New York and Miami.

At the time of Clinton's victory, the Democrats were aware that the Lavalas bourgeoisie expected a radical shift in U.S. Haiti policy. This, of course, was not the reality. Even before his inauguration, Clinton reneged on his campaign promise to undo what he called Bush's "immoral and illegal policy" of intercepting and repatriating Haitian refugees. In fact, Clinton strengthened the naval blockade against the small wooden sailboats fleeing Haiti's terror, in violation of peace-time international law.

While the Bush Administration did its best to undermine all progress toward Aristide's return, the Clinton team—in particular, new Secretary of State Warren Christopher—began cautiously working toward Aristide's return under the control of UN monitors and "peace-keeping" forces. Aristide, for his part, made the long-demanded promise of amnesty more explicit than ever, saying at a White House meeting with Clinton in March 1993 that "the departure of the authors of the *coup d'état* does not necessarily mean they would have to be in jail or have to leave the country." Clinton approved the statement, saying "that sort of attitude on the part of

President Aristide is the very thing that should enable us to resolve this in a peaceful way."

The beginning of the process was the deployment in March of a 250-member UN Civilian Mission to monitor and record human rights violations. Many popular organizations complained that the presence of the mission provoked more violence from the army. "Now instead of beating us during the day, they come and beat us even more savagely at night," a young militant from the Peasant Movement of Papaye (MPP) in Hinche explained in June 1993. "People who had returned to test the mission's effect have had to flee the area once again."[11]

On April 23, President Clinton announced a plan to send a "multinational police force" of 500-600 officers to Haiti to "professionalize" the Haitian army. This was the first concrete official proposal by the U.S. government for foreign military deployment in Haiti. In the face of the plan, Aristide remained enigmatic. This caused an outcry from the popular sector.

On May 17, a coalition of all the major popular organizations sent Aristide an open letter that put him on the spot. "You gave the OAS and UN authorization to send 'civilian observers' into the country, and even though it was strong medicine and a hard blow, we never officially protested because we always believed that you knew what you were doing and that there was a line you would not cross," the letter said. But, since the proposal "to send a military police force to occupy the country," it continued, "we cannot understand your silence and the silence of your government in this affair... We hope that you will immediately take an official public position that is crystal clear in denouncing and condemning this plan."

But the popular sector's warnings went unheeded, especially after the *de facto* government of Marc Bazin collapsed on June 8, 1993. Whether or not Bazin's resignation was orchestrated from Washington is still not known, but its effect was to lead Aristide and the Lavalas bourgeoisie to jump into the "void" supposedly created. The U.S. government pointed to the naked rule of the military in Haiti and, along with Haitian Ambassadors Long-champs and Jean Casimir, pushed the matter before the Security Council. On June 16, 1993, the body approved Resolution 841, which called for a mandatory global embargo on oil and arms supplies to Haiti to take effect June 23.

The day after the vote, President Clinton said in a press conference that he thought the sanctions would not be sufficient and that the only solution to the problem in Haiti was some kind of multinational peace-keeping force. The Security Council's sei-zure of the case of Haiti was the first time since the Korean War that the body had openly intervened in the internal affairs of a country since scenarios like El Salvador, Cambodia, Angola, Na-mibia and Bosnia were justified as "regional conflicts." The acting Security Council President had to emphasize the "exceptional" nature of the measures on Haiti. Cuba wrote a letter "opposing with the greatest energy the Security Council's adoption of meas-ures concerning the internal situation" in Haiti because it would create "a dangerous precedent...to give this body powers and a mandate which are larger than those granted in the Charter."

On June 23, Ambassador-at-Large Ben Dupuy, the govern-ment diplomat most identified with the popular sector, resigned from the government with a letter to Aristide that stated, "Without pretending to be more patriotic than anyone else, I think that it is extremely dangerous to put the national sovereignty of the country in the hands of an international organization whose real defense of the peoples' rights, and even its impartiality, can legitimately be put in doubt at this time."

In essence, this was the concern of the popular movement as a whole. The popular sector saw the gift of the Security Council's embargo as a trap for Aristide. "By requesting the Security Council to take up the case of Haiti, Aristide has surrendered his leadership and control over efforts for his own restoration to an international body controlled by the very nation which had a hand in the coup which overthrew him," the New York-based Haiti Commission of Inquiry into the September 30th Coup d'Etat observed in a June 26 statement. "Having usurped control of the crisis in Haiti, the UN and the United States have begun forcing Aristide into a corner....

The UN is trying to validate Cédras as a negotiating partner and force Aristide to bargain with him."

The UN now did bring the "two parties" of the Haitian conflict to the bargaining table. Having previously been branded an outlaw by the UN and OAS, Cédras was all too happy to be legitimized by negotiations. As for Aristide, he was now in so deep with the UN that he did not want to hesitate. "Haiti appeared like a country without a government, without a prime minister [after Bazin's resignation], without a president," said Chavannes Jean-Baptiste, the head of MPP and a member of the Presidential Commission, explaining why Aristide accepted the UN invitation. "Thus, you who are the constitutional government, [the UN] writes you to say 'Come, we are going to turn power over to you.' If you don't come, it's as if you refuse the power."[12]

The new round of negotiations began June 27, 1993 on Governors Island, in New York Bay, to avoid the massive demonstrations of Haitians outside UN headquarters in Manhattan. The two delegations occupied separate buildings, 100 yards apart, with Argentine diplomat Dante Caputo, the UN special envoy who took over from OAS special envoy Augusto Ocampo, shuttling between them.

The ensuing document—the "Governors Island Accord"—was "the direct result of consistent pressure and threats on President Aristide," according to a point-by-point analysis of the accord by the Haiti Reborn project of the Quixote Center. "There were never any real negotiations, but just the imposition of a plan designed by the international community."[13]

The essential sequence of this ten-point accord was that Aristide would name a new prime minister, the UN would lift sanctions, the parliament would undertake a series of reforms of the police and Armed Forces under the supervision of a UN force, Aristide would decree a blanket amnesty for those involved in the coup and then Cédras would voluntarily retire at some point before Aristide's return, which was set for October 30, 1993.

"The plan had been conceived with no input from the legitimate government and was shared with the press before reaching negotiators," Haiti Reborn explained. Caputo "threatened to have

UN sanctions lifted immediately if Aristide did not comply with the plan as proposed."[14]

Caputo called the accord "a model for the future," and President Clinton hailed it as "an historic step forward for democracy."[15] Still, Aristide withheld his signature for almost a full day, which sent UN and U.S. diplomats into a frenzy. One U.S. official called Aristide "a deal breaker."[16] "Don't think, Mr. President," counseled UN Secretary General Boutros Boutros-Ghali in one of the many pressuring phone calls Aristide received that day. "Just sign it."[17]

Even Aristide's own advisors, such as former ambassador Robert White pressured him. "It was more important [for Aristide]," said White afterwards, "to get back" in four months than to worry about what was essentially "a minor problem."[18]

The "minor problem" was that, in addition to many other concessions to the putschists, Aristide agreed to lift the embargo and name his prime minister before the departure of Cédras and his own return, leaving the putschists fully capable of sinking the process whenever they saw fit. The result was that Cédras was legitimized and Aristide's own return was rendered improbable. This was clear enough to the Duvalierists. When Cédras and his delegation returned to Haiti on July 3, he received a hero's welcome at the airport from cheering crowds of soldiers and coup supporters.

"This is not an accord between the military delegation and the constitutional government," said Chavannes Jean-Baptiste, who was part of the government's delegation at Governors Island. "This is an accord between the UN, the OAS, and the 'friends of the Secretary General,'" as the United States, France, Canada and Venezuela came to be dubbed during the Governors Island talks.[19] Although the Aristide delegation had stayed up all night on July 2 composing a counter proposal to what Caputo offered, they were given an "ultimatum" the next day to "take it or leave it," according to Jean-Baptiste.

The bourgeoisie, counting on U.S. good will and support, expressed guarded satisfaction with the accord. "The accord contains the elements of democracy, the return of the truly elected president of the Republic and the relinquishing of their command posts by the leaders of the coup," declared Ambassador Casimir.[20]

But an open letter to President Aristide from ten of the most established popular organizations called the accord "an affront to the heroic struggle of the Haitian people," noting in particular "points 5 and 10 of the accord which accept the entry of foreign troops into the country and give to the United Nations the right to control the governing of the country."[21]

In fact, the deployment of over 1,200 UN troops, including about 700 from the United States, was one of the State Department's key concerns in drawing up the accord. The soldiers were to be under UN Security Council command, not that of the legitimate government. In official statements the troops were referred to either as "instructors" to "professionalize" the Haitian Armed Forces or "technicians" to help "rebuild the country" by bringing their technical expertise to bear on problems such as road construction and reform of the justice system. The UN force, initially deployed for six months, was not restricted in how large it could grow or how long it could stay.

Aristide also went to great lengths to show the United States and Haiti's technocrats that upon his return he would be open to neoliberal economic policies. In July, his government hosted in Miami a "Haiti Government/Business Partnership Conference" in Miami, with the support of organizations such as CLAA, which had so vigorously fought the embargo. The meeting was well-attended by both the merchant and technocratic sections of Haiti's bourgeoisie. Many of the 200 businesspeople in attendance had helped finance the 1991 coup and break the ensuing embargo. The World Bank, International Monetary Fund, U.S. Agency for International Development (AID) and UN Development Project guided most on the conference with presentations on their plans to revive the Haitian economy and on the errors that Aristide had made in his first seven months as president. AID's $36.5 million "emergency recovery" package, which would largely go to repay bank debts run up during the coup, was the centerpiece of discussion.

Shortly after the conference, Aristide nominated U.S.-leaning Robert Malval as prime minister. Malval was a hybrid between the traditional bourgeoisie and the technocrats, a wealthy printer who was well-connected with the bourgeoisie, the oligarchy and the army. Malval was ratified in a ceremony at the Haitian Embassy in Washington, D.C. on August 30 and installed in Port-au-Prince on September 2. His cabinet reflected an opening toward the neoliberal technocratic sector.

All of Aristide's political retreats and make-overs had been for naught. He was still not trusted. The project derailed on October 11, when a U.S. troop carrier, the USS *Harlan County*, carrying the first major deployment of 200 American and Canadian soldiers, turned back from landing when about 100 armed anti-Aristide thugs affiliated with the Haitian military—called *"attachés"*—demonstrated at the port and threatened foreign diplomats.

The event opened a breach. Conservative sectors in the U.S. government, particularly from the Pentagon and CIA, completely distrusted Aristide and were opposed to the venture of controlling him and the mass movement he represented. Furthermore, if there were to be a U.S. military intervention, the conservatives favored the use of "overpowering force," as in Iraq, rather than piecemeal deployments disguised behind the fig leaf of UN command. After the devastating attack on U.S. troops in Somalia in early October, there was a backlash in U.S. public opinion against intervention overseas. The Pentagon and CIA used this backlash to try to scuttle the project of returning Aristide.

Many believe that this "hard-line" sector was behind the coup against Aristide in the first place. Some U.S. military generals were asked to put pressure on the junta to respect the Governors Island Accord, but in fact they gave reassurance. "An embassy official in Port-au-Prince has described his shock at seeing Marine Major General John Sheehan 'yucking it up' with Lieutenant General Cédras at a reception in September," columnist Christopher Hitchens wrote in the November 3 *Nation*. "'One shot and we're out of there,' a Pentagon spokesman helpfully said of the mission of the good ship *Harlan County*, almost advising the Haitian military of the paltry risk it would run in breaching the Governors Island accord."

There is other evidence that the Pentagon and CIA encouraged the *attachés* to rampage in order to justify the *Harlan County's* pull-out. *New York Daily News* columnist Juan Gonzalez was told of the October 11 port demonstration the day before at a Duvalierist meeting at which U.S. Embassy personnel were present. "How can two *Daily News* reporters who have only visited Haiti on a few occasions learn beforehand of secret plans to sabotage the landing of our troops, while our vaunted officialdom claims it was caught flat-footed?" Gonzalez asked on October 12. "In the weeks to come, we may find out who knew what, and when."[22]

The Clinton-Christopher policy to reconcile Aristide with the Haitian *de facto* military power was foiled by the U.S. *de facto* military power. "A member of President Aristide's entourage put it to me bitterly," Hitchens reported. "'All the world knows there has been a military coup in Haiti. But who would believe there has been a silent coup in the United States? This is the Bush Administration policy, determined by the military.'"

After the October 11 demonstration and the assassination of Justice Minister Guy Malary on October 14, Aristide's chances of returning on October 30, which had been slim to begin with, evaporated altogether. As Duvalierist violence grew in Haiti, right-wing campaigns in the United States—spearheaded by Senators Robert Dole, Sam Nunn and Jesse Helms—smeared Aristide's psychological health, human rights record and political affiliations. "The return of Aristide to Haiti is not worth even one American life," Dole said on October 24. Meanwhile, Clinton reimposed the trade embargo, this time backing it up with a naval blockade.

By early December 1993, the Lavalas bourgeoisie's strategy of selling Aristide to the United States seemed to have failed miserably. Not only was Aristide unable to return to Haiti on October 30, but the ministers of his entire government, including Prime Minister Malval, were unable to perform their duties or even occupy their offices. Headlines announced what the UN had decided to do about Haiti, while Aristide's calls were relegated to the footnotes.

Meanwhile, Aristide, in siding with the bourgeois sector, lost his political prestige in the popular sector. "Mr. President," Haiti's principal popular organizations wrote on July 9, after Governors Island, "today history places us, the popular organizations, at a crossroads where, with or without you, we are going to continue to struggle for the liberation of the country."

On November 9, Aristide seemed to have finally cast aside all pretense of pursuing the option he favored. When asked by a French journalist if he was ready to call openly for foreign military intervention, he responded: "I am sure that the Haitian people would be happy to be rid of the criminals, but if I ask for an intervention, I will be condemned by my Constitution."[23]

Since Aristide's return via U.S. or UN efforts seemed postponed, if not canceled, so did the military intervention that was needed to restrain the post-coup popular drive for justice. Should popular insurrection or guerrilla war break out and threaten the Duvalierists' grip on power, U.S. or UN intervention would be quickly mounted. For the time being, however, Warren Christopher said that the re-establishment of democracy in Haiti was not on the U.S. government's list of priorities.[24]

The coup of September 30, 1991, like all decisive historical moments, provides a litmus test of its actors' convictions. It revealed the true cynicism of the U.S. government and the U.S.-trained Haitian military, as well as the tragic ambivalence of Aristide. In the face of a bloody, unjustifiable coup, Aristide could have rallied the masses to rise up and organize outside of the legalistic confines imposed by the bourgeoisie. For the people of Haiti, and the people of the world, the lines demarcating democracy from dictatorship had never been so clearly drawn and the recourse to self-defense so justified.

But the Lavalas bourgeoisie convinced Aristide that strength lay in the halls of Washington rather than the mountains of Haiti. In two years of negotiations, the putschists gave nothing of their usurped power and the legitimate government traded away almost everything. "Meanwhile, Aristide, by sticking with these negotiations, has neutralized the only real weapon he has: the man in the street," a bitter Aristide supporter told the *New York Times.*[25]

These setbacks for the bourgeoisie's strategy should not be understood as a defeat for the people's movement overall, however. The tenacity and patience of the Haitian people have deep roots. In 1802, Toussaint Louverture, the leader of the successful 1801 revolution to abolish slavery in the French colony of Saint Domingue, was captured by French officers when he agreed to negotiate peace at Habitation Bréda. But the slaves of the colony, having tasted a year of freedom, rose up in fury at Napoleon's attempt to re-establish slavery. Within two years, the former slave armies had driven the French from the colony, proclaiming independence for the nation of Haiti in 1804.

Today, this past and Haiti's future lie within the Haitian people and their popular organizations, which have learned from the experiences of Habitation Bréda and of Cartagena, Washington and Governors Island. The popular organizations place their faith in the people who made Lavalas possible and continue to defend the movement's original ideals of national independence and democratic rebirth.

9

WHAT DO HAITIANS WANT FROM THE UNITED STATES?

CATHERINE ORENSTEIN

The infamous "Harlan County incident" was symbolic of the failure of the United States and the international community to live up to their formal commitments to create conditions necessary to ensure Aristide's return and the restoration of democracy in Haiti. The coup leaders' non-compliance with the Governors Island Accord on October 30, 1993—the scheduled date of Aristide's arrival—was somewhat of an anticlimax. This piece explores the question of foreign intervention in Haiti at that point in time. It depicts the range of attitudes among Haitians concerning the role of the international community in the aftermath of the ill-fated accord.

On October 11, 1993, the United States carrier ship USS *Harlan County* arrived in the bay of Port-au-Prince with a cargo of 200 "combat engineers and military trainers." But after a day-long standoff at the docks with a small gang of military *attachés* who brandished clubs and guns, and screamed "No U.S. intervention!" the troop carrier beat an ignominious retreat. Perhaps the course of events should have been foreseen, given the inconsistency of the troops' mission—to "restore democracy"—and their instructions to "run the other way" if they encountered any opposition. With the departure of the USS *Harlan County* and the pull-out of the UN observer mission shortly thereafter, the United States called on the remaining thousand or so Americans still in Haiti to register with the U.S. Embassy in the event of an emergency evacuation.

This sequence of events provided a unique opportunity to observe different Haitians' views of the role the international community and the United States should play in their country. From the wharves, through the sea-side slums, up the road past the *attachés'* hangout, *La Normandie*, up past the army headquarters, up past the mounds of trash into the wealthy hills of Pétionville, and over the seas to the suites of Washington, Haitians of every status were calculating the meaning of the most recent international maneuver. Some were gratified to see the ships and planes filled with foreigners depart. Some were wary of what might replace them. Others saw their last hopes retreating on the horizon.

On the docks, the rabble-rousers celebrated their victory, howling with glee at the boat's departure. The sight was sweetened by the memory of 1915, when U.S. ships had last come to Haiti and stayed for nineteen years. Waving a gun in the air with one hand and a bottle in the other, the *attachés* pounded on the car of a journalist not wise enough to stay away: *"Blan! Blan alé!"*—Whites! Whites go away! Most *attachés* were members of right-wing political organizations that had recently sprung up and proponents of extreme nationalism.

One group, the Front for the Advancement and Progress of Haiti, not only could turn the *Harlan County* around, but had effectively taken *de facto* control of the streets. The group's acronym, FRAPH, sounds like "strike" in French and its hand signal—fist clapped in fist over the head—is Nazi-esque. When joining, a member was given an identity card and the option to buy a gun. Although there was no formal link, FRAPH was said to work in close cooperation with, or as a front for, the army. Members of

FRAPH sometimes held rallies outside the Palace of Justice, near *La Normandie*, where they marched, waving the Haitian blue and red flag, the revived black and red flag of Duvalier and the U.S. stars and stripes. At one rally in November 1993 a group of men clustered around me, chanting, "America, yes! Intervention, no!" One of them, wearing dark glasses and a baseball cap, sported a rifle over his shoulder and two hand grenades on his belt. "Pssst, *blan!* Pssst," he said, juggling his hand grenades for me. "If Aristide returns, I will eat him—*eat* him!" he growled. "Americans, yes! Intervention, no!"

At his home, FRAPH's Secretary General Emmanuel "Toto" Constant sat on a balcony overlooking an empty pool, the butt of a guard's gun visible over the wall. "President Aristide is welcome back in my country," he said. "As a *citizen*. He cannot be president because, you know, he is unstable, as a CIA file has said." Earlier that week, at a press conference, Constant proclaimed, "Governors Island is dead... The international community must lift the embargo, because it is unimaginable and criminal to keep six million people hostage for one person...and we must have new elections according to Article 149 of the Constitution." Constant would have liked to see UN envoy Dante Caputo replaced by a U.S. mediator—"maybe Colin Powell." FRAPH's affinity for the United States indicated something about U.S. policy with Haiti—they knew what was in their own interest.

The popular movement leaders would also have been glad to see the USS *Harlan County* sail away with its anchor between its legs, so to speak, but for the fact that many of them were hiding out in the United States. The popular movement, which also has strong nationalist roots, opposed any form of foreign intervention, whether it was military troops or UN observers. It saw the solution to Haiti's crisis as a radical democratic change that must come from *within*.

Within the Lavalas coalition that brought Aristide to power, the popular movement was at odds with the more liberal bourgeois sector on the issue of international intervention, both diplomatic and military. The bourgeois sector saw the international community as a medium for resolving Haiti's crisis, reconciliation as necessary and intervention as a possibility. "Everyone who knows Aristide is absolutely amazed at the maturation that has occurred in the past two years," said Father Antoine Adrien, a close presidential advisor from the bourgeois sector. "His capacity for compromise has greatly expanded. He understands, in the transition from priest to president, it takes more patience, more willingness to compromise."[1] Adrien—like others in the reformist camp—was also less adamant on the issue of intervention. When the USS *Harlan County* turned around and sailed off last month, Adrien said, "the U.S. troops aboard...should have been ordered to land. Nothing would have happened because the vast majority of Haitians would have welcomed them."[2]

The majority of Haitians—the peasants who make up 90% of the population—had been excluded from diplomatic dialogue since the coup and cut off even from Aristide, who spoke only infrequently over the radio. But the hammer of diplomatic decisions hit them the hardest. In Cité Soleil, the poorest of the sprawling slums of Port-au-Prince, the empty streets offered up a daily quota of bloody bodies left for days as a warning of the penalty for hope. On November 4, the silence belied the continuing intensity of oppression, even as media attention dwindled. A group of boys played soccer in the empty street with deflated rubber balls.

"We know America is not afraid of the Haitian army. They could come in and shoot those guys," said Li-bon, whose name means "he's good" in Haitian Creole. He showed me his back, which was bruised. "When the military *attachés* came through the streets, they were looking for someone, a Lavalas man, but then they found me instead. So they beat me"—he demonstrated—"beat me. We hoped the Americans would come. They will get rid of the *attachés*. Everyone will be happy when they come."

"What about 1915?" I asked. "What about independence?"

"We are not independent," Li-bon said. "We cannot work, we cannot speak, we cannot live. We are in a moral prison. *Nou pa independan.*"

Farther on in Cité Carton, so named because the huts are constructed from cardboard and old U.S. Agency for International Development food cartons, Dieudonné sat on the ground with the metal bowls he makes. "I am for the embargo, because we have to get Aristide back," he said. "But the U.S. made a lot of promises, and where are they now? I believed them, and all I got was beatings. We are dying alone in the streets."

As I walked back, a woman I didn't know offered me her baby. "Would you take her to America with you? ... I had four babies, but two are dead already."

"What next?" I asked Li-bon. He said, "October 30 was only one date. We are in the middle of a long struggle."

How Haitians saw the role of the international community in the Haitian struggle was determined by what they perceived to be its goal. Some asked for peace, others demanded power, and some called for democracy. The military junta and its Duvalierist allies sought to maintain and consolidate their control, seeing in the United States an ally to prevent Aristide's return. For the popular movement, the "solution" was radical democratic change—a social revolution with no room for compromise with the "U.S. imperialists or Macoutes." The bourgeois sector of Lavalas, on the other hand, saw diplomatic dialogue, reconciliation and integration of the opposition as the primary components of a new democracy. Meanwhile, among the poor masses who didn't have the luxury of idealism, many hoped for peace at almost any cost.

1 0

AN INTERVIEW WITH
BEN DUPUY

CATHERINE ORENSTEIN

Ben Dupuy is one of Haiti's foremost radical journalists. In 1984 he founded the Committee Against Repression in Haiti. From 1983 until 1991, he was the director of Haiti's leading opposition newspaper, Haïti Progrès. By the late 1980s, Haïti Progrès had become the voice of Lavalas, the political movement that swept Jean-Bertrand Aristide to power in the December 16, 1990 elections. When Aristide took office in February 1991, Dupuy was named ambassador at large. After the coup, Dupuy remained ambassador at large for Aristide's government in exile until his resignation after the Governors Island Accord. He was interviewed in his Brooklyn, New York office in June 1993 by NACLA staff member Catherine Orenstein.

What is the background of the post-coup political situation in Haiti?

There are several classes struggling in Haiti. The old elite, or so-called oligarchy, has its base in the agricultural structure of the country, which is semi-feudal. Haiti has always been presented as a country of small property holders, but, in fact, the oligarchy is composed of large landowners. What created this myth of Haiti being a country of small peasant landowners is the very feudal type of social relations, where the large land holdings are divided into small plots and the peasant works those plots for the landowner.

Historically, the elite was composed of two sectors. On the one hand, there were the landlords, who in Haiti are called *gwandon*. At the same time, we had a bourgeois sector. It was not a capitalist sector *per se;* it was more merchant capitalism. This sector would export agricultural products and import manufactured goods. Historically, these two sectors of the elite have been fighting for political control. The very tumultuous history of the country is a result of that struggle *within* the elite.

But things have changed in recent years.

The focus is no longer on the simple securing of raw materials. Capital's need to compete in the world market, and the fact that the cost of labor in developed countries had increased in spite of high technology, led to the creation of a new form of industry—assembly industry—in which foreign capital could be imported into countries like Haiti at much less risk. Before, when there was a capitalist venture, the possibility of it being nationalized existed, such as the sugar industry in Cuba. But the new assembly industry receives its material from the outside and the market is also outside. So what is isolated is the domestic labor force. This type of industry is *outside* the economic structure of the country.

The one handicap was the need for infrastructure. These countries lacked sufficient electricity, ports, roads, etc. And that is where the international institutions and the private banks took a role in lending to those governments. This was the beginning of our debt crisis.

Did this affect the power base of the merchant class in Haiti?

Yes. This created a division within the merchant class. Certain merchants became involved in the assembly industry. Another part remained in traditional commerce. Because of this development, some in the elite felt the need for a new political structure. Power had always been monopolized by the oligarchy who were very backward. They didn't even conceive of modern management and were more concerned about living a sumptuous life and using political power to exploit and to enrich themselves. This was not compatible with the developing assembly industry.

The international investors and the assembly entrepreneurs began to realize that Haiti needed elections, democracy. So it was necessary to remove political power from the traditional oligarchy. There were two objectives: on the one hand, to diffuse the possibility of a mass movement that could wind up in a radical revolution; and, on the other, to create a political structure more in tune with these new types of investment and development.

How was this agenda pursued and to what effect?

The struggle to destroy the oligarchy was not only a political power struggle to modernize the state, but also a struggle to destroy the oligarchy's economic base. It coincided with the food aid program, which created a situation in which the country became more and more dependent on the outside world. Dumping surplus food on the Haitian market was a sure way to destroy the economic base of both the agricultural oligarchy and the traditional merchant class, those who had not invested in the new assembly industries.

Aristide was the first presidential candidate who came not from the powerful, but from the people. What were the political alliances behind the elections? Who supported Aristide, and who opposed him?

Well, in the arena you had the United States trying to change the political structure and fighting the oligarchy, but, at the same time, allying with the same oligarchy in order to oppose the masses, the people. It was a tricky situation, where, on the one hand, the United States and the international institutions wanted to change and mobilize the society and, on the other hand, there was the risk that the people might have their own agenda, at odds with U.S. policy.

The people's agenda is rooted in a nationalist ideology, which espouses safeguarding the country's independence from its economic partners by promoting self-sufficiency in agriculture. The

Lavalas movement that brought Aristide to the presidency is an alliance of the masses—the peasantry—and the traditional merchant bourgeoisie, which was on the verge of bankruptcy. This alliance defeated the oligarchy, the assembly entrepreneurs and the U.S. agenda.

Lavalas overcame the type of electoral process where money is the determining factor. In most Latin American countries, the candidate who can sell himself, just like any merchandise or product, wins the election. It didn't work that way in Haiti. That's why the Haitian process is so unorthodox. This is probably why the United States is putting so much emphasis on solving the crisis in Haiti. It's not because of Haiti's importance in international terms, but if Aristide is restored to meaningful power, it could derail the whole democratic process in all of Latin America—where, until now, leaders have emerged with a different political agenda in line with the United States.

The coup was a response to this attempt by the masses to control the political process and to create conditions for reforms—agrarian reforms and political reforms. We can see how the coup is another tactical alliance, in this case between the assembly industry sector, Marc Bazin [the *de facto* government], the United States and the Tontons Macoutes.

After the elections, the United States officially supported Aristide. Where do you see evidence of the role of the United States in the September '91 coup alliance you describe?

Without a doubt, the U.S. ambassador to Haiti, Alvin Adams, was active in the coup. The United States was caught in a contradiction. On the one hand, the United States was the biggest promoter of the elections and facilitated the presence of the United Nations (UN) and the Organization of American States (OAS). And, if we look at U.S. policy in Latin America, it has been to replace military dictatorships with civilian governments. But most of the civilian governments are very much in tune with the U.S. political agenda in this part of the world. So, on the one hand, the U.S. had to accept the legitimacy of Aristide's election. They could not dispute it because the OAS and the UN supervised the election, everybody agreed that the electoral process went fine, and Aristide was duly elected. On the other hand, Aristide's government was not in tune with the U.S. agenda.

So the United States faced a dilemma. To accept the coup would be to send a signal to all the oligarchies in Latin America that the time of coups is not over. The United States could not accept the coup, even if they engineered the coup. They had to accept the necessity of Aristide's return, but under conditions in which he would be totally unable to fulfill his own political agenda and the political agenda of the masses.

If the United States was sincere in its opposition to the coup, it would have been easy to get rid of the military by enforcing the UN embargo. If Haiti did not receive petroleum for one or two months, that would be the end. Everything would come to a standstill. But that would have meant a victory for the masses, a victory for Aristide. And most probably the oligarchy would have lost completely. It would have meant restoring Aristide with even more power than before.

You think the leaky embargo was a conscious part of U.S. policy?

Yes, it was a question of not letting the embargo force the *de facto* government to leave. It allowed the United States to put pressure on Aristide to compromise. In fact, I think the ultimate goal of the United States is to get militarily involved in Haiti—to do it through international institutions like the OAS and the UN.

If so, why now? There have been other occasions for such an action.

I think that the United States can't really rely on the military, who have represented the oligarchy. The United States had an alliance with the oligarchy, but don't want the oligarchy to remain in power. My feeling is that the United States would like to restructure the army; in that case, their goal would be some form of occupation of the country. The only peculiarity in the case of Haiti is that most probably it will done under the auspices of the UN and the Security Council.

Why didn't Aristide immediately oppose an intervention?

He has decided to play the game, probably hoping that once he gets back he can mobilize the people and change the situation. But I think he's totally wrong.

What are the odds of Aristide accepting this arrangement, going back under the auspices of UN troops?

I have no idea, but the very fact that he remains silent leaves the door open. I think that he could have made a statement. This is one of the things that I have told him time and again. He should say to the United States: "Okay, if you want those people out, don't let the tankers go to Haiti. But instead you use your boats to stop the refugees, which is totally illegal. No one has the right to police international waters in time of peace."

I'd like you to comment on the change in U.S. administration and the change in the outlook for Aristide's return.

I think the Bush Administration was involved in the coup. But I think that because Clinton was embarrassed about not being able to let the refugees in, he had no alternative but to say, "Okay, we'll solve the problem by orchestrating Aristide's return." So I think there is more readiness from this administration to bring Aristide back, but under certain conditions—surrounded by foreign troops and dependent on foreign protection.

If Aristide accepts this arrangement, what would the new government look like?

Well, I doubt he would have a government. He would have a prime minister, who would run the government. He already said he would choose a prime minister from the opposition. So it would be somebody who would be acceptable to the private sector—the sector that financed the coup and is connected with the assembly industry. And that would create a very conflictive situation, because the people would still be convinced that Aristide was in control and that now they could go out and demand their rights. And I think they would be very surprised to see that they were not welcome.

What is Aristide's role in Haiti's future?

I recall that in Haiti's fight for independence, Toussaint Louverture fought for something that didn't occur during his lifetime. The people afterward had to fight for total independence. So, in this sense, Aristide may be just a step in the struggle of the people.

HAITI IN THE
MAINSTREAM PRESS

CATHERINE ORENSTEIN

This brief analysis of Haiti coverage in the mainstream U.S. press was written in June 1993. These patterns in media coverage remained substantially unchanged until the Clinton Administration's putative policy shift in May 1994, when the media—taking their cue from Washington— suddenly "discovered" and began to report some of the background and analysis presented throughout this book. Certainly, in the period immediately prior to the U.S. intervention in Haiti in October 1994, the New York Times, among others, began to report extensively on the massive human rights violations that were occurring under military rule.

At a demonstration in October 1994 against *New York Times* coverage of Haiti, Haitian protesters accused the newspaper of being "the voice of the State Department." Their argument had some credibility: a three-month tracking of the paper from September through December 1991 shows that over 35% of sources who gave information or commentary in *Times* news articles were U.S. officials. Another 10% were unidentified diplomats. This total

is almost double the count of all Haitian sources—military, peasant, elite and Lavalas—combined. Preferential sourcing greatly
affects not only the perspective printed, but also the "facts." For
example, numbers of deaths attributed to the September 1991
military coup ran from "dozens" (U.S. Embassy), the most frequently reported number, to 500 for the week following the coup
(international human rights groups), to 1,000 (Aristide, citing unreported mass graves). By depending on State Department sources,
the mainstream media runs the risk of becoming its mouthpiece.

One of the subtle ways mainstream media coverage of Haiti
imposed a U.S.-centric perspective was through an unbalanced use
of epithets and adjectives. The media sobriquets pinned on then-
exiled President Aristide played heavily on North American political stereotypes. Aristide was called a "populist demagogue" (*Los
Angeles Times*, 3/18/92) and "a mix of Khomeini and Castro" (*New
York Times*, 11/12/90). His politics were said to "come from Robe-
spierre" (*Washington Post*, 10/2/92). In addition, political labels—
valid and dubious ones alike—were exclusively applied to Aristide
and his movement as an unobtrusive and repetitive way of express-
ing disapproval. In contrast, the *de facto* government was not
referred to as rightist. *De facto* prime minister Marc Bazin, who was
the U.S.-backed candidate for president in the December 1990
elections, was labeled, if at all, with the ironic sobriquet, "Mr.
Clean" (*Los Angeles Times*, 6/3/92).

There was also an imbalance with respect to which topics the
media chose to emphasize. In the days after the coup, newspaper
attention focused not on the violence of the army, as one would
expect, but rather on Aristide's human rights record. During the
two-week period after the coup, the *New York Times* spent over
three times as many column inches discussing *Aristide's* alleged
transgressions than it spent reporting on the ongoing military
repression. Mass murders, executions and tortures that were later
reported in human rights publications earned less than 4% of the
space that the *Times* devoted to Haiti in those weeks. The *Washington Post* (10/6/91) claimed that Aristide organized his followers
into "an instrument of real terror," but declined to note the National Coalition of Haitian Refugees (NCHR) report citing a 75%

reduction in human rights abuses during Aristide's seven months in office.

If the media reveal themselves in their excesses, what they *don't* report is just as telling. The failure of the embargo and the deplorable conditions at the Guantánamo Bay refugee camp in Cuba are two examples. The U.S. sanctions imposed against Haiti and the Organization of American States embargo were represented in the mainstream press as forceful blows against the military government. The mainstream press gave little attention to early reports of blatant disregard for the embargo. According to the National Labor Commitee, for example, $67 million of apparel was imported to the United States from Haiti in 1992 despite the trade restriction.

In addition, even as the refugee crisis saturated the press, there was virtually no media coverage of the "temporary" refugee camp at Guantánamo. The little coverage available gave the impression of a vacation camp. One *New York Times* article had the preposterous headline, "U.S. Base is Oasis to Haitians" (11/28/91). Mainstream media coverage of Guantánamo suggested a high degree of self-censorship. Unreported events at Guantánamo included a hunger strike on January 29, 1993; an escape by eleven "inmates" on March 11, 1993; and a military crackdown on March 13, 1993, in which women were subjected to vaginal searches and twelve barracks were burned down. These unreported incidents indicated that Guantánamo was more of a prison camp than an "oasis," and cast a dark shadow on the U.S. "solution" to the refugee crisis.

In its coverage of Haiti, the mainstream media has essentially functioned as the public relations arm of the U.S. State Department. The mainstream press increasingly painted the Haitian situation as intractable, with a choice of likely outcomes "between mob revenge and anarchy...hence the necessity of the U.N. force" (*Newsday*, 5/13/93). The unwillingness of the international community to enforce the embargo against the military regime was forgotten. By denying the possibility of an internal Haitian solution, the U.S. media suggested that Haitians must once again bow to the traditional "necessity" of a U.S.-determined solution "for their own good."

12

HAITI'S SECOND U.S. OCCUPATION

KIM IVES

The spectacle was surreal, especially in this corner of the Caribbean, which has remained so resistant to Americanization over the past century. Thousands of Haitians, taut with anticipation, thronged the streets outside the green iron fence in front of the National Palace. Inside the fence and across the broad lawn studded with a mix of Haitian and U.S. soldiers, scores of hand-shaking dignitaries, ear-touching security personnel and eye-roaming journalists swarmed around the palace's wide steps. With Black Hawk helicopters thumping overhead, hundreds of heavily armed U.S. troops snaked through the crowds with walkie-talkies or surveyed the scene with binoculars from towering armored vehicles, windows or rooftops.

In the middle of it all sat Haitian President Jean-Bertrand Aristide, a small figure on a regal chair in a bullet-proof glass cage, exhibited for the crowds like an animal in a zoo. The date was October 15, 1994. After three years and fifteen days in exile, President Aristide was finally back in Haiti but surrounded, in every sense, by the putschist Haitian military and the occupying U.S. forces.

One year earlier, Aristide's first projected homecoming had been foiled. After a surge of Duvalierist violence and a well-orchestrated U.S./UN retreat, the return date of October 30, 1993 fixed by the July 1993 Governors Island Accord came and went.

In November and December 1993, the United States pressured Aristide through his second prime minister, Robert Malval, a wealthy printing press owner, to hold a "national reconciliation conference" to meet and compromise even more with the Duvalierist sector that had reneged on the Governors Island agreement.

"I would like for you to tell me without any ambiguity if you agree with the proposal for an Assembly for National Salvation," Malval impatiently wrote to Aristide on December 5. "I must know before 10 a.m. tomorrow," at which time Malval was to meet with President Bill Clinton. Malval had already unilaterally visited UN Secretary General Boutros Boutros-Ghali in New York to get his benediction for the conference.

"The present insecurity [in Haiti] prevents the pursuit of such a project," Aristide shot back in a letter the next day.

A bitter public rift between the president and prime minister emerged. Malval formally resigned as prime minister on December 15, as he had said he would when nominated in August, but he continued on as "acting" prime minister, remaining an ace in the hole for the U.S. government.

Burned by the October 30 fiasco and piqued by Malval's insolence, Aristide delivered a speech on January 1, 1994, that seemed to augur a change of strategy. "In 1993, it was negotiations which were favored," Aristide said. "In the course of 1994, the people will march more to the rhythm of [Jean-Jacques] Dessalines," the general who led the revolution for Haitian independence in 1804. The message seemed to be that mobilization and resistance on the ground in Haiti would be the new line of march.

The legitimate government even had a concrete plan. It called for an "International Conference on Refugees" in Miami on January 14 to attack Clinton's most vulnerable point, the policy of forcibly returning Haitian refugees to the terror in Haiti.

But, once again, the now-familiar Aristide pattern reasserted itself. After strong words and initial defiance to gather popular support, Aristide capitulated.

The planned conference on refugees was transformed through State Department pressure into a virtual "national reconciliation conference," where the centerpiece was a closed session in which the Governors Island participants wrangled over how to install a new compromise prime minister and strike a new deal with the putschists. The conference buzzed with back-room bargaining with pro-coup participants, who were applauded by Aristide for their presence. The refugee battle, for which many activists had come girded, was completely skirted.

In early 1994, the coup leaders, emboldened by U.S. pressure on Aristide, launched a savage new wave of repression and took over the parliament's leadership offices from elected lawmakers.

On March 18, Aristide relaunched his refugee offensive, calling Clinton's refugee policy "racist and criminal" at a meeting of the Congressional Black Caucus (CBC) in Miami. In public appearances, Aristide also began telling the joke about why there has never been a *coup d'état* in the United States. Punch line: "Because there is no U.S. Embassy in Washington." It's just a joke, he would apologize afterwards.

On March 30, *Haïti Progrès* broke a story about Yvon Desanges, a refugee returned to Haiti from the Guantánamo Bay detention center who had been hacked to death by a military death squad. Five days later, Aristide gave six months notice that Haiti was abrogating (belatedly, according to refugee advocates) the interdiction agreement signed by presidents Jean-Claude Duvalier and Ronald Reagan in 1981 that supposedly permitted the United States to intercept and return fleeing Haitian refugees on the high seas (in violation of international law). On April 12, TransAfrica's Randall Robinson, after strategizing with Aristide and the CBC, launched a twenty-seven-day media-intensive hunger strike urging Clinton to change his repatriation policy.

In response, on April 26, Clinton ditched his Haiti envoy Lawrence Pezzullo, who had a blatant style of arm-twisting, replacing him with the suave head of the United Negro College Fund, former U.S. Representative William Gray III on May 8. Clinton also announced a retreat from automatic repatriation to the Reagan-era policy of interviewing refugees aboard U.S. cutters, with the difference that those who were "screened in" would be taken to "safe havens" in any country in the hemisphere other than the United States. The refugee issue was now pushing the Clinton Administration to resolve the Haiti question once and for all.

From May through August 1994, events quickly accelerated toward invasion. Clinton began to "carry out a series of diplomatic, public, and other steps that would allow him to assert all other avenues had been exhausted," according to the September 25 *Washington Post*. In short, the United States needed to justify the invasion.

This made for a series of almost humorous about-faces. The U.S. Embassy, for instance, reported in a secret memo in early 1994, that "the Haitian Left, including President Aristide and his supporters in Washington and here, consistently manipulate and fabricate human rights abuses as a propaganda tool" and that the right-wing paramilitary Front for the Advancement and Progress of Haiti (FRAPH) "has essentially the same modus operandi [of terror] as the Lavalas' *Comités de quartiers'* [neighborhood committees]." But, by June, the U.S. government was itself using human rights abuses "as a propaganda tool," issuing strongly-worded daily statements to decry putschist violence. The U.S. Agency for International Development (AID) began searching for Haitian and U.S. human rights groups to give more than $1 million drawn from a new "Human Rights Fund."

Most important to the justification process, however, was the UN Security Council. On May 6, 1994, the United States pushed through Security Council Resolution 917, which stiffened the embargo against Haiti on paper, but not really on its borders. The 1993 sanctions targeted oil and weapons, while the new ones cut all trade (except for food and medicine) and all non-commercial air traffic with Haiti. The measures did little to pressure the putschists from power. Instead, they just increased the flow of

Haitian commerce across the Dominican border, which remained wide open throughout the crisis, despite regular announcements of resolve issued from Washington and Santo Domingo.

"These [UN] sanctions are being drafted in a way that sets them up for failure," said Berton Wides, one of Aristide's lawyers, on May 4. "They are so half-hearted that they almost seem designed to fail so that the Administration can say 'I told you so.'"

During June and July, the United States, followed by Canada, the Netherlands, the Dominican Republic, and France, stopped its commercial flights to Haiti. The United States also went after coup participants and supporters, banning their international financial transactions (which were long since completed) and freezing their assets and bank accounts (which were long since emptied). Money transfers from Haitians in the United States to their families in Haiti—which account for the vast bulk of the country's foreign revenue—were slashed to $50 per person per month, helping to fuel escalating desperation.

On July 31, the Security Council passed Resolution 940, which gave the United States authority to carry out a military intervention in Haiti on the UN's behalf, an arrangement now being dubbed "sphere of influence" peace-keeping.

The Haitian putschists issued ridiculously defiant, transparently phony, nationalist calls for resistance, thereby playing their role in intervention theatrics. To further provoke reaction, the military installed a second *de facto* president, Duvalierist chief justice Emile Jonassaint, on May 11, and cranked up repression a few more notches. By late May, record numbers of refugees were again fleeing Haiti.

As intervention approached, Aristide's ambiguity increased. On June 3, he began to call for the United States to carry out a "swift and determined action" in Haiti, and even asked for a "surgical strike," alluding specifically to the 1989 Panama invasion as a model.

Haitian popular organizations and U.S. solidarity groups were aghast, prompting Aristide to backtrack and issue an open letter on June 22 saying, "I have never asked for military intervention, nor will I. We have no illusion that a military intervention would serve the purpose of restoring democracy, or justice to Haiti." When asked in a National Public Radio interview on June 25 if he would agree to be restored to power through foreign military intervention, Aristide replied "Never! Never! And never again!"

But it was obvious by now that, despite his denials, Aristide had placed all his hopes on the United States. On July 29, Aristide clearly endorsed intervention in a letter to the UN Security Council urging passage of the resolution authorizing U.S. military action.

Support for intervention was by now the hallmark of the "Lavalas bourgeoisie." This section of Haiti's import-export bourgeoisie and its fringe of doctors, lawyers and engineers had rallied to the anti-imperialist platform of Haiti's popular organizations to form the Lavalas alliance that brought Aristide to power in 1990. At that time, the Lavalas bourgeoisie was looking to stop the political and economic march of the "technocrat" sector of the bourgeoisie, which was more closely tied to U.S. capital and the expanding assembly industries and agribusiness. Due to the coup, however, the Lavalas bourgeoisie now felt that a pact with the technocrats and the United States was in order. Central to the deal was intervention, which violated a key commandment of the old alliance.

Faced with questions or criticism about intervention, members of the Lavalas bourgeoisie responded that Aristide had no alternative. It was a choice, they argued, between continuing the reign of terror under Cédras or inviting U.S. military intervention. Aristide had to choose the lesser of two evils.

But the two evils were, in fact, one. The U.S. government, in collaboration with the putschists, was carrying out a classic good cop/bad cop routine: the bad cop to abuse and terrorize; the good cop to offer comfort, escape and a solution. The "bad cop" death squads of FRAPH were conceived, recruited and funded by the CIA and the Defense Intelligence Agency (DIA), *The Nation* revealed in October, and Cédras and most of the Haitian high command had been on the CIA payroll.

The countdown for the inevitable intervention of the "good cop" began on August 19, 1994. But now came the trickiest part of all: how to transfer the apparatus of repression from the "bad cop" to the "good cop" without creating an opening for insurrection? If Cédras and other putschists were to flee before the U.S. force was in place, the people might take to the streets and "get the idea that they can do whatever they want," as one U.S. Army psychological operations official put it.

Clinton made his nationally televised address on September 15 to set the stage for intervention. "Cédras and his armed thugs have conducted a reign of terror, executing children, raping women, killing priests," Clinton said. "We must act."

But Clinton still had a plan to converse more with the thugs to create a "permissive entry"—in Pentagon parlance—for U.S. troops. That way, the U.S. military could take over smoothly and avoid casualties in an intervention that was widely unpopular in the U.S. Congress and among the U.S. population at large. There was nothing "eleventh hour" about the planned mission. The administration had intended to send its own officials but settled on former President Jimmy Carter, former chairman of the Joint Chiefs of Staff General Colin Powell and Aristide critic Senator Sam Nunn (D-GA). They held two days of talks with Cédras in Port-au-Prince, which resulted on September 18 in a deal for "a peaceful, coopera- tive entry of international forces into Haiti, with a mutual respect between American commanders and the Haitian military com- manders," as Carter reported on September 19.

The essence of the deal, signed by Carter and *de facto* Haitian President Jonassaint, was two-fold: 1) to keep Cédras in power until October 15, while the U.S. occupation force was "inserted," as Secretary of State Warren Christopher characterized it; and 2) to ensure that "a general amnesty will be voted into law by the Haitian Parliament."

To soothe Aristide's initial misgivings about Carter's "Port- au-Prince Accord," the Pentagon gave him a twenty-one-gun sa- lute in Washington on September 21. "The ceremony of the Pentagon showed us very clearly that our president was recog- nized, that he had been returned his legitimacy," said close Aristide advisor and former Planning Minister Renaud Bernadin, who had severely criticized the Carter deal only days before. In the ceremony, Aristide profusely thanked Clinton, Carter and the Pentagon.

U.S. troops entered Haiti on September 19 and quickly "interfaced"—in military-speak—with their Haitian counterparts. The three designated coup villains—Cédras, Brigadier General Philippe Biamby and Colonel Michel François—were all spirited out of Haiti, away from justice, to comfortable exiles, thanks to U.S. government largesse. While under-the-table payoffs are also likely, the U.S. government has openly admitted that it will use U.S. taxpayers' money to pay Cédras $5,000 a month for rental of his three luxurious homes in Haiti.

Members of the Haitian parliament who had been living in exile were flown in on U.S. planes. Overseen by U.S. guns, the legislators passed a law on October 8 that granted amnesty for "political matters."

Thirteen other Haitian officers who were instrumental in the coup were transferred to tranquil embassy duties overseas by "interim commander in chief" Lieutenant General Jean-Claude Duperval, himself implicated in the September 1991 coup, the attempted coup of January 1991 and drug trafficking.

The U.S. government also unfroze $79 million in assets of the coup-makers and their wealthy supporters and announced a plan to provide $5 million for stipends and civilian retraining of Haitian soldiers who are so infamous for repression that they cannot be recycled in the "new" Haitian military.

In Grand Goâve, Cap-Haïtien and Jérémie, large demonstrations took place to demand that members of the military and *attachés* responsible for human rights abuses during the dictatorship be brought to justice. Crowds captured dozens of Haitian soldiers and paramilitary gunmen around Haiti and brought them to U.S. soldiers, as they had been instructed to do by the U.S. military over sound systems mounted on Humvees and helicopters and by President Aristide himself in his October 15 address at the National Palace.

"The American soldiers then handed them over to the remnants of the very Haitian police with whom the gunmen had collaborated in terrorizing the population during the three years of military rule," reported John Kifner in the October 18 *New York Times*. "No one seems able to say exactly what will happen to the gunmen, called *attachés*, who murdered, robbed and raped with impunity. One strong possibility is that their friends in the Haitian police will simply let them go."

The *de facto* protection by the U.S. high command of the former repressive forces is becoming clearer daily to ordinary Haitians, and also to the American GIs, who often sympathize with the Haitian people's struggle. "These people are really believing in us now," a U.S. police monitor/retrainer told Kifner. "But if these guys just walk free, it's all going to turn sour. It will be like Somalia."

In 1991, the Haitian people wanted to see a definitive end to the Duvalierist legacy. "*Makout pa ladann*"—which, loosely translated, means no dealings with Macoutes—was one of the principles of the December 16, 1990 coalition. "How can one extend a hand to those who stand on a mountain of corpses, feet in the blood of victims, with arms open to welcome assassins?" asked President Aristide in his 1992 autobiography *Every Person is a Human Being*. One wonders if Aristide remembered these words in 1994 when he received putschist criminals, embezzlers and collaborators at the National Palace, as he did on October 27 to talk about future elections.

With the watchword of "reconciliation," the United States is remodeling and shoring up the entire Duvalierist apparatus, in both its military and civilian incarnations. The "separation of the police and the armed forces" is the magic formula offered by U.S. reforms. Its goal is as cosmetic as the repainting of the infamous Cafeteria police station of Colonel François from mustard-yellow to white. The Cafeteria police used to best symbolize the union of Haiti's police and army, wearing blue police shirts and green army helmets. Now they and the rest of the police will wear new uniforms with inoffensive yellow and maroon baseball caps.

Although the figures keep changing, as of mid-November 1994 the army was slated to be reduced to 1,500, while the police—who will handle internal "law and order"—were planned to number about 6,000. Thus, the old "unseparated" armed forces of about

7,000 and the new "separated" ones will barely differ in size, contrary to the message sent by the mainstream media.

On the "civilian" demilitarization front, despite a much vaunted weapons "buy back" program, the U.S. occupying force retrieved only a small percentage of the tens of thousands of firearms in the hands of *attachés* and has even returned arms to rural section chiefs and their thugs, prompting popular demonstrations that have been in turn repressed.

Aristide wanted to fire the entire army high command and manage the formation of the new army and police with his government. The U.S. military, however, vetoed the move. For "retraining" the Haitian Armed Forces, the U.S. government wants to employ exclusively its own International Criminal Investigations Training and Assistance Program (ICITAP), which is staffed by current and former agents of the FBI, Drug Enforcement Administration (DEA), Secret Service and U.S. police departments. The new "professionalized" police and army will be—if all goes according to plan—more responsive to central (and U.S.-guided) control, not as prone to arbitrary and indiscreet violence and better versed in focused surveillance and repression of democratic and popular organizations. For good measure, the new forces will be supervised indefinitely by the yellow-capped International Police Monitors, the most multinational component of the United States' "multinational" occupation.

Candidates for "professionalization" are to be drawn largely from the "previous" Haitian Armed Forces, many officers and specialists of which have already been trained in the United States, mostly at the School of the Americas in Fort Benning, Georgia.

With the United States in complete military control, Aristide has jettisoned his nationalist program for the revitalization of Haiti's state industries, which had begun to show profits after just a few months of non-corrupt administration in 1991. Those industries are now to be sold to private capitalists, both Haitian and American, who backed the September 1991 coup with their heads, hearts and wallets.

"You have to remember that the coalition that brought [Aristide] to power is not the same coalition that brought him back now," said a prominent Haitian intellectual in the October 23 *New York Times*. The new coalition is between the Lavalas bourgeoisie and the technocratic bourgeoisie and U.S. capital. The new program is to bring about neoliberal "structural adjustment" of the Haitian economy.

Allan Nairn summarized this new IMF-World Bank "Strategy of Social and Economic Reconstruction" in the July/August 1994 *Multinational Monitor*: "Haiti commits to eliminate the jobs of half of its civil servants, massively privatize public services, 'drastic[ally]' slash tariffs and import restrictions, eschew price and foreign exchange controls, grant 'emergency' aid to the export sector, enforce an 'open foreign investment policy,' create special corporate business courts 'where the judges are more aware of the implications of their decisions for economic efficiency,' rewrite its corporate laws, 'limit the scope of state activity' and regulation, and diminish the power of Aristide's executive branch in favor of the more conservative Parliament. In return, Haiti is to receive $770 million in financing, $80 million of which goes immediately to pay the debt accrued to foreign banks over the past three years since the coup."

The plan so emphasizes privatization that even the Aristide government's role in administering funds becomes superfluous. "U.S. officials acknowledge that they will have direct control over most of the hundreds of millions of dollars worth of aid which will bypass Aristide's team and the central government altogether," reports the Haitian Information Bureau. The aid will instead be funneled directly to an array of organizations and individuals closely linked to the U.S. government through such organizations as the National Endowment for Democracy (NED).

Just as they justified foreign intervention, ideologues of the Lavalas bourgeoisie are now justifying neoliberalism. "You have to understand, the world has changed in these three years [since the coup]," said Father Antoine Adrien, former head of Aristide's Presidential Commission, to James Ridgeway of the *Village Voice*. "What was good in 1991 is not necessarily good in 1994. First of all, no country can survive without capitalism." Of course, Aristide's 1991 program was not anti-capitalist. It simply proposed "Justice, Openness, and Participation" in the running of the government and state industries and sweeping out corruption and inefficiency. For Adrien, however, it is "better to privatize them. It would ultimately be to the benefit of the state because we can collect taxes from them and have money to do other work. I really do not think this has been foisted on Aristide. With very few exceptions, state-owned enterprise is not in the benefit of the people."

However, Antoine Izméry—one of Haiti's largest merchant capitalists and the principal funder of Aristide's 1990 campaign, who became a martyr for democracy he was executed by *attachés* on September 11, 1993—would have strongly disagreed. "This mafioso private sector [in Haiti] has robbed the Haitian people through smuggling, drug-dealing, government subsidies, non-payment of their taxes, and all that, so that now they have the capital to buy up the state industries with the money they have stolen," he explained to *Haïti Progrès* after the Haiti Government/Business Partnership Conference in July 1993 in Miami. As for foreign buyers of Haitian industries, he said, "Haiti is virgin territory and very cheap right now. So there are several [foreign] companies interested in controlling the Haitian economy.... Now we are going to have the Americans controlling us completely and imposing their financial system which, in fact, has never had good results."

Ironically, Aristide was elected to fight against the very two processes he has now been returned to legitimate: reconciliation with Duvalierism, and neoliberal reforms. Whether he is a prisoner or player, or something in between, is not totally clear. Nor does it really matter. His government is only a portrait; the real regime is American.

Part III

Haitian Development and U.S. Economic Policy

HAITI'S NIGHTMARE AND THE LESSONS OF HISTORY

MICHEL-ROLPH TROUILLOT

❝The Haitian mind, you know, is just different," said Robert
McCandless, a Washington lobbyist described as "the most
vociferous advocate" of the civilians and military leaders behind
the coup that toppled President Jean-Bertrand Aristide in September 1991. "I mean they don't understand why we react to things
that they don't, and why we don't react to things that they do."[1]
Aristide's own prime minister, Robert Malval, seemed to agree, at
least in part. Referring to McCandless' employers, he warned U.S.
reporters in November 1993: "We are not talking about rational
people."[2]

These statements rest on weak evidence. The Haitian high
brass has been quite "rational" in pursuing its interests since 1985.
More disturbingly, however, statements such as these lead us to
search for the wrong *kind* of explanation. They reflect the tendency
to resort to exceptionalism. Haitian exceptionalism takes many
forms.[3] The most dangerous and resilient is the idea that the Haitian

political quagmire is due to some congenital disease of the Haitian mind. Such a conclusion makes Haiti's political dilemma immune to rational explanation and therefore to solutions that could be both just and practical.[4]

As soothing—and rewarding—as such analyses may be to their proponents in Port-au-Prince and Washington, if history reveals anything it is the extent to which the stakes have long been different for various groups in Haiti. The history of Haiti is one of sharply opposed interests, of competing visions of state and nation. If "the Haitian mind" is a short-cut phrase to signify the political will of the majority, Haitians can be said to have been of one mind only twice in their history. Their first—and only unquestionable—gesture as a people was in 1791-1804, when they stood *en masse* against slavery and French colonialism. Their second gesture as a people was in 1990, when a 67.5% majority elected Jean Bertrand Aristide to the presidency in the country's first free elections. The aftermath of that election, however, suggests the depth of the divisions that had ripened between the two events.

Even sympathetic U.S. policymakers find Haiti hard to explain, mainly for two related reasons. First, for most of them, as for many other Americans, history is rarely a serious explanation—especially history that runs deep. Analyses that go back a decade, let alone a century, seem moot—at least until the latest exercise in myopia reveals a new disaster. Second, class remains the capital taboo of U.S. political analysis, a divide not to be mentioned except as a measure of income. Yet class structure, rather than mere income, and history, rather than the immediate past, are at the roots of the current Haitian crisis.

The product of a revolution against slavery and colonialism, Haiti emerged in 1804 from the ashes of the French colony of Saint-Domingue on the western part of the Caribbean island of Hispaniola. By 1789, Saint-Domingue was arguably the most profitable colony of the Western world, setting world production records for both sugar and coffee. It was also the worst place in the world to be Black. The colony imported many more enslaved

Africans than most plantation societies of the Americas, including the United States. It also killed them at a much faster pace, through mistreatment and harsh labor. In August 1791, the slaves of Saint-Domingue revolted. Under the successive leadership of Toussaint Louverture and Jean-Jacques Dessalines, they defeated Napoleon's army after twelve years of struggle. In this way, the first independent state of the Americas—where "freedom" meant freedom for everyone—was born.

The Haitian victory exemplified the best of the age of revolutions. Like the French Revolution, it was a revolution for social justice. Like the American Revolution, it was a victory against colonialism. It foreshadowed the independence of Latin America and the demise of African-American slavery. But it was ill-timed precisely for these reasons. In 1791, European powers held Caribbean colonies and accepted African slavery as a matter of fact. Similarly, representatives of the southern states in the U.S. Congress argued vehemently that recognition of Haitian independence would encourage Blacks elsewhere to revolt. Thus France, England, the Netherlands and the United States traded with Haiti, but only on terms that they themselves imposed. The United States provided most of Haiti's imports but bought little in return. It only recognized Haitian independence almost sixty years after the fact, in 1862, when the Civil War created an unexpected need for cotton and silenced the South in Washington. While Haiti was ostracized diplomatically, it also represented "the world's first experiment in neo-colonialism." If, in retrospect, the Haitian revolution appears to have been a failure, it is in part because Western powers—notably France, England, the United States and the Vatican—wanted it to fail. But it is also because the new Haitian elites treated the rural masses pretty much the same way that the West had treated them.

Haitian leaders vainly tried to restore the plantation economy immediately after independence. The majority of the former slaves, however, abhorred plantation labor and settled as small peasants on land bought or reconquered from the state or abandoned by large landowners. The urban elites countered with a dual strategy, set up during the presidencies of Alexandre Pétion (1807-1818) and Jean-Pierre Boyer (1818-1843).

The first leg of that strategy was economic. The elites turned the fiscal and marketing systems of the country into mechanisms that would allow them to siphon off the wealth produced by the peasants. As traders, politicians and state employees, they lived off the peasants' labor. An import-export bourgeoisie, dominated by foreign nationals and unconcerned with local production, garnered profits from the labor of the peasantry. Taxes collected in the urban markets and at the customhouses—and ultimately paid by the peasants—provided the bulk of government revenues. In 1842, more than 90% of government revenues were collected at the customhouses. In 1891, import and export duties accounted for 98.2% of state income.[5]

Coffee, Haiti's main agricultural export, was the favorite target of these elites and the centerpiece of Haiti's fiscal policy. The direct and hidden taxes imposed on that peasant crop accounted for 60% to 90% of government revenues from the late 1800s to the first half of this century. Until recently, the various charges on coffee amounted to a 40% tax on peasant income in a country where, after almost 200 years of independence, the government has yet to collect income tax from most merchants, civil servants or middle-class employees.

Successive Haitian governments also heavily taxed food and other necessities such as flour, oil, candles, kerosene and matches. Meanwhile, luxuries consumed by the elites entered the country free of charge. At the turn of the century, for example, import duties on a pair of opera glasses were equal to those on five gallons of kerosene. Eighty years later, as coffee exports fell during Jean-Claude Duvalier's regime, taxes on flour, sugar, petroleum, tobacco and matches provided as much as 25% of government revenues.[6] Meanwhile, the number of luxury cars in the streets of Port-au-Prince reached an all-time high.

The economic response of the Haitian elites to the emergence of an independent peasantry refusing to labor on the plantations guaranteed that they would get their surplus one way or another, even if it meant squeezing the nation to death. The state reproduced itself by exploiting the peasantry; the urban classes reproduced

---

themselves by exploiting the state *and* the peasantry. For a century and half, successive governments have prolonged the agony.

Death and ruin were foretold in these choices. So was political instability.[7] To limit the political turbulence that was an inevitable outcome of their economic designs, the Haitian elites added a second leg to their strategy. They used the very isolation that the peasantry enjoyed on its small mountain plots to keep it away from the political scene. While the state turned inward to consolidate its control, the urban elites gravitating around that state pushed the rural majority toward the margins of political society. The very peasants who subsidized the state had no say in the running of the state. Once in a while, they joined one or another regional landowner to attack Port-au-Prince, the ultimate site of power. Most often, however, they were kept at bay legally and illegally, through manipulation of election laws or through repression. It's doubtful that any elected official in Haiti ever received a thousand legitimate votes before the twentieth century.[8] Before the François Duvalier dictatorship, many peasants would not have been able to name the president. They encountered the state mainly through two dubious characters: the *preseptè*, who collected their market taxes, and the *chèf seksyon* (section chief), who acted as the sole representative of the three branches of government in the deep countryside. That countryside was—and remains—a class colony of the urban elites. To wit, as befits occupied territories, the infamous *chèf seksyon* is a member of the army.

The Haitian Creole language registers the enormous distance between the elites and the peasantry. The word *leta* in Creole means both "the state" and "a bully." Urbanites, in turn, often refer to rural dwellers as "*mounn andewò*" (outsiders). Few have bothered to ask how or why rural people can be *mounn andewò* in a country that is 70% rural.[9]

Haitian culture also registers this distance, although in complex ways. To take only the example of language, all Haitians speak Creole, which evolved during the Haitian colonial period and matured in the nineteenth century. Less than 8% of the population, however, is comfortable speaking French, a competence acquired mainly through the school system. Only a tiny minority within the elites can be said to be truly bilingual in both French and Creole. Similarly, practices and beliefs associated with Haitian folk religion—referred to as *"vodoun"* (Voodoo) mainly by non-practitioners—can easily be found among the elites, in spite of their formal adherence to Christianity. At the same time, most peasants see themselves as Roman Catholic Christians, practice Roman Catholicism as much as possible (that is, to the extent that priests and churches are accessible) and follow the annual cycle of Roman Catholic events. If prompted and willing, they may add, however, that they are also "servants of the gods."

Thus, while it would be wrong to suggest that elites and masses fully share the same culture, it is equally misleading to divide Haiti into two separate cultural spheres. The fundamental cultural divide is not based on huge differences in cultural repertoire but on the use of those differences that exist to create a social wall that few can cross. Culture works as a dividing force because of the value added to the rather small part of that repertoire that is not accessible to the majority. More important than bilingualism *per se* is the number of times an elite child is told *not* to speak Creole. More important than the elites' uneven competence in French is the number of times that privileged Haitians make a point of using French and the fact that the use of French in the school and court system denies majority participation. More important than the elites' mixed adherence to Christianity is the number of times privileged Haitians publicly associate *vodoun* with evil and the number of times successive governments persecuted the servants of the gods, often with zealous help from the Catholic Church.

Two structural features emerge from this sociohistorical sketch: the total rejection of the majority by the groups that exert political and economic control and the role of the state as the key mechanism of both rejection and control. Simply put, the Haitian elites made a choice early on that the maintenance of their lifestyle was more important than the survival of the majority. That choice, in turn, meant using the state both to exploit the economic output of the majority and to stop the majority from crying out too loudly.

Seen from this perspective, the Haitian state has never represented government *for* the people, let alone *by* the people. The Haitian state is inherently predatory: it has always operated against the nation it claims to represent.[10] It is a closed world over which civil society has no hold. The 1915-1934 U.S. occupation of Haiti left the country with two poisoned gifts: a weaker civil society and a solidified state apparatus.[11]

The first outcome was largely unintentional, the second deliberate. The U.S. Marines who occupied Haiti professed a desire to create a U.S.-style middle class. They failed in that attempt—in part because the goal was set too late and too timidly, and in part because the occupation did little to change Haiti's economic structure. Haiti's trade dependence on coffee increased during the occupation. So did its fiscal dependence on custom revenues. Export duties, in fact, increased in relation to the value of merchandise, imposing an even greater burden on the average consumer.[12]

The occupiers did train a few craftspeople, enlarging Haiti's small crew of urban independent producers. More importantly, the Marines improved the material infrastructure of the country, most notably by overseeing the construction of roads. The political cost was heavy: peasants, at times bound in ropes, provided forced labor for these projects. The economic returns were meager. The minor improvements did not lessen the elites' historical aversion to production. They were used to "making money" as merchants or as state officials. Why would a few roads make them risk the hassles of manufacturing or petty commodity production? The elites considered making things a lower-class venture. Rich people, they believed, made profit only by buying and selling, usually with the connivance of the state.

The U.S. occupation failed to strengthen Haitian civil society, but it did strengthen the arm of the state. First, the Marines reinforced the fiscal and economic power of the capital city, Port-au-Prince, notably by centralizing the customhouses. Second, and more damaging, the occupation deliberately contributed to the centralization of political power in Port-au-Prince. It did so by "pacifying" the countryside, "modernizing" the so-called rural police (the infamous *chèf seksyon*) and creating a new Haitian army, the very one now at the center of the current political crisis. Whereas the first Haitian army, because it was born of the war against the French, could claim a patriotic mission, the Haitian *Garde* was created specifically to fight Haitians. Up to now, indeed, this force has never fought anyone but Haitians. Finally, by contrast to the first Haitian army, whose allegiances were primarily regional, the army created by the Marines was heavily centralized.

As a result of this centralization of power, it became easier for would-be dictators to control the state. However brutal they were, Haitian dictators of the nineteenth century knew that they might have to pay for power with their lives. However crude the system of checks and balances, it limited the ambitions of the generals. Military centralization, however, afforded full protection to the rulers of the day and removed the tenuous right of the majority to revolt. Hereafter, as Hans Schmidt notes, "political strongmen in Port-au-Prince were able to control the entire country more effectively than ever before."[13]

Thus, the cadets of the Military School set up by the Marines took part in the removal of President Elie Lescot (1941-1946) and the nomination and removal of his successor, Dumarsais Estimé (1946-1950), before ultimately placing one of their own, Paul Magloire (1950-1956), in the presidency. By the time Magloire left, the army had become the final arbiter of Haitian politics and its dominant factions imposed the presidency of François "Papa Doc" Duvalier. Duvalier learned the lesson: he gradually discharged most senior officers, but he relied heavily on their successors to build the most centralized power Haiti had ever seen. Then, he closed the Military School.

François Duvalier was a cunning and ruthless politician who enjoyed the fruits of Washington's "realistic" policies at the very moment his regime seemed to run out of steam. Yet neither his ruthlessness nor U.S. support fully explain the longevity of Duvalier's dictatorship, the fact that his son Jean-Claude lasted even longer, nor that Duvalierism is now going through a revival of a sort, years after Jean-Claude Duvalier's exile in 1986. To be sure, the first Duvalier regime exercised state repression with a swiftness hitherto unknown in Haiti. To be sure, in 1963 U.S. Army doctors reportedly revived a comatose Papa Doc, lengthening by decades the agony of average Haitians. To be sure, in 1971 U.S. Ambassador Clinton Knox personally supervised the transition from one Duvalier to another. To be sure, current wavering in Washington has provided much-needed fuel to the Duvalierist machine.

None of these facts, however, should mask the fact that Duvalierism has its roots in the socioeconomic organization set up by the Haitian elites and the centralization of the state and army brought about by the U.S. Marines. Using the full power of the centralized state, the elder Duvalier formalized a system of absolute individual power. At the center of the system stood an all-powerful and personalized Executive branch that dominated all activities of the state, from military training to the writing of national school exams. That modified state apparatus, in turn, attacked or marginalized all the groupings and institutions of an already weak civil society: extended families, schools, neighborhoods, clergy, press, villages, trade unions, soccer teams and carnival bands. At one point, François Duvalier even outlawed the Boy Scouts. In sheer Mussolinian fashion, the Duvalierist state aimed to become "total"; its means became totalitarian.

But Duvalier could achieve his aim only because of the role played by the state in Haitian history since independence. Indeed, Duvalierism invented very few formulas of power. Rather, it systematically codified old-fashioned practices of the Haitian state. Government-sponsored paramilitary groups, such as the "Zenglen," had terrorized Haitians a century before the Duvaliers. The difference in the Duvalier era was that the *Volontaires de la Sécurité Nationale* (VSN) enjoyed total and official support from an all-powerful Executive. That systematic backing turned the VSN into the most feared militia of Haitian history. The methods of the dreaded Tontons Macoutes—the secret police, whose members and function overlap with those of the military—reflect the systematization of practices honed by the death squads of earlier years.

Similarly, the Duvalierists systematized the extractive power of the state, multiplying the number of points at which the government could siphon off money from the average citizen. Duties and charges multiplied, varying in form from additional stamps on official papers, transcripts or documents to booths set up for no other purpose than the enrichment of a local strongman. More importantly, the government centralized the management of coffee exports and increased taxes in the process, creating new fortunes. In addition, the Executive and its proxies took control of the import and distribution of a number of basic commodities, such as oil, flour, matches and tobacco. The Duvalierists also declared open season on the Treasury. Not only did they—like their predecessors—misuse public funds, they made their personal fortune the very *raison d'être* of state revenues. An infamous operation suggests Duvalierism's extremes: while previous Haitian governments always fed—at least metaphorically—on Haitian sweat and blood, in the 1960s the Duvaliers and their cronies literally sold Haitian blood to the U.S. market.

In systematizing both the extractive and repressive power of the state, Duvalierism gravely worsened the Haitian situation. Predatory policies accelerated the speed of environmental degradation. Impoverished peasants rushed in greater numbers to urban centers, especially the shantytowns of Port-au-Prince. Following U.S. advice to bypass the peasantry, Jean-Claude Duvalier's regime tried to take advantage of this urban labor force to spark an "economic revolution." The rapid spread of light-assembly industries, subcontracted to U.S. firms, only reinforced economic polarization in Haiti. As imports rose in both quantity and value, so too did the already huge gap between the haves and the have-nots. The intense economic polarization and the unmediated distance between the regime and the swollen urban masses contributed to urban rebellions in the mid-1980s. In the midst of that popular agitation, Jean-Claude Duvalier was forced into exile in February 1986, leaving behind a much more depleted country and much more desperate elite.

Regardless of the deals that led to Jean-Claude Duvalier's departure, the end of that dictatorship was an obvious victory for the Haitian people. But it did not and *could not* mean the end of Haiti's nightmare. Haiti begot two Duvaliers. It could beget more or worse dictators if the structures that bred Duvalierism remained unchanged. The elimination of known Duvalierists or officers was no guarantee whatsoever that Duvalierist behavior would not immediately resurge within the state apparatus.

The conversion to a non-Duvalierist regime is only one of the transitions that Haiti now faces. A second transition is the passage to the rule of law. The two somewhat overlap, while, in other ways, they cancel each other out. Attempts to get rid of Duvalierism by legal means have failed. The 1987 Constitution—which banished prominent Duvalierists from the political process—is a dead letter; the 1988 elections resulted in a massacre; the presidency of Aristide was disrupted with a coup.

If Duvalierism impedes the advent of the rule of law, the weakness of democratic institutions, in turn, keeps Duvalierism alive. Right-wing allegations to the contrary, Aristide's presidency showed the lowest level of human rights violations by the state in recent Haitian history. At the same time, the perception—never proven, though sincere—that President Aristide might not even *try* to control Port-au-Prince's masses if that human flood decided to take the law in its hands helped the coup leaders. Individuals who were not Duvalierists—including some who had voted for Aristide—honestly believed that their lives were in danger. That they are now in more immediate danger only exemplifies the paradoxical overlap of the two transitions.

This overlap stems from the transformations that Duvalierism imposed on Haitian society. The elder Duvalier achieved the near destruction of Haitian civil society. Civilities that had bonded otherwise divided citizens tumbled under the weight of a totalitarian apparatus that made political polarization a fact of daily life. The younger Duvalier's reckless wager on light industry added the weight of a huge, desperately poor urban underclass to this breakdown of social norms. Port-au-Prince and its immediate environs now counts anywhere between 1.2 and 1.8 million people split between two extremes: an increasingly nervous wealthy minority, desperate to hold on to its privileges, and an anonymous mass that has nothing left to lose and that occupies front stage by sheer virtue of its size. The temptation to use this *"lumpen"* for political leverage is almost irresistible.[14] But, as the Duvalierists demonstrated when they staged a made-for-television protest against the landing of the USS *Harlan County* that forced a U.S. president to back down, this *lumpen* can cut many ways.

Duvalierism's legacy of extremes means that neither changes in the state apparatus nor institutional reform are enough to compel real change in Haiti. Relations between the state and civil society have deteriorated to the point that any government, regardless of its popularity, can maintain itself only by force of arms, at least until the state gains some legitimacy. The Haitian problem is not merely political. It is in the class structure of the country, in the military organization of a society at war with itself, in a fiscal system that discourages production and investment and, finally, in sociocultural elitism.

Legitimacy of the state, in turn, requires a social contract—that is, the participation of Haiti's majority in deciding the fate of the country. It requires the recognition by the urban elites and their foreign partners that Haiti fundamentally remains a country of poor peasants. But old habits die hard. The negotiations concerning Aristide's return to Haiti all but forgot the fact that Aristide himself was possible in part because of deep political changes in the countryside, rooted in the rural churches and the emerging peasant movement.[15] To emphasize the peasantry as the most repressed actor on the Haitian political stage is not to fall into romanticism. It is, on the contrary, to acknowledge that Haitian democracy will happen in the deep hinterland or it will not exist at all.

14

MODEL UNDERDEVELOPMENT

MICHAEL S. HOOPER

This chapter describes the U.S. response in terms of development assistance and economic policy to the overthrow of Baby Doc, and the end of the Duvalier dynasty. It is noteworthy that the architect of the anti-corruption and deficit-reduction crusade in 1987, Leslie Delatour, has reemerged as one of the designers of the new International Monetary Fund/World Bank structural adjustment scheme for Haiti, which was foisted on Aristide's government at a Paris meeting in August 1994.

A month after Jean-Claude Duvalier's fall in February 1986, the Catholic Church called for a massive literacy campaign, aiming to reach two million adults over the next five years. Numerous radio stations spontaneously offered their equipment, and soon thousands of volunteers in slums and villages across the country were teaching the poor to read and write Creole.

When the Church launched an appeal to help rebuild schools damaged during the mass demonstrations to oust Duvalier, Haitians at home and abroad responded with $600,000 in small donations; the Haitian community in New York City provided more than $150,000.

Another $75,000 was collected to rebuild Radio Haiti Inter, which had been destroyed by Duvalier's security forces in 1980.

Dozens of neighborhood committees were flourishing in the poorest areas of Port-au-Prince, organizing clean-ups to improve sanitation and tapping into water lines that previously bypassed their communities.

Clearly, the Duvaliers' flight created new opportunities to tackle the country's overwhelming economic difficulties. Haiti seemed ready to mobilize human resources—its biggest capital— to rebuild the economic infrastructure so badly neglected during the dictatorship.

Despite this flurry of grassroots activity, the possibility of renewed public confidence in government development efforts was stymied by the failure of General Henri Namphy's National Government Council (CNG) to stop the mismanagement of public monies. Pervasive official corruption continued to siphon off scarce public funds and foreign assistance into extra-budgetary expenditures for the elite, feeding the inequality that was responsible for so much of Haiti's political instability. While the half of 1% of the population who earn 46% of the national income continued to jockey for political access to even greater wealth, nearly all Haitians remained trapped in unimaginable misery.

It would be difficult to exaggerate the depth of Haiti's poverty. In 1987, one Haitian child died every five minutes from malnutrition, dehydration and diarrhea.[1] According to the U.S Agency for International Development (AID), in 1985, the average Haitian consumed 20% fewer calories and 30% less protein than levels recommended by the United Nations. In rural areas, where 75% of the population lives, these deficiencies climbed to 40% for calories and 50% for protein.[2] At least one-third of children under the age of five suffered chronic malnutrition, which along with gastroenteritis accounted for 90% of child deaths. The infant mortality rate—135 per 1,000 births—was the hemisphere's highest, while average life expectancy was just 53 years.[3]

Ninety percent of the population earned less than $150 in 1985.[4] Fewer than 20% of full-time workers actually received the official urban minimum wage of $3 per day; even government employees often earned less. In the countryside, wages averaged only a little more than half the official minimum of $2.64 per day.[5]

Like other underdeveloped nations, Haiti was continuously *underdeveloping,* as reflected in the traditionally minuscule state expenditures on public education, health and agricultural extension services, which were the lowest in the hemisphere. Almost 80% of the population was illiterate, and most of the 18,000 children ready to enter school each year could not be accommodated for lack of facilities, teachers and funds.[6] The educational system was virtually privatized through neglect, and consisted mainly of Church-run schools. Sixty percent of all teachers worked in urban areas, the majority in Port-au-Prince, while student-teacher ratios in the countryside reached 60 to 1 or worse.

Haiti continued to import almost twice as much as it exported, with the deficit exceeding $160 million in 1985.[7] Disaster was averted only because of the substantial amount of money sent home by Haitians living abroad, about $125 million yearly. The value of one of the country's largest foreign-exchange earners, coffee, continued to plummet, down another $6 million in 1985 alone. By that year, the balance of payments deficit reached $25 million, while total debt was estimated at between $519 million and $833 million by August 1987.[8]

Le siphonage—the "siphoning off" of public monies by the Duvaliers and their close associates—had a devastating impact on the Haitian economy. In the four years before their flight, Jean-Claude and his entourage stole much more than the country's annual national budget. Canceled checks and bank transactions show that Jean-Claude, his wife Michèle Bennett and their agents alone lifted more than $505 million from public monies and treasury revenues.[9] Their system of expropriation was shockingly simple, although more sophisticated schemes were constantly coming to light.

Prior to their departure, the Duvaliers had begun to monopolize spoils that were once more equitably distributed among a larger retinue. In addition to his salary, a $2.4 million expense account and a $2 million supplementary account, Jean-Claude stole

$120.5 million and Michèle $94.6 million between 1981 and 1985. $59.8 million went to Finance Minister Franz Merceron and $109.1 million to Jean Sambour, Michèle's fashion consultant. Courier Auguste Douyon made off with $120 million.

The Duvaliers and favored guests skimmed funds from the treasury and a number of quasi-governmental entities. Payments were made into irregular, non-fiscalized accounts. These weekly or monthly payments were listed as "expenses" or as "profits"; checks were made out either to the Duvaliers or to front accounts like "Social Projects of the President-for-Life" or "Social Projects of the Guardian of the Revolution." The checks were then endorsed by Jean-Claude or Michèle and deposited in private bank accounts or used to purchase dollars.

But the Duvaliers did not stop at skimming profits off state-owned businesses. They often resorted to crude political pressure, forcing ministers to write checks for their "special projects." Between 1982 and 1985, Merceron, for example, authorized payments to the Duvaliers exceeding $22 million. The largest amounts went to fictitious projects like the Michèle Bennett Duvalier Foundation, the Bon Repos Infant and Maternal Health Hospital—her pet charity, which in fact received little money—or directly to the president or first lady.[10] The Bank of the Republic of Haiti or the National Bank of Credit was then coerced into cashing the checks or converting them into dollars for transfer to foreign accounts.

Eight quasi-governmental enterprises—completely dominated by the Duvaliers—provided the best opportunities for embezzlement. These included: the Regie du Tabac; Minoterie d'Haiti, the state flour mill; and TELECO, the state-owned telephone company. All eight enterprises were headed by Duvalier appointees, and each had its own accounting procedure, independent of the public budget or the Ministry of Finance.

Each used a slightly different "siphoning" technique. The Regie du Tabac collected all taxes on the sale of basic commodities, depositing over $30 million in the Duvaliers' private accounts between 1978 and 1984; the Regie issued checks worth an average of $109,500 per month to non-existent social agencies.

An additional charge of 93 cents was levied on each bag of flour ground by the state flour mill. These "taxes" went into a special account from which the Duvaliers would order checks made out to "Public Works of the President-for-Life." From early 1981 to late 1985, it is estimated that over $4 million was siphoned from the public treasury in this fashion. In addition, the Duvaliers charged 93 cents per sack of flour donated or subsidized by U.S. taxpayers under the PL 480 Food for Peace Program.

The pattern of corruption for the other quasi-governmental entities was equally efficient, with various "charitable institutions" taking turns laundering funds. If not transferred directly to the Duvaliers, money would be assigned to fronts such as Michèle's favorite charities or "Cultural Activities." Between 1983 and 1985 alone, a total of almost $40 million in hard currency was removed from the central bank, which the Duvaliers left with just slightly over $1 million.

To the degree that it acted at all to reform the nation's finances, the CNG followed the recommendations of the World Bank and other international financial agencies, whose investment funds were the mainstay of the Haitian economy. The largest bilateral contributor consistently was AID, with total U.S. support rising from $54 million in 1985 to $110 million for fiscal year 1987.

The International Monetary Fund (IMF), which assigns primary importance to keeping a country solvent, so as to meet external debt and balance-of-payments requirements, mandated severe budget cuts. As a consequence, the Haitian government's meager contribution to development declined to nearly nothing. On IMF recommendation, the government also raised taxes on consumer goods, further undermining the standard of living.[11]

The development strategy for Haiti encouraged by the World Bank and AID was based on agribusiness and assembly-industry exports to northern industrialized countries, mainly the United States. In a 1985 "Strategy Statement," the World Bank was upbeat about Haiti's growth potential:

> Haiti could enjoy a better place in the world than 1983 per capita GNP of U.S.$320 would indicate. It is close to the

North American market, especially attractive since the advent of the U.S. Caribbean Basin Initiative. It has untapped agricultural possibilities [including] comparative advantage in a number of crops.... Industry as a whole can take advantage of the factors that have so attracted the largely foreign assembly firms: productive low-cost labor, proximity to the United States, functioning basic infrastructure, pro-business atmosphere, and political stability.[12]

Haiti's "attractiveness" and "untapped possibilities" were not lost on Washington, which also recognized the island's strategic military importance:

First, the U.S. has significant security interests in Haiti which shares the windward passage to the Caribbean Sea and the Panama Canal with Cuba. Haiti is strategically located only 700 miles from Florida and the existence of a non-hostile government and populace in Haiti is a fundamental security interest.... In recent years, almost 50% of all imports into Haiti have been of U.S. origin (estimated at $267 million in 1986) and more than half of Haiti's exports are to the United States.[13]

According to plans laid out in 1982, "AID proposes to shift 30% of all cultivated land from the production of food for local consumption to the production of export crops."[14] Washington's experts were surprisingly candid about the consequences of their development plans for the hemisphere's poorest nation:

AID anticipates that such a drastic reorientation of agriculture will cause a decline in income and nutritional status, especially for small farmers and peasants... Even if transition to export agriculture is successful, AID anticipates a "massive" displacement of peasant farmers and migration to urban centers.[15]

Haiti had the capacity to meet its own needs for rice, vegetables and many cereals, yet—in large part due to AID and government policies—Haiti's food situation was reaching crisis proportions. A rapidly expanding population increased demand, while agricultural productivity seriously declined.16 Food imports rose steadily over the years to $89 million in 1987 (up from $62 million in 1984), constituting some 20% of total imports.[17] This may have filled part of the gap, but it did not address the problem of malnutrition.

Food imports were also encouraged by U.S. programs such as Food for Work and Food for Peace. By bringing wheat in to Haiti at concessionary prices, these programs made it less profitable to grow cereals locally, since they could easily be replaced with subsidized imports. Wheat imports increased 11% per year from 1970 to 1983; by 1984, they constituted 32% of grain consumption.[18] These percentages continued to increase considerably thereafter.

Haiti's inequitable distribution of wealth was dramatically illustrated by its virtually feudal patterns of land ownership, exacerbated by the existence of large tracts of underutilized land. Haiti's total arable land in 1989 was approximately 2,161,000 acres, 60% of which is comprised of small holdings under three acres; large farms (250-750 acres) numbered about 1,000.[19] Many major landowners lived in the capital, doing little to encourage increased output. Sharecroppers lacked the means to invest in the land and were typically limited to technology such as the machete and hoe; few had horses or oxen to haul a cart. Many peasants were relegated to poor plots on steep hillsides where primitive farming techniques yielded little produce and greatly increased soil erosion. About 45% of the agricultural labor force were independent farmers and peasants; the remaining 55% were wage laborers or sharecroppers. Farmworkers earned an average of $1.45 per day, far below the government-mandated minimum.

The most dramatic issue in the countryside in the 1980s centered on the devastating effects of an international program to eradicate and replenish the entire pig population after the detection of African Swine Fever in 1981. Questions persist as to whether the program, which destroyed almost all of Haiti's one million native pigs, was primarily intended to protect the U.S. pork industry or was actually necessary.

The loss of pigs—often the Haitian peasant's only savings and insurance, and a source of at least 50% of the protein consumed annually—was a harsh blow to the already fragile peasant economy. While the eradication program had been completed by late 1983, the great majority of peasants who lost their pigs never received any of the partial compensation provided to the Haitian government by international agencies and the United States and had no reason to expect they would ever receive replacements.

AID did provide 500 Iowa breeding stock, avowedly to assist those farmers and peasants who suffered the greatest losses. Many agronomists, however, believed this plan would result in agribusiness producers gaining control of the pork market.[20] The pink and plump Iowa pigs demanded constant and meticulous care: special pens, vitamin- and protein-laced feed, cool cement floors, clean water and constant fine showers to withstand Haiti's environment.[21] Dubbed "four-legged kings," they were only allowed visitors who wore disinfected boots and overalls.

An impoverished Haitian peasant could never afford such luxuries for himself, let alone for his pigs. And the continued dependence of even fifth- and sixth-generation pigs on grain feed made them unaffordable to most.

The reluctance of both Haitian and U.S. authorities to comply with peasants' demands for the importation of "black pigs" from Jamaica and Martinique—which would have been more suitable to the environment and to scavenging for food—became a powerful focus of anti-government feeling. On the sensitive eve of the first anniversary of Jean-Claude Duvalier's fall, thousands of peasants threatened to slaughter the Iowa pigs if black pigs were not brought in quickly. While the government officially gave in to the demand, little substantive action followed.

Pushed off the land by hunger, Haitians migrated to the cities *en masse*. Port-au-Prince grew from 150,000 in 1950 to 720,000 in 1982.[22] By the late 1980s, the capital housed approximately one million people, with the outlying slums of Cité Soleil, La Saline, Carrefour, Martissant and Bizoton absorbing the biggest influx. The country's second largest city, Cap-Haïtien, had 80,000 residents; Les Cayes had 50,000.

This vast internal migration was also accompanied by an equally vast migration overseas. Between 1970 and 1987, at least 25,000 Haitians per year left for other countries, mainly the United States and the Dominican Republic.[23] Overall, the number of Haitians residing abroad by 1987 was estimated to be one million, with more than half of this diaspora residing in the United States. Haiti also witnessed a massive brain drain, with more Haitian nurses and physicians practicing in Montreal, where the Haitian community numbered about 40,000, than in all of Haiti.

Those displaced farmers who remained in Haiti were key actors in the AID/World Bank development model, which saw them as a cheap labor force for the assembly industry.[24] By 1987, manufactured goods—with clothing, electronics and baseballs leading the way—rivaled agricultural exports in value. Assembly-industry exports averaged $53.9 million yearly between 1980 and 1984, while coffee—a major export crop—earned $53.2 million.

But even the World Bank admitted that the "assembly industry is largely outside the Haitian economy: it provides employment but purchases few Haitian inputs and makes almost no fiscal contribution."[25] Most assembly firms were "shelter operations" in which a Haitian investor or speculator provided workers, a plant and equipment (often leased from the United States) and the foreign buyer provided all raw materials and purchased all output. In the women's underwear industry, for example, all inputs were flown in from the United States, most managers were foreigners and none of the products were even available in Haiti.

The government offered "tax holidays" to prospective assembly-industry investors, for periods generally no less than ten years through an elaborate system of loopholes and kickbacks that continued even after the "holiday" was over.[26] In addition, the government provided the basic infrastructure necessary for efficient operations: roads, low-cost energy, telecommunication services and even buildings. Haitian security forces were always available to place severe restrictions on labor organizing and guarantee low wages.

"Haitians need jobs and the assembly industry provides them," said Finance Minister Leslie Delatour.[27] Yet assembly plants absorbed a minimal portion of the workforce, employing about 40,000 workers, while some 39,000 new workers entered the labor market every year.[28] Moreover, assembly-industry operations required a politically stable environment and a docile labor force. In 1970, assembly workers earned $1 per day. Wages were officially increased to $3 per day in 1985, and some assembly workers earned $5-$7 per day. But, due to the rising cost of living, real earnings decreased 20% between 1981 and 1986.[29] To dampen workers' calls for higher wages and recognition of trade unions, the government claimed that 14,000 jobs were lost because of such "unreasonable" demands.[30]

The key figure in CNG economic policymaking was Leslie Delatour. Labeled Haiti's own "Chicago boy" in reference to his cold-bath approach, the finance minister was rapidly becoming as unpopular with the anti-Duvalierist forces (for slashing state expenditures and dismantling some state-owned industries) as with the Duvalierist Right (for eliminating opportunities for graft).

Some of the controversy around Delatour was due to his brash personality and nonchalance in the face of charges that he was no more than a tool for U.S. investors. Yet much of the opposition to him was quite substantive. Delatour was despised by many for continuing to serve a military junta that had little remaining credibility. And, when confronted by Haiti's very immediate economic crisis, his frequent backsliding into neoliberal rhetoric indicated to many his lack of a concrete strategy for development.

Delatour nonetheless made many changes during his ten months in office. He slashed spending in several departments and closed the state-run edible oils processing plant (ENAOL) and one of the country's largest sugar refineries, Darbonne. While few doubted that these state enterprises were inefficient and provided golden opportunities for graft, public opposition to their closing was vociferous; The closings caused both a direct and derivative loss in employment while increasing dependence on imports. Haitian cane growers, mostly peasants, were particularly hurt, as they had nowhere to sell their crop.

The finance minister slashed taxes on the production of coffee and basic commodities, began to reform the income-tax system and reduced many of the tariffs that favored national consumer-goods industries. As these tariffs had made many consumer staples produced in Haiti far more expensive than in the United States, Delatour's action and *laissez-faire* approach to the contraband now flooding the Haitian market resulted in a notable reduction in the cost of some basic goods. While Delatour conceded that opening the borders to consumer goods from the Dominican Republic and Miami also resulted in a massive increase in food imports, he ignored the long-term effects on local peasant economies, urban migration and overall dependency.[31]

Nevertheless, the short-term benefits from these policies combined with a virtual doubling of U.S. economic assistance in 1987 to produce a little breathing room for an economy that otherwise would have collapsed. And, on the basis of increased international aid and reductions in other departments, Delatour actually increased the education budget by 11% over 1986.[32]

According to the *Washington Post*, Delatour discovered early in 1987 that some employees of his ministry were erasing funds from checks and then redepositing them, netting over $400,000 per month.[33] This was particularly embarrassing in light of the finance minister's highly publicized campaign against corruption.

Little headway had been made in ending the systematic fraud fostered by the dictator's example. Large quantities of U.S. food donations continued to be sold for profit on the open market. And illegally imported goods, such as cigarettes, sugar, flour and rice were blatantly hawked in streets and markets. Over 60% of the medical supplies of the country's main hospital were sold off by corrupt administrators; as a result, patients went without penicillin, sterile syringes and even sterile gauze.[34]

The World Bank reported that some 57,000 salary checks were issued by the Haitian government in April 1986, when there were only 32,500 public employees, the difference being phantom employees who received what are known as "zombie checks." The report also confirmed that influential employees were not expected to perform on the job; some never showed up to work.[35] The World Bank team was unable to trace almost one-fifth of the budgeted government spending, while 22% of the money spent was not budgeted. Due largely to nepotism, the telecommunications company had five times the number of necessary staff, and the Port-au-Prince water works more than twice as many employees per 1,000 connections as the average for Latin America and the Caribbean.

Perhaps the CNG's most meaningful effort at economic recovery was its attempt to repatriate some of the $800 million stolen from the public treasury by the Duvaliers and a small coterie of former public officials and friends. On March 19, 1987, amid much fanfare, the Duvaliers' assets in the United States were frozen. Yet even this task was poorly coordinated. Part of the work was handled by the governmental Commission of Inquiry, while the more detailed and successful work was undertaken by a U.S.-based law firm; but nothing was ever returned.

The end of the Duvalier dynasty provided an opportunity for trying new development approaches in the poorest country of the Western hemisphere, especially ones based on mass participation in self-help schemes. Widespread nationalist sentiment—a product of the anti-Duvalier movement's success—seemed to make such an attempt feasible.

International lending agencies, however, fixed their gaze on developing Haiti's export potential, channeling resources into agribusiness and assembly plants to compete for the U.S. market. Even in the unlikely event that this top-down approach could convert Haiti into the "Taiwan of the Caribbean," the pressures to maintain the country's "comparative advantage"—a poorly paid and malleable workforce—would keep the benefits of such growth from trickling down to the poor.

Other than accelerating the crisis in agriculture, the government showed no sign that it intended to undertake *any* coherent development plan, much less one that would buck foreign economic interests. Clearly, the CNG and its friends in AID could not solve Haiti's crushing poverty, while the young and diverse mass movement's potential was as yet untapped.

THE U.S. ECONOMIC AGENDA

A Sweatshop Model of Development

BARBARA BRIGGS
and CHARLES KERNAGHAN

In the North American Free Trade Agreement (NAFTA) debate on "Larry King Live" between Vice-President Al Gore and Ross Perot in November 1993, there was a particularly lively exchange about the threat of jobs moving south to where wages are cheapest. If U.S. companies are only interested in a low-wage labor force, Gore asked, why aren't U.S. companies flocking to Bangladesh and Haiti? The question caught Perot off guard; in typical fashion, he turned defensive and scoffed that the answer was obvious. Neither man seemed to know that Haiti has indeed caught the U.S. government's eye. Over the last decade, the U.S. Agency for International Development (AID) has worked hard to promote Haiti as a low-wage site for U.S. companies fleeing offshore. This is more than just talk. AID poured over $100 million into Haiti's corrupt and tiny business elite to enlist its support in this effort.

The United States has a significant economic presence in Haiti. Prior to the September 1991 coup (the most recent figures available), U.S. investment was estimated to represent over 90% of total foreign investment in the country; 95% of Haiti's light-manu-facturing exports were destined for the U.S. market. According to the U.S. Commerce Department, the United States had "an esti-mated $120 million [$90 million excluding inventory] invested in Haiti as of early 1991. With the exception of several oil companies and banks (Texaco, Exxon, Bank of Boston, Citibank), U.S. invest-ment is almost entirely in the assembly sector."[1]

In 1986, AID put $7.7 million into an Export and Investment Promotion Project "to recruit assembly contracts and attract over-seas investors" to Haiti. AID felt that "medium and smaller sized American compan[ies]…, which often do not have overseas offices, have to be reached through aggressive outreach efforts." Haiti's "large pool of productive, competitive, labor-seeking employ-ment" would be one of the "factors enhancing" this promotional effort.[2]

According to AID, one of its primary objectives was to help Haitian women. In a 1986 report, the agency observed that "assem-bly industries in Haiti have a tendency to create a relatively greater demand for female workers who are believed to be better qualified for work which requires detail, dexterity, and patience. This carries a particular advantage in that increased employment for women in urban areas provides additional income which will more directly bear on the welfare of infants and children."[3] AID took this position despite their caveat that "the conditions under which [women] work are not generally conducive to realizing their productive capacities nor adequately safeguarding their children's welfare."[4]

The agency's public stance is that its real goal has always been to create decent paying jobs that would allow Haitian families to live in dignity and health. In a 1991 report, the agency noted that "most of these jobs will be for low-income citizens, with a large proportion of these going to women. As citizens enjoy employment opportunities, they can then secure their shelter, provide necessary nutrition for their families, place their children in schools and provide adequate health care for their families. With improvement in the social status of its citizens, Haiti's new democracy will be strengthened and the participation of its population assured."[5]

Despite this professed concern, AID has no empirical studies documenting the number of jobs created in Haiti's assembly-export sector; nor has it conducted any studies on what percentage of these jobs went to women, whether or not the minimum wage was paid, how many hours were worked, whether overtime and benefits were paid, what working conditions were, how people traveled to and from work, what transportation cost and how long it took or how families could afford to live on the wages paid. In 1984, the agency observed, "Haiti has no reliable work-force data."[6] In 1992, the U.S. Commerce Department again noted that "no reliable data exists" on wages and that "reliable data on employment are non-existent in Haiti."[7] AID never documented the most basic working and living conditions of the very people whom the agency was supposed to be assisting. What little information exists on these subjects has to be culled from between the lines or sought in places other than AID reports.

On the other hand, there is no shortage of AID-sponsored studies about the advantages that Haiti offers U.S. business interests. As early as 1980, AID was funding studies that showed that it was far cheaper for U.S. companies to produce goods in Haiti than in the United States, even taking into account the costs of relocation, setting up production, freight and customs. A survey of Haitian and U.S. electronic-assembly plants operating in Haiti established that 38% of the companies enjoyed savings of 20-40% over U.S. production, while 20% enjoyed savings of 40-60%.

This study may also have pinpointed the real interest in women assembly workers: "Women workers tend to be quieter." The study went on to state that "traditional management prerogatives such as the right to hire and fire are respected by the government. There are no profit-sharing schemes or featherbedding requirements." Only quiet women, who "are young and highly motivated" and "who adapt easily to industrial discipline," are strong candidates for employment.[8]

Concerned about working conditions in plants closely linked to the U.S. economy, a delegation of U.S. trade-union leaders visited Haiti in 1991, just after the military coup. Their business-sector hosts took the delegation to a "model" apparel factory in Haiti's export-assembly sector. At the factory, where fabric is sewn into clothing to be exported to the United States, the highest paid workers receive the equivalent of U.S.$1.48 a day. These workers' average transportation cost to and from work is 44 cents a day. A meager breakfast and lunch comes to 33 cents. This leaves 71 cents to bring home at the end of the day. Multiply this by the six days of the Haitian work week, and working people have $4.26 to meet their family's expenses for a week. Since a working family needs about a third of this to cover rent and other expenses, family members have approximately $2.75 a week with which to feed themselves.[9]

Not one single collective-bargaining agreement is in effect in Haiti's export-assembly sector. According to the U.S. Labor Department, "It appears that many employers of the export industry are not in fact willing to bargain with trade unions." Further, "many employers, domestic and foreign, still question the legitimacy of unions."[10] While freedom of association, the right to strike and the right to organize are legally provided to all workers in Haiti, few workers actually enjoy such rights, whether employed in export-processing operations or local firms.[11]

A ristide's unexpected victory in the 1990 elections threw a wrench in AID's well-laid plans. Under the Aristide government, observed AID, "Businesses are postponing investment and reducing inventory while waiting to see the future directions of the new government before making significant business growth decisions."[12] AID, which had spent tens of millions of U.S. tax dollars since 1980 to foster offshore investment in Haiti's low-wage assembly sector, stopped promoting investment when Aristide took office in 1991.

An AID/Haiti Mission internal staff assessment concluded that the incoming Aristide government "could benefit from position papers staking out the issues" and suggesting "possible policy solutions" for economic development. "However," continued the study, "in view of legitimate political sensitivities, greater policy ownership by various Haitian interest groups may be more important than more donor-produced studies and reports." The "donor"—AID—was supposed to go backstage. "Enhancing indigenous policy dialogue capacities within the private sector," the study concluded, "may be the most productive course of action."[13]

In country after country throughout Central America and the Caribbean, AID's development strategy is based on working with local business elites to help them more efficiently utilize their large pools of low-wage labor. Accordingly, AID's next move was to quickly allocate $26 million to the "ad-hoc committee of business organizations," which was under AID's control, to help keep "Haitian production competitive in world markets."[14] An internal working paper recommended that the ad-hoc committee be organized and placed "under the umbrella of AID's export and investment promotion project (Prominex)." Prominex—which, after a series of scandals, changed its name to PROBE (Promotion of Business and Exports)—receives 99% of its funding from AID and is, in fact, an AID front group. AID allocated $7.7 million to Prominex, $12 million in loans to business and $7 million to foster democracy "from a business perspective." After 67.5% of the Haitian people had voted for change in the 1990 presidential elections, AID worked with the Haitian business elite to keep things the same.

The refurbished Prominex/PROBE operation was supposed to "work with local business organizations to develop internationally competitive local production, build constituencies for open-market policies and move Haiti toward becoming a full partner in the hemispheric free-trade block [sic]." Of course, it was Haiti's "highly productive, low-cost labor" which was to be the engine for integrating Haiti into this bloc.

By the middle of Aristide's first seven months in office, AID was declaring that "signals" from the constitutional government "to the business community have been mixed." AID went on the attack saying that "decisions have been made which could be highly detrimental to economic growth, for example in the areas of labor and foreign-exchange controls."[15] The agency was displeased with the fact that Aristide wanted to place temporary price controls on basic foodstuffs so people could afford to eat.

But AID's real wrath was targeted at labor reform efforts. They opposed the Aristide government's attempt to raise the pitifully low minimum wage in Haiti's export-assembly industry. According to the agency, the proposed minimum-wage increase would price Haiti right out of the low-wage assembly market. "Wage systems," AID said, "should not be the forum for welfare and social programs." It warned that "high distortion in labor costs"—the 50-cent hourly wage increase proposed by the government—"can lead to capital-intensive, rather than labor-intensive responses to opening of markets."[16] Haiti, the agency seemed to fear, might turn into Switzerland or Denmark.

Three months before the coup, the agency mused: "If Haiti's investment climate can be returned to that which existed during the CNG [the National Government Council headed by Lieutenant General Henri Namphy, a Duvalier loyalist, who took power after the Duvaliers fled] or improved beyond that, and the negative attitude toward Haiti appropriately countered, Haiti stands to experience significant growth."[17]

In April 1992, as the military regime that ousted Aristide became increasingly intransigent, the U.S. Commerce Department calmly noted:

> After an internationally recognized government is reestablished, the best long-term prospect for U.S. business will continue to be investment in export-assembly operations. Haiti's proximity to the United States, its access to Generalized System of Preferences (GSP), Caribbean Basin Initiative (CBI) and Section 807 U.S. Customs benefits, as well as its abundance of low-wage, productive labor should make it a good location for assembly operations when the country achieves some level of political stability.[18]

While AID's projects may be a boon for U.S. and Haitian business interests, they have done little to alleviate the devastating poverty of residents of Port-au-Prince. The poor continue to live in miles and miles of broken-down shacks made of rough concrete, mud, straw, cardboard and scrap sheet metal. When the wind blows in off the ocean, the metal roofs strain and rattle. It's like being inside a tin can. Open sewers flow down the dirt streets, which are deeply rutted by erosion. When it rains, the sewage overflows into people's homes. There are no bathrooms, no running water. Thousands depend on a public faucet or a broken water main where people scoop up water. Children can be seen playing and washing in the open sewers. The government doesn't collect garbage. It piles up everywhere in great mounds that people periodically burn to reduce the volume and to check the spread of disease.

The most common meals for working families are cornmeal with onions or boiled plaintains with beans—when they can afford beans. Almost everyone eats only one meal a day. Many working families have only bread to eat and rely on sugar cane water to fill themselves up.

The poor are barely surviving, and they are getting sicker. While the consolidation of Haiti's elected government is an urgent and necessary first step, the economic development strategy that Haiti pursues has great significance for the growth—and sustain-ability—of democracy. AID and other "donors" might consider that the foundation for a viable development strategy must be more than the comparative advantage afforded by "cheap labor."

16

FRAPH AND CDS

Two Faces of Oppression in Haiti

DEIDRE McFADYEN

The stretch of land was gray and pock-marked like a desolate moonscape. A swath of 1,000 shanties in Cité Soleil, Port-au-Prince's largest slum, had been burnt down on December 27, 1993, in retaliation for the death of Issa Paul, a militant of the right-wing Front for the Advancement and Progress of Haiti (FRAPH), the day before. The January afternoon that I visited the site with NACLA's fact-finding delegation, two weeks after the fire, some people were camped out on the plots under the blazing tropical sun, afraid the government would use the opportunity to take away their land.

According to residents, a gang of *attachés*—paramilitary troops in civilian clothes—had descended on the area at eleven in the morning and set houses alight with gasoline and fire grenades. As the fire took its deadly course, the men fired shots into the air to prevent people from fleeing it and neighbors from dousing the flames. In one particularly gruesome incident, a six-year-old girl trying to escape a burning shanty was allegedly shot in the arm and pushed back into the inferno. Witnesses testified that police stood idly by and that the fire department was kept away. According to the Catholic human rights group Justice and Peace, about seventy people, half of whom were children, died or "disappeared" in the arson attack. The Haitian Press Agency reported that at least thirty were killed by gunshot. *Haïti Progrès* estimated that 10,000 people lost their homes.

Investigations by Justice and Peace and by Haitian journalists revealed that in the days preceding the fire, rumors that FRAPH "had decided to empty Cité Soleil of its residents" had been spreading through the slum, home to 200,000 residents. *Attachés* identified as FRAPH members had begun a campaign that week to force the drivers of Haiti's colorful tap-tap minibuses to change their placards from Cité Soleil to Cité Simone. The community was named Simone, after François Duvalier's wife, until 1986. It was rechristened Cité Soleil after Baby Doc's ouster in honor of the Catholic radio station Radyo Solèy, which had been a catalyst for the liberation struggle.

Justice and Peace also reported that it had not turned up any evidence to support the allegation that Lavalas supporters were to blame for Paul's death. More likely, the death of the FRAPH militant can be attributed to a settling of accounts within the paramilitary organization itself. "The offensive seems to have been planned," concluded the group's report. "The death of Issa Paul merely furnished a pretext."

AID-funded Centers for Development and Health (Centres de santés et de développement, CDS), were promptly on the scene after the fire to distribute aid. According to U.S. Ambassador William Swing, the United States decided to give CDS a $100,000 special grant for "disaster relief" "to permit Doctor Boulos and the personnel of CDS to continue the excellent work that they have undertaken to relieve the suffering of the victims of the fire."

Each homeless family was supposed to be allotted some food and fifteen Haitian dollars (about U.S.$6). Attesting to the intricate web of repression, people in Cité Soleil claimed that many of those handing out food aid were among those who started the fire. On the day of our visit, virulent arguments broke out among the residents about how some families were denied assistance, while other people received more than their fair share. Still others claimed that they did not even try to register for aid because they were afraid of being apprehended by members of FRAPH who could be found at the CDS offices. Justice and Peace also found that aid was being sold to local merchants and given to others not affected by the fire. CDS said plans were in the works to rebuild homes in the area. Cité Soleil residents were nonetheless worried, unsure what the future held and distrustful of CDS' intentions.

CDS—run by wealthy Lebanese businessman Reginald Boulos as his personal fiefdom—played a key role in the effort to stifle dissent during the dictatorship. Like the good cop/bad cop routine, CDS' social work complemented FRAPH's iron hand. Founded twenty years ago with funds from 100 privileged Haitian families, the center has grown over the years. Today, AID is the principal backer of CDS' $2-million-a-year operation. The center operates three multi-service clinics in Cité Soleil and sends volunteers into the neighborhoods to do a census and register children in preventative health care program.

At the "Brooklyn" clinic, mothers with their infant children held cards issued to them by CDS and made their way among the stations set up for immunizations, weighing and vitamins. One room was full of bassinets for 100 malnourished children who were brought to the clinic each day for feeding. In an interior courtyard, children dressed in neat red-aproned dresses and matching bows frolicked. These were the "post-malnourished" children in the center's kindergarten program.

No one disputes the fact that CDS was providing a useful service. It's only in the broader context that its potentially pernicious effects became apparent. Because the clinics could not possibly provide full health services for everyone, a selection process was inevitable. "The poor who are compliant and docile get health services," explained Gérard Blot, a progressive doctor who is familiar with CDS. "Those who are more militant have trouble getting services." A select 100 malnourished babies were showered with attention and care, but what about the thousands of other impoverished children in the slum? CDS director Doctor Joseph Mazouka, when asked if there was a waiting list, shrugged his shoulders and dismissed the question. Moreover, the user fees that patients must pay precluded the very poorest from receiving treatment.

People went to the private clinics because they have no other choice. The Haitian state has a nominal presence in health and education programs. According to Boulos, 70% of health services are provided by private charities and 85% of education is privately run. In Cité Soleil, there are no public hospitals, one public school and two army barracks. During the dictatorship, the state was totally absent except for repression.

Because CDS tracked the movement of families into and out of the neighborhood, the organization's records would have been useful to the army in its efforts to monitor and control the population. Members of one grassroots organization in Cité Soleil complained that Boulos' operation was full of "recycled Macoutes"; and there was fear that the extensive dossiers that CDS kept on each family might fall into the wrong hands.

Suspicions that CDS and FRAPH were in cahoots were borne out eight months later in the disarray at the time of the U.S. military's "permissive entry." In a report in *The Nation* in October 1994, Allan Nairn reported that four senior *attachés* worked for CDS. Boulos acknowledged to Nairn that one of the four, Fritz Joseph—who, according to FRAPH leader Emmanuel Constant, is the key FRAPH recruiter in Cité Soleil—had worked at CDS for many years. According to sworn testimony, CDS also regularly made cash payments to two others—Marc Arthur and Gros Fanfan—who were implicated by the UN in the September 1993 murder of prominent pro-Aristide businessman Antoine Izméry. Finally, Constant insisted that he regularly spoke on the phone with Boulos, a charge the latter denied.

As Haiti languished in its third year of military dictatorship in January 1994, the protracted, often brutal work of consolidating the military regime was underway. Cité Soleil, along with other Aristide strongholds, was targeted by the army in an effort to obliterate all opposition to the regime—whether through the overt repression of FRAPH or the more subtle methods of CDS. By funding such organizations as CDS that were probably aiding the *de facto* regime, the U.S. government ended up undercutting its professed goal to kick out the putschists. This funding, however, may in fact have fit perfectly into the unspoken agenda of the U.S. government, which did not want to dirty its hands by associating publicly with the paramilitary thugs but nevertheless approved of more passive forms of repression and control.

Part IV

Resistance and Human Rights

Fighting over a poster mocking Jean Claude "Baby Doc" Duvalier shortly after he fled. (Port-au-Prince) *Photo by Maggie Steber, 1986.*

THE MONKEY'S TAIL STILL STRONG

The Post-Duvalier Wave of Terror

MICHAEL S. HOOPER

Reagan Administration spokesperson Larry Speakes was only slightly premature in announcing the Duvaliers' departure on January 31, 1986. Although Baby Doc declared that his rule was "as strong as a monkey's tail," the end was in sight. Up against the wall, Jean-Claude Duvalier had declared a state of siege, ordering the Tontons Macoutes (Volunteers for National Security, VSN) and the army into the streets, where they killed hundreds. By February 6, however, Baby Doc had passed into the pages of Haitian history and into a luxurious exile abroad.

The *coup de grâce* was delivered to the dictatorship by two of its closest allies, the Army High Command and the U.S. Embassy. The Army High Command deserted the President-for-Life in part because of protesters' appeals, in part because of the wanton character of the slaughter, and in part because of the chance to rid itself of the Tontons Macoutes, which had become the single most pervasive force in rural Haiti.

Created soon after François Duvalier ("Papa Doc") took power, the VSN grew to at least twice the size of the armed forces. Although the blue-uniformed Macoutes carried out the bulk of the repression, others worked as civilian government employees, businessmen, Voodoo priests and transportation workers. Almost all rural section chiefs and other local officials were Macoutes, as were members of the more powerful secret societies. The military high command, therefore, joined the U.S. Embassy in abandoning Baby Doc to avoid a greater blood-bath and to consolidate what was left of the regime.

Beyond the army's desertion of Baby Doc, Haitians with access to the Duvalier inner circle agreed that a crucial factor in bringing down the dictator was dissent and fragmentation within the ranks of the old-guard "dinosaurs." Even as they deserted Jean-Claude, these cronies of Papa Doc remained loyal to the latter's widow, Simone, and to strongman Roger Lafontant, who as minister of the interior and national defense dominated Haiti until September 1985. Men such as Clovis Desinor, who served in Papa Doc's cabinet for thirteen years, felt pinched by the new elite. While living lavishly himself, Desinor deplored the "money everywhere and the lining of pockets."[1] Toward the end, he took to denouncing the policies of the young Duvalier as "an insult to misery."

The continuity of the "Duvalier revolution" was not only based on sowing terror among all perceived opponents, but also on the creation of a political class to monopolize government posts and state contracts. Negritude, or Noirisme, provided access to previously unimagined wealth and arbitrary power to a relatively small black middle class, for whom continued privilege presupposed complete loyalty to the Duvaliers.[2] By the end of the Duvalier era, 700 families dominated Haitian economic and political life.

Michèle Bennett's behavior after her 1980 marriage to Baby Doc did much to offend the old guard of Noirisme. The mulatto Bennett clan lived ostentatiously—the wedding celebration cost some $1 million—and resentment grew as they successfully monopolized access to the spoils of power. Behind gossip about mulatto/black tensions, it should be remembered that the old Duvalier elite only became seriously disenchanted when the Duvalier-Bennett clan so dominated the corruption network that little was left for the faithful. In December 1985, the French press published accounts of Michèle's "astronomical" spending spree in Paris, even as Haiti "reeled from a shortage of fuel and foreign exchange."[3] After the Bennetts' ascension, the Duvaliers' claim to have made a political revolution to benefit middle-class blacks was difficult to sustain.

This tension between the old guard and the Bennetts also played itself out on the stage of daily politics, particularly during Lafontant's harsh tenure. A physician, Lafontant took pleasure in personally interrogating and beating detainees in the Dessalines barracks. He boasted of his role in crushing the infant Christian Democratic Party of Sylvio Claude and forcing the League for Human Rights to halt all meaningful activity.

As Catholics became increasingly outspoken, Lafontant initiated a campaign of intimidation against the Church and insisted on harsh edicts banning opposition political activity and muzzling what was left of the press. The personal and institutional excesses of Lafontant and secret police chief Albert Pierre drew international condemnation. Arguments broke out within the regime over who was best serving the interests of Duvalier and his "revolution." This resulted in a whirlwind cabinet reshuffling and public recriminations between ministers, especially between old-guard Duvalierists and the newly ascendant merchants and businesspeople around the Bennetts. Buckling under Haiti's increasing diplomatic isolation, some within the power elite began to withdraw overt support for the President-for-Life.

Whatever the differences between their regimes, by the time nineteen-year-old Jean-Claude Duvalier succeeded his father in 1971, there was no clear distinction between the Duvalier family and the Haitian government. The Duvaliers eliminated all institutions representing meaningful ideological pluralism: political parties, free press and trade unions.

Over the years, Washington officials encouraged Baby Doc to allow the winds of liberalization to blow periodically. These openings were followed by harsh crackdowns, as the population tested his promises of participation and democracy. By mid-1985, what had for twenty-nine years seemed an unassailable fortress turned up riddled with fault lines. A deepening economic crisis and defections of close Duvalier supporters feuding over government spoils had already done serious damage. Even so, few experts predicted the Duvaliers' imminent ouster when, on November 28 of that year, troops shot and killed four schoolchildren in the coastal city of Gonaïves. In retrospect, this last blood-bath washed away Baby Doc's remaining legitimacy and united the population in taking unprecedented risks to oust him.

The army officers to whom Baby Doc passed the baton on February 7, 1986 were all familiar figures. Most of the officers who dominated the National Government Council (CNG) after Duvalier's fall were among those responsible for enforcing his reign of terror. Nominally led by Duvalier's army chief of staff, Lieutenant General Henri Namphy, real power was exercised by Colonel Williams Regala, appointed to the crucial post of interior and defense minister, and Colonel Prosper Avril, Duvalier's personal military adviser, who held no formal government position. Also prominent initially was Alix Cineas, Duvalier's minister of public works, a civilian whom insiders simply called the "bagman" because of his knack for transferring misappropriated funds overseas.

The inclusion of Professor Gerard Gourgue as minister of justice and Professor Rosny Desroches as minister of education initially lent the cabinet considerable credibility. Gourgue, as president of the Haitian League for Human Rights, and Desroches, as a widely respected educator, had both earned solid reputations working to curb the worst excesses of Duvalierism. Three days after taking power, junta president Henri Namphy declared that his regime would be based on "absolute respect for human rights, press freedom, the existence of free labor unions, and the functioning of structured political parties." Namphy regularly reiterated these promises.

Yet the CNG inspired little confidence in its human rights policies. The council took few demonstrable steps to transcend the Duvalier legacy of terror, cronyism and corruption. Although the Tontons Macoutes were formally dissolved after Duvalier's departure, in practice they remained armed and continued to dominate many rural areas. There was no attempt to determine the extent of past human rights violations, the identity of those who committed them or the role of the security forces in such violations. Moreover, there was no indication that security forces would be prosecuted for future abuses.

With few exceptions, only officers loyal to Duvalier and his inner circle had traditionally wielded any real authority within the military. Early in the Duvalier years, Macoutes replaced commanders they considered unreliable. At times, officers had to bow to lower-ranking Duvalierist cadres, while soldiers were rewarded for fidelity to the President-For-Life and zeal in combating his opponents.

The Army High Command exercised only nominal authority over the officer corps. Real military power rested, as it did in 1987, with the commanders of the Dessalines barracks, the U.S.-trained elite batallion known as the "Leopards," the Fort Dimanche barracks, the presidential guard and the military police, each of which had effectively independent command structures stemming from the presidency. In creating islands of military power, the Duvaliers were able to exploit their overlapping and conflicting roles, thereby preventing the regular army from establishing any independence. After Duvalier's fall, it appeared that the army was unwilling or unable to challenge the arbitrary power of these groups.

On March 19, 1986, five civilians were shot to death and another nineteen were severely beaten in Martissant by the "Leopards." The soldiers were attempting to disperse a crowd angered by the arrest of a tap-tap driver who was accused by an army captain of illegally passing his vehicle.[4] The following day, a Leopard unit killed two more civilians in Carrefour, where roadblocks had been erected to protest the killings.

After less than two months as justice minister, Gourgue resigned under pressure to protest the army killings and the CNG's uncanny ability to look the other way as Duvalierist criminals slipped out of the country. Within six weeks of the dictator's flight, all his closest associates had left Haiti, many with considerable fortunes. Secret police head Colonel Albert Pierre and notorious Macoute executioners such as Elous Maitre and Lyonel Wooley were all allowed to flee.

Mounting opposition forced the CNG to regroup on March 24, 1986. Cineas was ousted and François Latortue—who had established solid anti-Duvalierist credentials in exile—replaced Gourgue as minister of justice.

On April 26, army troops fired on peaceful, unarmed marchers outside Fort Dimanche, the infamous military barracks where thousands of political prisoners were held during the Duvaliers' twenty-nine-year rule. Six civilians were reported dead and more than fifty wounded. Military police at Fort Dimanche prepared for the demonstration by assembling heavy automatic weapons atop the two-story building. Some troops took up posts behind bushes while others stood in formation in front of the main gate, loaded rifles in hand. Contrary to claims made by Fort Dimanche commander Captain Isidore Pognon, no stones were thrown at officers before the first shots were fired. Newspaper accounts and eyewitnesses reported that the march was among Haiti's most peaceful and best organized.[5]

The demonstration, which followed a mass and prayer march, was called by the League of Former Political Prisoners to commemorate the 1963 massacre of Benoît family members in Jérémie. The Benoîts had been granted permission to lay a wreath paying tribute to the many prisoners who died at Fort Dimanche. Despite the clearance, the family was turned away, and the crowd began to chant in protest. In response, the military police fired into the crowd. Only after scores lay dead or injured was tear gas used to disperse the remaining protestors.

In a communiqué released the next day, the Ministry of Interior and National Defense characterized the actions of the armed forces as a "normal reaction of the troops who were defending access to the Fort Dimanche barracks against an invasion effort."[6] Namphy expressed regret, but declined responsibility, blaming the incident on "agitators and *provocateurs*." He also criticized human rights activists such as Gourgue, who had condemned the killings. Junta strongman Colonel Regala told a visiting U.S. human rights delegation that this kind of response was appropriate "if people demonstrated and didn't behave correctly."[7]

During the summer of 1986, the CNG moved to eliminate Haiti's infant trade-union movement. At least 14,000 workers were fired or locked out in the assembly industry alone, most of them because of efforts to unionize. In urban areas, workers' demands for pay increases and improved working conditions were met with hostility from employers and intimidation by thugs believed to be former Tontons Macoutes. The Ministry of Social Affairs, charged with mediating worker-management disputes, worked closely with employer organizations and refused to defend workers' constitutional right to organize.

Companies producing goods for the U.S. market, including shoe, sportswear and electronic assembly operations, were among the first to fire scores of employees attempting to unionize. The U.S. Embassy remained silent, despite Caribbean Basin Initiative requirements that internationally recognized labor rights be respected.

Much less was known about continuing human rights abuses in the countryside, where 75% of the Haitian population lived. Many rural areas were still controlled by Tontons Macoutes and other Duvalierists; and serious human rights violations continued, despite the fact that the 22,000-member Macoutes were officially disbanded and forced into hiding after Duvalier fled Haiti.[8]

After they had legitimized the junta, cabinet ministers Latortue and Desroches were forced out by Colonel Regala on January 5, 1987 in what marked the beginning of a sharp turn to the right by the government.

Regala, who promoted himself to brigadier general in March 1987, personified the current leadership's close ties to the old regime and its repressive ways. After graduating from the Military Academy in 1959, he quickly climbed the army ladder, becoming increasingly influential in a group of officials who acted as a secret police force. He was believed to have taken part in the mass murder of unarmed civilians at Jérémie in 1964.[9] Regala also appeared to have played a key role—along with secret police chief Luc Désyr and Dessalines barracks commander Breton Claude—in the bloody "drive against the communists," which began in 1969. Several hundred Haitians were shot outright or killed in prison during the two-year campaign, which targeted anyone even loosely associated with the Unified Haitian Communist Party (PUCH).

In the summer of 1987, soldiers from the Dessalines barracks, as well as members of the Leopards strike force, began shooting down demonstrators without provocation and carrying out nightly raids on the crowded slums outside Port-au-Prince. At least twenty-eight Haitians were shot dead and 110 were wounded in late June. In the last week in July, twenty-four were killed and many others were seriously injured.[10]

The Army High Command broke its silence in a July 30 communiqué explaining the wave of killings. "Certain demonstrators approached the soldiers, evidently intending to disarm them," the statement said in regard to the killings in Port-au-Prince. "Some individuals identifying themselves as journalists, and others identified with 'Press' signs, circulated with bags of rocks on their backs. These journalists carry weapons and shoot at demonstrators." Further, it claimed that "certain terrorist elements...trained in Cuba, have re-entered the country as boat people and are using weapons previously smuggled in...or hidden in bags of rice brought from abroad [sic]."[11]

The July 23, 1987 massacre of at least 300 peasants in the barren hills near the northwestern city of Jean-Rabel—an impoverished region from which many Haitian refugees in the United States had fled—was a particularly horrifying incident. Traditional property holders, supported by peasants and former Tontons Macoutes in their employ, were pitted against the *Tet Ansam* (Heads

Together) peasant collective, supported by activist Catholic clergy. The violence exploded over the cooperative's increasing demands for land reform and the return of land allegedly stolen by local Tontons Macoutes under the Duvaliers.

Tet Ansam had grown in strength, successfully organizing a number of alternative irrigation and marketing projects, which encroached on the *gwandons* (landowners) economic monopoly. The group organized the July 23 march to protest landowners' efforts—enforced by Macoutes—to hold on to choice lands and harass its members. Several thousand marchers were attacked by a large group of machete-wielding peasants and former Tontons Macoutes as they walked near the Jean Rabel River. In addition to the 300 believed dead, many more were seriously wounded. The same goons later tried to remove wounded *Tet Ansam* members from the local hospital.[12] Clergy and reporters who tried to visit the area were blocked for five days by the same gangs.

These killings accompanied a crisis that had begun on June 22 when a clique of army officers controlling the government took over the pending electoral process and banned Haiti's most active trade union, the Autonomous Haitian Workers Union (CATH).

The army resumed the Duvalierist practice of threatening foreign and Haitian journalists—with bullets. On July 29, 1987, journalists from CBS, CNN and the *Christian Science Monitor* were targeted. Soldiers routinely confiscated film and fired shots to scare journalists away from gruesome security force murders; and, on June 28, a regular army unit had killed a crew's guide outright.

Prior to these incidents, public pressure had resulted in a considerable increase in the range of freedoms for both the press and political parties. The March 1987 Constitution formally guaranteed freedom of the press and political parties. Even so, the CNG insisted that its restrictive press and political parties laws, passed in July 1986, were still on the books. These decrees paralleled the Duvaliers' 1980 press law and the political parties law of 1985. Article 1 of the law extended the definition of press—as did the 1980 version—to bookstores and printing facilities, so that book vendors and printers could be prosecuted for selling material that violated the statute. Article 6 required journalists to reveal their sources, limiting their ability to collect news and information by subjecting informants to possible arbitrary reprisal. Article 10 stipulated that print and broadcast media could only hire licensed journalists. Critics feared this provision might be directed at the many fledgling newspapers and magazines had sprung up after the Duvaliers' ouster, making it impossible for many of them to operate.

Leading journalists reported that the Duvalierist system of government subsidies and inflated advertising fees for "cooperative and responsible publications" continued under the CNG.[13] Similarly, many of the best-known editors supplemented their earnings with government jobs that required little effort. One independent editor, Dieudonné Fardin, of the weekly *Le Petit Samedi Soir*, said this system of journalistic self-censorship was an inevitable legacy of decades of political repression.

Like the press statute, the July 1986 political parties law was a refurbished version of Duvalier's restrictive decree. The new law granted the justice minister power to accredit political parties or order their suspension. All parties had to be registered to participate in elections scheduled for November 1987. Each party was required to submit the names and addresses of some 5,000 members to be legalized; previously 18,000 members had been required. Parties with any religious or trade union affiliation were proscribed. In addition, the military government set the by-laws under which a party could function and established rules that would allow the government to take over the property of parties declared suspended or dissolved.

The Port-au-Prince Bar Association, alarmed by efforts to censor the press and limit political activity, suggested that military authorities were overstepping their boundaries, since no laws should have been passed before the new constitution was adopted. "When a political regime does not know the limits of its actions, it becomes an autocratic regime," the attorneys observed.[14]

In spite of the violence, the hopes of many were focused on local elections scheduled for November 1987, which were also seen as a test of the CNG. Yet the public also viewed the electoral process with deep mistrust, particularly given the track records of the parties and candidates involved, as well as the June 22 takeover of the Provisional Electoral Council (CEP), the only structure to suggest that elections might in any way reflect the popular will. The popular refusal to work with existing political parties and candidates soon became absolute. Instead, the popular movement concentrated on grassroots education and elections from below to prepare the population for local and parliamentary polls. This was to lay the groundwork for the eventual development of national political groupings.

This popular movement developed into *Operation dechoukaj,* the Creole term for the movement to uproot and sweep away the old order. Largely peaceful, this campaign of refusal and regeneration was led by unknowns and ignored by the elite and foreign embassies until it could not be stopped. Much of the intrigue that ensued in 1986-1987—involving a broad spectrum of political leaders and the middle class—can perhaps best be understood as an attempt to catch up with and control this amorphous and effective popular revolt.

"Rache manyòk, bay te-a blanch"—"we will pull up the deepest roots of Duvalierism until Haiti is finally cleansed"—said Bishop Willy Romulus of Jérémie during a sermon. This phrase perhaps best symbolizes the parameters of the popular movement in Haiti in 1987: consensus on the need to uproot the system of privileges, corruption and terror became the yardstick by which all politics were judged and for which many were clearly making extraordinary sacrifices.

By eliminating independent political parties, unions, media and rule of law, Duvalierism gave birth to a new form of passive resistance. With no leaders to eliminate, no program to seize, and no formal means of communication, the movement proved the catalyst for Baby Doc's ouster and eventually demanded the replacement of the CNG. This popular movement initially called for the *dechoukaj* of Duvalierists, but then unified around the notion of *rache manyòk*, the total uprooting of Duvalierism itself. The movement found expression in the Catholic Church, especially the *Ti Legliz* (Christian base communities) and in a range of increasingly militant youth groups throughout Haiti.

Demands for *rache manyòk* and the rejection of the presidential candidates led to the development of two interrelated coalitions, indirectly supported by the Church and youth groups, which gave a national voice to the movement. Comprised of 284 national and local organizations, the National Congress of Democratic Movements (Konakom) was founded in early 1987. Army efforts to take over the electoral process in June then spawned the Group of 57, which was pushed to the forefront of the opposition by continuing official violence and disregard for the March 1987 constitution.

Meanwhile, the international press continued to overplay the "leading presidential candidates" and their parties. In fact, they were without exception self-appointed and largely without social base. Many had coexisted with Duvalierism for much of their lives, and the best-known internationally were all friendly to the CNG and Washington. Reagan's snub of the popular movements while he actively supported the CNG partly explained the growing anti-American sentiment in Haiti.

After Duvalier's fall, U.S. policy toward Haiti was designed to keep a lid on popular demands for profound structural changes by overtly supporting the military junta. Prior to Baby Doc's departure, Washington praised his referenda and excused his human rights record. Afterwards, the United States was said to want elections at any cost, an ultimatum understood in Haiti to mean that the U.S. trump cards had all been handed to generals Regala and Namphy and that support for the junta would not waver, human rights violations notwithstanding.

Privately, U.S. diplomats argued that this one-dimensional policy furthered U.S. interests and encouraged the long-term development of democracy in Haiti. These "interests" were usually expressed as maximizing stability and obtaining the cooperation of the Haitian government in halting the continuing flight of refugees to the United States.

When Congress resumed military aid to Haiti in September 1986, its authorization was conditioned on ending human rights abuses by the armed forces, ensuring freedom of speech and assembly, investigating and prosecuting those responsible for past rights violations and requiring former Tontons Macoutes to turn in their weapons.

The Reagan Administration continued to certify that the CNG was "liberalizing" the government and improving respect for human rights in order to justify continued foreign assistance to Haiti. After February 7, 1986, U.S. aid virtually doubled to $1.10 million. In 1986, U.S. military advisors were sent to train Haitian security forces.[15]

Yet violence by uniformed armed forces escalated. In an August 6 letter to U.S. Secretary of State George Shultz, Senator Edward M. Kennedy called for an immediate end to military aid to Haiti, to be followed by a suspension of economic aid unless progress was made. At the same time, Kennedy urged that the United States not certify that human rights had improved in Haiti. A bipartisan appeal also called for an end to military aid.

Congressional concern, however, was not echoed by the State Department. On June 30, 1987, Assistant Secretary of State for Inter-American Affairs Elliott Abrams spoke at length about the sanctity of the electoral calendar in Haiti without once mentioning the recent wave of killings.[16] The Haitian military seemed to have interpreted this as a sign that U.S. support for the junta was unflagging, so long as elections were delivered.[17]

The United States was seen in Haiti as promoting the *forms* of democracy—such as symbolic elections—without encouraging significant efforts to promote the democratic institutions required to give substance to these forms. In refusing to require that the CNG respect fundamental human rights during the pre-election period, Haitians felt that U.S. policymakers undermined the very electoral process they championed.

18

PÈRE LEBRUN IN CONTEXT

ANNE-CHRISTINE D'ADESKY

The cruelties of property and privilege are always more ferocious than the revenges of poverty and oppression. For the one aims at perpetuating resented injustice, the other is merely a momentary passion soon appeased.
—C.L.R. James, *The Black Jacobins*

After the military coup that overthrew his government, President Jean-Bertrand Aristide found himself the object of intense scrutiny in the international media for alleged human rights violations during his brief administration. Accusations that Aristide had condoned and even advocated mob violence and class war continued to dog him during his exile, and "Père Lebrun"—the practice of necklacing political opponents with burning tires—became a rallying cry of those opposed to his restoration to power. Meanwhile, the coup leaders engaged in wholesale slaughter with seeming impunity. This article on Aristide's human rights record and the incidence of "popular justice" during his seven months in office sets the record straight and places the controversy in proper perspective.

The September 1991 military *coup d'état* that overthrew Haitian President Jean-Bertrand Aristide shone a new spotlight on the issue of justice and human rights in Haiti. Aristide's great popularity stemmed from his outspoken commitment to human rights and to ending Haiti's legacy of dictatorship. But, in the aftermath of the coup, critics accused Aristide of failing to uphold these very principles.

Aristide's detractors charged that he supported mob lynchings, or "popular justice," whose grisly symbol is *Père Lebrun*, a gasoline-soaked tire that is "necklaced" around a victim and set on fire. *Père Lebrun* (the name comes from a local tire dealer) was used by angry crowds against known or suspected Duvalierists after the fall of the Duvalier dictatorship in 1986. During a failed coup attempt on January 6, 1991, a month before Aristide's inauguration—led by Duvalier's former Interior Minister and Tontons Macoutes chief Roger Lafontant—crowds again used tires and gasoline to stop the coup from succeeding.

"You have to see Père Lebrun in the actual context of the country," explained former soldier Patrick Bochard before the coup. "If the Haitian people hadn't fought back, Aristide wouldn't be in office, and we would still have a dictatorship."

In a July 1991 interview, Aristide claimed that "without a system of justice that is not corrupt, the people must remain vigilant." He was careful to talk about Père Lebrun as a means of assuring respect for the Constitution, which he called "our only guide to justice." According to a post-coup survey of Père Lebrun incidents by the New York-based National Coalition for Haitian Refugees (NCHR), twenty-five people were killed in mob lynchings during the seven months of Aristide's tenure.

In an impromptu September 27, 1991 speech to supporters gathered in front of the National Palace that has been widely disseminated in the international press since the coup, Aristide appeared to condone, and perhaps even encourage, the practice of Père Lebrun. Using strong language, Aristide told the upper class that it must invest in Haiti and give food and jobs to the poor. He exhorted the poor and unemployed to "turn your eyes in the direction of those with the means." And, in an indirect reference to Père Lebrun, he said: "Your tool in hand, your instrument in hand, your Constitution in hand. Don't hesitate to give him what he deserves."

In this speech, as in prior ones, Aristide specifically named the Tontons Macoutes as legitimate targets of popular vigilance. But, in a subtle shift, he added to the list of fair targets the vague term "false Lavalassien" (a reference to certain members of Lavalas, his own political organization), which could have been interpreted as "non-supporters of Aristide."

Many in the country's economic elite and opposition political parties complained that the president was inciting the poor to attack the rich. They also felt that Aristide, contrary to his call for national unity, was emphasizing the gap between the two classes. Finally, critics felt that Aristide was strengthening his already cult-like status to the point that dissent and free speech were threatened.

"There is no excuse or justification for the army coup," said Jean-Claude Bajeux, a human rights advocate and member of the Konakom opposition party, as the coup unfolded. But, he added, "mistakes were made by Aristide and his entourage. By refusing to condemn Père Lebrun, he is seen as tolerating this kind of violence."

"He should have spoken out," admitted a close aide to Aristide, who requested anonymity. "You have to understand that the climate was hostile; there were constant threats. But that does not excuse what I consider an error of judgment. He is not responsible for the violence, but neither should he give the impression of having accepted or supported it."

Under pressure after the coup, Aristide tried to clarify his position on Père Lebrun, condemning the violence and again stressing his support for the Constitution. But his tacit acceptance of lynching as a political tool and his failure to speak out earlier lost him the unqualified faith of some and planted a damaging seed of doubt in many.

This mixed record, however, ought to be reviewed in the context of his efforts at reform. In his electoral campaign, Aristide made it clear that justice would be a priority for his administration. At the top of his agenda was the immediate need to curb the threat of a coup and reduce everyday street violence by armed gangs. Aristide planned to initiate vast reforms in the army, police, judiciary and state-run industries, among them to separate the army from the police, a goal set forth in the 1987 Constitution. This was viewed as part of a longer-term effort to demilitarize Haiti and create a new role for the country's uniformed men—and, for the first time, women.

"The idea is to retrain the army and the police. Why does Haiti need such a big army?" asked Constitution author Dr. Louis Roy in February 1991. "We need the army and police for ports, customs and border control. We need to put these people to work rebuilding the country, like a civil police."

Aristide also sought to purge the army of former Duvalierists. In his inaugural speech, Aristide replaced six of the seven members of the powerful army high command, considered "the old guard." He declared "a new marriage" between the army and the Haitian people, and courted the army rank and file by allotting $6 million to improve working conditions for soldiers.

That same day, Aristide forbade over 150 members of the previous Trouillot regime to leave the country, pending an audit of the state's accounts. The order was eventually dropped, but not before alarming the military and political establishment, which was long accustomed to corruption and patronage.

In a more symbolic effort, Aristide presided over a moving ceremony for the Duvaliers' victims at the notorious Fort Dimanche military prison on February 8, 1991. Later, he appointed a cabinet-level commission, followed by an independent one, to review human rights abuses committed during the 1957-1990 period, with an eye toward prosecution.

Under the Constitution, Aristide was legally entitled to a six-month "grace period" during which he could make major reforms without the approval of the legislature. Duly empowered, he arrested a dozen top officers linked to Duvalier, including the powerful Fort Dimanche commander, Isidore Pognon. Aristide also rehired pro-democratic soldiers who had been fired under previous regimes.

In another blow to army power, Aristide put the country's 555 section chiefs, or rural sheriffs, under the jurisdiction of the Justice Ministry, rather than the military, and ordered them to turn in their weapons. But, in the absence of a functioning legal system, the move backfired in some areas. Some residents complained that the unarmed sheriffs were unwilling to intervene to stop violent disputes. Meanwhile, other section chiefs held on to their weapons and remained in the pay of local landowners, firing on peasant groups during land disputes.

These reforms would lead nowhere without a justice system to enforce them. Aristide replaced four Supreme Court justices who were considered "compromised" and initiated a similar cleanup of judges in the countryside. In an effort to educate public officials about the Constitution and human rights issues, the president planned to open a magistrate's school for judges and a police academy in 1992.

Aristide has been criticized for his handling of the Justice Ministry. His minister, Baynard Vincent, resigned in May 1991, after being indirectly implicated in a scandal. His replacement, Karl Auguste, was unable to organize effectively the government's case against several Duvalierists accused of plotting against the state.

The most important of the cases against the Duvalierists was the July 27, 1991 trial of ex-Macoutes leader Roger Lafontant, jailed after his failed coup attempt in January of that year. Though Lafontant was convicted and sentenced to life in prison with hard labor, the marathon twenty-one-hour trial seemed more a political event than a judicial procedure. Aristide supporters kept a twenty-four-hour vigil outside the court; following the announcement of the verdict, Aristide declared a national holiday, thanking his supporters for assuring "that the Macoute trial went ahead without problems."

"There was no trial. There was a travesty of justice," said Jean-Jacques Honorat, a lawyer and head of the CHADEL human rights organization at the time. Honorat, a strong Aristide critic who later became a prime minister of the post-coup government, complained about the unwillingness of local lawyers to defend

Lafontant. "They are afraid of reprisals by Aristide's people," he said. "They are afraid of being lynched, and for good reason."

On August 13, some 2,000 Aristide supporters threatened legislators inside the National Assembly in an attempt to stop a motion of no confidence against Prime Minister René Préval. Later that week, Aristide supporters burned the headquarters of the CATH labor union to protest an anti-Aristide campaign by CATH organizer Jean-Auguste Mesyeux. Summing up public opinion prior to the coup, left opposition leader Bajeux said: "There's a mounting frustration in the parliament with Aristide and a fear among the elite. Aristide is doing nothing to change that."

"Aristide started to become president for 70% of the people and wanted to forget the other 30%," said a top aide looking back over events. "After a while, they rebelled."

Ironically, opponents have pounced on Aristide's mixed human rights record to justify a coup that led to an escalation of human rights abuses. The army massacred and wounded hundreds of civilians during and after the coup. Dozens of Aristide officials and supporters were jailed; many were tortured. The right to public assembly was gone, along with free speech and a free press. Soldiers also looted businesses, extorted money from civilians and pillaged private homes. During the three years of military rule that followed the coup, more than 5,000 Haitians were killed or disappeared, over 300,000 were internally displaced and another 50,000 fled the country.

The army used Aristide's Père Lebrun threat as a justification for several raids on poor neigborhoods where support for Aristide and resistance to the coup were strongest. Many poor youths from the Cité Soleil and Carrefour districts of Port-au-Prince are still reported missing. Others were arrested without charges or evidence on the grounds of plotting Père Lebrun-type actions. Slum residents who fled the cities in terror remain in the countryside, while those who are unable to leave fear for their lives.

"Who are the real perpetrators of the terror? Who are the real criminals?" asked Antoine B. from Cité Soleil. "It is the army and the bourgeoisie. They are trying to blame Aristide, but they are the ones coming to kill us."

I 9

HAITI'S POPULAR RESISTANCE

MARX V. ARISTIDE and LAURIE RICHARDSON

On a chilly Washington weekend in October 1993, Haiti's grass-roots leaders huddled with exiled President Jean-Bertrand Aristide to take stock of their country's popular movement. Their reflections yielded a mixed assessment. To its credit, the movement's resistance and mobilization had kept the restoration of democracy to Haiti high on the international agenda for two full years since the September 1991 *coup d'état*. Yet, as painful reminders of the movement's limitations, the military junta remained entrenched in power, a wave of brutal repression threatened to drive popular organizations completely underground and strategies to resolve the crisis were being worked out in diplomatic suites without the input or participation of the grassroots.

As the often-invoked Haitian adage says, "*Dèyè mòn, gen mòn*"—beyond these mountains lie more mountains. Such is the saga of Haiti's popular movement. Having emerged from the Duvaliers' twenty-nine-year reign of terror with little organizing experience, the movement is still struggling to overcome a seemingly inescapable legacy of marginalization. Made up of a wealth of base ecclesiastical communities, peasant groups, labor unions, student organizations and neighborhood associations, the popular movement espouses mass mobilization as the means to institute revolutionary changes in the country's traditional order and establish a truly participatory democracy. Through demonstrations, strikes, land takeovers, written and audio publications and the occasional use of "popular justice," popular organizations have advanced demands ranging from agrarian reform to university autonomy.

The movement's effectiveness has been mitigated by brutal repression, a chronic lack of resources and political opportunism. Add to these a U.S. offensive aimed at coopting grassroots cadres and the absence of a political party or united front capable of concretizing popular demands, and the challenges facing the movement are revealed.

In addition to these obstacles, the popular movement is embroiled in a dialectical struggle with the reformist sectors of Haiti's broader "democratic" movement. This reformist camp—consisting of certain politicians, intellectuals and members of the business elite—remains preoccupied with establishing formal democracy through elections and superficial reforms. The tension between these two currents remains the most formidable impediment to the success of the popular movement. Although the reformists oppose hard-line Duvalierism, they do not share the popular movement's more radical long-term vision for a new Haiti.

Despite these challenges, Haiti's popular movement has grown bigger and stronger over the past decade. Through its exuberant emergence in 1986, its often painful debates about strategy from 1987 to 1989, its triumph at the polls in 1990 and its scrappy resistance to three years of military dictatorship, the popular movement began to come into its own—gaining force with each victory and learning lessons from each defeat.

MARX V. ARISTIDE and LAURIE RICHARDSON

After months of sustained popular mobilization, Jean-Claude "Baby Doc" Duvalier was finally whisked away to France on a U.S. jet on February 7, 1986. As the Haitians say, *"Baboukèt-la tonbe"*—the horse was unbridled. The masses once again took to the streets, this time to celebrate. The make-up of this collective victory party reflected the broad tactical unity that had formed in opposition to the dictator. Landless peasants danced alongside large landowners, and slumdwellers celebrated beside industrialists.

With the bit of the brutal Duvalier dictatorship out of the people's mouth, everything seemed possible. This new-found taste of liberty whetted an appetite for justice and a desire to organize collectively for fundamental change. For the first time in nearly three decades, the voices of Haiti's poor majority found expression in a myriad of grassroots organizations, some newly formed and others emerging from clandestinity. These groups began to articulate a range of concrete demands—from land reform to Creole literacy programs. Uniting virtually all sectors across ideological and class divides, however, was the clarion call to banish the hated Duvalierists from the political scene.

Clearly, there was more to Duvalierism than the Duvaliers themselves. Despite Baby Doc's departure, the pillars of Duvalierism remained intact. Baby Doc had passed the baton to the Duvalierist National Governing Council (CNG), a six-member junta headed by General Henri Namphy. Brutal section chiefs still ruled the countryside with impunity, the public administration remained bloated with corrupt civil servants, and the Tontons Macoutes still held powerful government posts. Explained "Fritz," a well-known militant who has spent over twenty years in the struggle, "We all witnessed Duvalier's departure. Theoretically, there was no more dictatorship and the era of repression was over. Then, we began to realize that Duvalier was just the tip of the iceberg and that we had to start mobilizing on all fronts."[1]

One of the strategies employed in this mobilization was *dechoukaj*. Translated literally as "uprooting" and often equated singularly with "necklacing"—execution by means of a burning tire—the concept of *dechoukaj* embraced much more than popular street justice. In fact, its most potent dimension was political. In the process of "uprooting" Duvalierism, peasants organized to eliminate the brutal section-chief structure, students fought to end state control of the university and the masses were galvanized to dismantle not just the Tontons Macoutes themselves, but the political machine that created and sustained them for nearly thirty years.

Popular militants were convinced that *dechoukaj*, left to gain momentum, could successfully transfer real power from the Duvalierists and the elites to the poor majority. Indeed, it was this possibility that most unnerved the reformist camp, many of whose adherents benefited at least indirectly from the status quo and would—if political *dechoukaj* were allowed to run its course—ultimately be held accountable to the more militant bases.

Echoing the Duvalier-appointed Catholic bishops, the reformists launched a propaganda offensive highlighting the street justice aspect of *dechoukaj* and calling for national reconciliation. By virtue of money and control of major media outlets, the reformists were able to bring *dechoukaj* to a halt by mid-1986.

"Whenever the people were highly mobilized," lamented Fritz, "instead of having a clear and unified call to action, you would find those guys ready, behind closed doors, to talk to [hard-line junta General] Regala, to talk to Namphy. Instead of urging the population to keep pressing with their demands, they acted like firefighters, making conciliatory declarations. Sometimes we felt that they considered us more of an enemy than the Macoutes."[2]

Haitian wisdom warns that *"kay koule twonpe solèy; men li pa twonpe lapli"*—the leaky house may fool the sun, but not the rain. In early 1987, merely one year after Duvalier's downfall, tensions between the revolutionary ideals of the militant camp and the petit-bourgeois tendencies of the reformists flared. While a general consensus had emerged around the need to eventually replace Haiti's Constitution and hold new elections, there was debate about whether or not such steps could be taken in the repressive climate under CNG rule. As testament to its complexity, this period elicits divergent assessments within the popular movement even to this day.

In January 1987, a broad spectrum of democratic groups was invited to participate in the Congress of Haiti's Democratic Movements (Konakom). The Congress produced a platform endorsing the constitutional referendum and laying the groundwork for a center-left political party. The more militant sector of the popular movement was skeptical. It saw the focus on the referendum and elections as a maneuver designed to stave off more radical change. "We were in the streets yelling, 'Namphy is going to fall!'" said Fritz, "so [Namphy] sent everybody back home to study the Constitution."[3] In March of that year, the newly formed National Popular Assembly (APN) called for a boycott of both the referendum and the elections. Others, such as the Peasant Movement of Papaye (MPP), took a more nuanced position, endorsing the Constitution despite certain misgivings.

After the Constitution was approved in March, debate shifted to the November 1987 elections. Even many who endorsed the elections doubted the will of the CNG to play fair. "*Rache manyòk*"—literally "pull out your roots"—became the order of the day as the junta was urged to exit the political scene. The July massacre in Jean-Rabel of over 300 peasants advocating land reform reinforced this mistrust in the electoral process and fueled calls by militants for a total boycott. Port-au-Prince's *Ti Legliz* coordinating committee urged the people to "remain mobilized against these elections, whose results—no matter what—will not resolve the fundamental problems of the people."[4] As election day neared, however, "*rache manyòk*" was modified to encourage the masses to shift their energies from street mobilization to an "electoral clean-up"—voting Duvalierists out of office.

The army responded with a "cleanup" of its own, massacring voters as they turned out to cast their ballots. While temporarily forcing the movement to retreat, the aborted elections paradoxically advanced the popular movement's long-term struggle by highlighting the limitations of the reformist strategy in confronting the Duvalierists. The reformists "need the popular mobilization when they are under fire," said Fritz, "but once they get the

Macoutes off their backs, they make an alliance with the bourgeoisie to block any deeper change. They always say it's not to block
you. They say you are unrealistic, you are extremist, you are a
purist. They have all kinds of names for you. But when the Macoutes come back to haunt them, they are quick to cry for help."[5]

Two coups and one bogus election later, the popular movement emerged to reclaim the streets in March 1990 to force dicta-
tor-of-the-hour General Prosper Avril from power. Yet, once again,
their victory was cut short. In a familiar scenario, the newly opened
political space was monopolized by traditional reformists who
made an unholy alliance with interim President Ertha Pascal-
Trouillot, a Duvalierist.

"After we braved the army's bullets and riot gear to force
Avril out, the suit-and-tie types took over," explained Calixte, a
leader of the Coordination of Popular Organizations. "They essentially informed us that our involvement in the process was over
and that the affair had moved to air-conditioned suites where we,
the masses, were not welcome."[6] A twelve-member interim State
Council, co-governing with Trouillot, was created to prepare for
new elections in December 1990. Popularly denigrated as being
"two-headed," the government was quickly discredited for its
complete inability to respond to the demands of the masses.

Yet, as with past setbacks, many within the ranks of the
popular movement were further radicalized by this experience. As
political elites positioned themselves for the 1990 elections, most
people refused to take the bait, remaining indifferent to the process.

Aristide's last-minute entry into the presidential contest in-
stantly changed this equation. Only seven months earlier, reformists had ignored calls by the APN and the National Front Against
Repression to install the populist priest as interim national leader.[7]
Faced with the return from exile of hard-line Duvalierist Roger
Lafontant and the slick U.S.-funded campaign of Marc Bazin, it was
now the reformists who asked Aristide to join with them to stave
off these threats. The strategy worked brilliantly. Within a week,
electoral rolls doubled as over a million new voters flocked to
register.

This marked the birth of "Operation Lavalas." Since its incep-
tion, Lavalas was an arranged marriage between the popular
movement, from which Aristide sprang, and anti-Macoute elites,
characterized by the National Front for Change and Democracy
(FNCD), whose legal status Aristide used in his run for the presidency. "What is important," Aristide said when announcing his
candidacy, "is to know the moment when history calls upon us to
forge a tactical unity...in order to stop the Macoutes."[8]

Not surprisingly, the Lavalas alliance was marred by internal
friction from the outset. The previous favorite for the FNCD presidential nomination, Konakom's Victor Benoît, quickly dubbed
Aristide's bid "political adventurism" and called on party members to suspend all electoral activities.[9]

This time, however, the militant camp had the upper hand.
With a legitimate representative of the masses shaping the political
debate, the reformists could not control the outcome. And, while
FNCD sought to usher candidates into other offices on Aristide's
coattails, the popular movement saw the elections only as a vehicle
for mobilization and reiterated its readiness to boycott them if
necessary. "We will either take it all the way," warned Aristide, "or
reject it categorically."[10]

On February 4, 1991—a month after he swept the elections
and three days before his inauguration—Aristide announced the
replacement of the "Lavalas Operation" with the "Lavalas Organization." His motive was clear: to build an independent political
structure around the mass mobilization of the people. This signi-
fied a divorce from the FNCD, which became threatened by the
prospect of a rival party that would inherit Lavalas' glory. Because
FNCD reformists could not control the alliance, they became Aristide's most bitter enemies; many actively participated in destabilizing his government.[11]

Shortly after his inauguration, President Aristide welcomed
MPP to the National Palace. After an arduous six-hour drive from
the Central Plateau, the 100-member delegation from Haiti's oldest
peasant group presented its demands, talked with the president
about their future and joined him in an animated chorus of MPP's
theme song: "Let's join forces to liberate Haiti."

With a democratically elected popular government in power for the first time in Haiti's history, the climate was ripe for grassroots organizations to solidify their structures, empower and expand their bases and advance their demands. "During Aristide's presidency," explained Ben Dupuy, co-director of the weekly *Haïti Progrès* and a founder of APN, "APN's concern was to...make people aware that even though they were formally in power...the forces against progress were still very strong and there was no guarantee the present situation would last. So, the people had to take advantage of this space and period to consolidate themselves, instead of looking for quick solutions or individual benefits."[12]

Yet, in spite of the advantages offered by the presence of one of their own in the National Palace, the movement was also faced with a new set of challenges. First, lured by prestige or money, some grassroots leaders left the popular sector to take positions in the government. Second, although numerous self-proclaimed popular organizations were taking shape, particularly in Port-au-Prince, many were devoid of any real base and were headed by opportunists merely seeking power and status. Finally, some militants opted for a leave of absence from their organizing activities to indulge in the Lavalas euphoria.

The September 1991 coup came mercilessly. One of its primary objectives was to destroy the popular movement and drive the masses away from the political arena. To withstand the repression, the Haitian people revived the concept of *mawonaj* (marronage), a form of clandestine resistance deeply rooted in the Haitians' historical rebellion against slavery.[13] Haiti's contemporary maroons have replaced the conch shell, used by the revolutionary maroon leader Boukman to call the slaves to action, with underground bulletins, leaflets and cassette tapes. They disguise meetings as games of dominoes or *konbit*, the traditional cooperative work teams used in rural areas. They use the vehicle of the popular church to spread the message of hope.[14]

Yet, with President Aristide in exile and isolated from his popular base after the coup, reformist elements within Lavalas came to dominate its policymaking structure. They chose to rely almost exclusively on internationally sponsored negotiations to resolve the crisis. Many within the popular movement were leery of this strategy, warning, in the words of MPP spokesperson Chavannes Jean-Baptiste, that "only the heat of mobilization will make the pot of negotiations boil." Nathan, a student from Petit-Goâve, summed up the frustration: "Every time we were ready to turn up the heat, the international community intensified negotiations, and everyone was sent back underground to 'wait and see.' If it wasn't leaky sanctions, it was the Organization of American States/UN Observer Mission, and the waiting game continued."[15]

As the international community extracted deeper concessions from the Aristide government, criticism of the negotiating process grew. The popular movement found the deafening silence of the reformists in the face of increasing threats of military intervention particularly alarming. When the Governors Island Accord was signed, popular organizations expressed support for President Aristide, yet denounced the document's content and voiced skepticism that the military and the international community would deliver on their part of the bargain.

The failure of the accord reinforced the popular movement's conviction that it could no longer wait for deliverance and must mobilize its own forces to topple the coup regime. Discussions of "a new formula of struggle" and a more active resistance were multiplying as militants strategized about how to turn disillusionment into defiance and rejuvenate international solidarity.

For their part, the reformists came to a dangerous crossroads where they had to choose between a deeper alliance with a self-interested international community or tactical unity with an increasingly militant popular movement. While the reformists have historically used the masses to tip the balance of power at such junctures, they were hesitant to revert to this strategy during the period of military rule. Aware that the empowerment Lavalas instilled in the masses was being reinforced by ongoing popular resistance, the reformists feared that they would not be able to contain the pressure for deep and sweeping change that would inevitably be liberated if the military regime were to be ousted through mass mobilization.

The U.S. government sees Haiti's popular movement as a threat, which it has attempted to contain and counter using the National Endowment for Democracy (NED), the U.S. Agency for International Development (AID) and the Central Intelligence Agency (CIA). Under the guise of "democratization," "development" and "the war on drugs," these agencies have funneled millions of dollars to Haitian military and intelligence agencies, political parties and non-governmental organizations to destabilize genuine popular organizations and build conservative alternatives.

An April 1992 report on Haiti from the Inter-Hemispheric Education Resource Center details how "NED and AID have tried to craft a carefully tailored electoral democracy based on conservative interest groups."[16] Funding for such activities began in earnest with the fall of the Duvalier dictatorship in 1986 and increased sharply in 1989 in preparation for the December 1990 elections. After President Aristide's victory, support for political projects in Haiti soared again with the addition of a five-year, $24-million package for "democracy enhancement." The aim of the program was to strengthen conservative forces within the legislature, the local government structures and civil society at large. And, as summed up by the Resource Center report, "to unravel the power and influence of grassroots organizations that formed the popular base of the Aristide government." The U.S. government went to special lengths to counter the demands of Haiti's labor movement. According to research conducted by the National Labor Committee, "U.S.AID used U.S. tax dollars to actively oppose a minimum-wage increase from $.33 to $.50 an hour proposed by the Aristide government."[17]

The main conduit for "democracy enhancement" funding in Haiti is the Integrated Project for the Reinforcement of Democracy in Haiti (PIRED). Established by the United States in 1991, PIRED is directed by U.S. anthropologist Ira Lowenthal. Lowenthal maintained in an interview that PIRED does not oppose the Aristide government, but he confessed that he believes the U.S. government does. Lowenthal gave three reasons: "A basic U.S. reflex against populism; the U.S. does not like Aristide's vision of redistribution; and Aristide is a small black man talking trash."[18]

Although evidence has yet to be unearthed proving U.S. involvement in the coup that ousted Aristide, the list of junta members or supporters who received substantial amounts of U.S. funding is rapidly growing. Recent reports in the *New York Times* have exposed the CIA's nefarious role in propping up Haiti's corrupt military rulers.[19] Not only did the CIA and the U.S. military establishment forge ties with the most anti-democratic elements of Haiti's military—training these officers and paying them for information—but the agency also actively participated in establishing and maintaining repressive structures inside Haiti. In 1986, for example, the CIA set up and provided funding for the National Intelligence Service (SIN) under the guise of fighting narcotics. Yet, according to a U.S. Embassy official cited by the *New York Times*, SIN "never produced drug intelligence" and instead used the $500,000 to $1 million they received annually from the United States "for political reasons, against whatever group they wanted to gather information on." A Haitian official concurred, saying SIN was "heavily involved in spying on so-called subversive groups.... They were doing nothing but political repression.... They targeted people who were for change." After the *coup d'état*, the CIA used the distorted data it obtained in a vociferous attempt to discredit President Aristide and his supporters in the popular movement.

With the restoration of Aristide in October 1994, the debate between the reformist camp and the popular movement is bound to intensify. It is the popular movement, however, that gained strength, insight and stamina during the long journey up this mountain range and on to the next. In the words of one peasant organizer: "With the increased repression, the struggle just takes different forms depending on the circumstances. If the road has thorns, we know what shoes to wear; if there's a river in our path, we are prepared to swim. But, above all, we keep struggling because that's our only chance for a brighter tomorrow."[20]

Profiles of the Popular Currents in Haiti

Ti Legliz—the Little Church

Many of Haiti's popular organizations trace their roots back to the *Ti Kominote Legliz* (TKL), for it was in these ecclesiastical base communities that activists found cover during the repressive Duvalier era. Springing from the current of liberation theology, the *Ti Legliz* movement took off in the mid-1970s, providing a common thread to link catechists, peasants, students and workers. The use of church-based training programs and the emergence of the church-funded popular radio station Radyo Solèy further politicized and fortified the *Ti Legliz* sector.

After Baby Doc's downfall in 1986, the movement sought to formally structure itself. A National Coordinating Committee was established with representatives from diocesan TKLs throughout the country. Other religiously based groups cropped up, including Solidarite Ant Jèn and Veye Yo. The new political opening allowed activists to spin off and build peasant, student and other popular organizations.

Peasant Groups

The seeds of Haiti's peasant movement were planted in the late 1960s in the form of farming cooperatives, or *gwoupman*. Consisting of ten to fifteen members, *gwoupman* gave peasants a collective base of resistance against the rural structures of exploitation and repression.

By 1986, *gwoupman* had become widespread and extremely politicized. After Duvalier's fall, they developed into a myriad of local and regional peasant organizations. Relying on tactics such as marches and land takeovers, peasant groups demanded agrarian reform, elimination of the repressive section chiefs, repopulation of Black pigs eradicated by AID between 1981 and 1983, tax reform and promotion of Haitian Creole.

Founded in the early 1970s and operating in semi-clandestinity until 1986, the Peasant Movement of Papaye (MPP) is Haiti's oldest peasant organization. In March 1987, MPP formed the National Peasant Movement of the Papaye Congress (MPNKP), which reported a membership of 100,000 Haitians before the 1991 *coup d'état*. Another national movement is *Tèt Kole Ti Peyizan* (Heads Together Little Peasants), which has its roots in meetings held by peasant delegates beginning in September 1986. Tèt Kole has *gwoupman* in each of Haiti's nine departments and is strongest in the northwest town of Jean-Rabel.

The Student Movement

Although Haitian students have been active since the beginning of the U.S. occupation in 1915, François "Papa Doc" Duvalier dealt a serious blow to the movement by eliminating the leadership of the National Union of Haitian Students (UNEH) in the late 1960s. Although student participation in the ouster of Jean-Claude "Baby Doc" Duvalier was massive, it was largely unorganized. Not until late 1986 did the movement begin to restructure itself.

UNEH's successor is the National Federation of Haitian Students (FENEH), formed in March 1987, and based in Port-au-Prince. Calling for university autonomy and the removal of Duvalierists from the educational system, FENEH's methods of organizing include boycotts, demonstrations and building takeovers. A variety of high school and youth organizations have also emerged, key among them *Zafè Elèv Lekòl* (ZEL). Founded in November 1986, ZEL has campaigned to demand free basic education for all.

Labor Unions

Haiti has a rich tradition of cooperative and union organizing. Yet, until Duvalier's downfall, virtually all unions—with the exception of the U.S.-backed Federation of Workers Union (FOS)—operated underground. The Autonomous Central of Haitian Workers (CATH) emerged out of clandestinity in 1986 to become the most powerful federation of unions in the country. However, a series of internal crises, compounded by a stepped-up U.S. destabilization campaign, split CATH into various factions.

Today, the Central Workers Union (CGT), founded in October 1986, is the most militant of Haiti's three union federations. The other two—FOS and OGITH (Independent General Organization of Haitian Workers)—both receive funding from the National Endowment for Democracy (NED) and toe a more moderate line.

Neighborhood Committees

Primarily organized in poor urban areas, neighborhood committees emerged as marginalized residents sought to improve the lot of their communities. Committees have organized to demand potable water and electricity, protest the high cost of living and defend themselves against crime and extortion.

Committees often formed "vigilance brigades" that erected barricades and interrogated and searched suspicious individuals in an effort to provide security to residents. The brigades also served as dynamic networks for sharing information and for political organizing.

Today, various neighborhood committees are loosely linked under the umbrella of the Federation of Neighborhood Committees (FEDKKA).

Other Popular Organizations

Not all of Haiti's popular organizations can be easily classified into categories. Many have broad-based constituencies that include workers, peasants, students and others. One such example is the National Popular Assembly (APN). Founded in March 1987 as a popular alternative to Konakom, APN is represented throughout the country in the form of local popular assemblies. One of the more militant organizations within the popular movement, APN was the first to propose Aristide as a national leader. More recently, the organization has been a vocal critic of the reformist sector within the Lavalas camp.

THE 10th DEPARTMENT

JEAN JEAN-PIERRE

When, at a campaign planning session in October 1990, President Jean-Bertrand Aristide referred to Haitians living abroad as the "Tenth Department," he had little idea how indelible a mark this new concept would leave on the Haitian sociopolitical landscape. Although the then-priest of Saint Jean-Bosco, one of the poorest parishes of Port-au-Prince, was well known as a consummate neologist, even some of his closest advisors dismissed the new term as another passing fad in the colorful Haitian Creole language.

Haiti is divided into nine regions known in French as "departments." Aristide christened as the Tenth Department the estimated 1.5 million Haitians residing in major cities such as New York, Boston, Miami, Chicago, Montreal and Paris, as well as in Africa, the Dominican Republic and elsewhere in the Caribbean. Nearly one out of every four Haitians now resides in the diaspora. Its size and strong ties with the homeland have made the Tenth Department a political and economic force that every Haitian government must reckon with.

Haitian immigration began when laborers started traveling to Cuba to harvest sugar cane in the 1920s, in the midst of the U.S. occupation of Haiti. By the 1930s, due to deteriorating working conditions in Cuba, these *braceros* started moving across the border into the Dominican Republic to work in the sugar fields there. Within a few years, tens of thousands of Haitians of varied professions followed the cane cutters and successfully integrated into Dominican society. Although these Haitian workers were crucial to the Dominican economy, some Dominicans—mainly politicians and intellectuals—saw their presence as a second occupation of their country. (Haiti had occupied the Dominican Republic from 1823 to 1844.) This deep resentment culminated in the massacre of 30,000 Haitians in 1937 by Dominican dictator Rafael Leonidas Trujillo, who felt the migrants threatened his country's security. This incident temporarily halted the migration of Haitians to the Dominican Republic; but, by the early 1950s, it had resumed, and continues to this day.

When the brutal dictator François "Papa Doc" Duvalier took power in fraudulent elections in 1957, the ensuing repression changed the nature of Haitian immigration. Intellectuals were the first group to be targeted as the Tontons Macoutes—Duvalier's private militia—brutally suppressed academia's opposition to his rule. Papa Doc openly encouraged the Haitian intelligentsia to leave the country. In fact, he invited the UN to open offices in Haiti to recruit Haitian professionals to go to Zaire and other newly independent African nations that were in dire need of doctors, nurses, teachers and lawyers. Haitian journalist André Charlier refers to that early wave of Haitian exiles, in which he was included, as the "first Haitian brain drain." In subsequent years, a systematic terror campaign orchestrated by Duvalier, combined with U.S. labor shortages, generated a substantial flow of immigrants to the United States.

In December 1972, a group of Haitian refugees landed on the shores of Miami after braving the high seas in a flimsy craft. These Haitians were not truly the first Haitian boat people. After all, the first boat leaving Haiti for the United States sailed in 1776, carrying recently freed Haitian slaves who had volunteered to participate in the War of Independence against England. Furthermore, prior to 1972, hundreds of Haitians had sailed to the Bahamas, where it was easier to obtain a U.S. tourist visa. The Bahamas' open immigration policy and its proximity to Miami made it a perfect corridor to the United States.

The new "boat people" phenomenon, however, was a direct result of the unremitting hardship wrought by a rudimentary economy and a repressive dictatorship. These conditions were reinforced by the passing of power from Papa Doc to his nineteen-year-old son, Jean-Claude "Baby Doc" Duvalier in 1971. It did not take long before this new wave of refugees became an integral part of the Haitian community living in the United States. They participated in weekly church services, in music dance parties and other community activities. But all did not go smoothly. The Haitians who immigrated to the United States during Baby Doc's reign tended to be blacker, poorer and less skilled than the earlier generation of immigrants. The new mix was a microcosm of Haitian society.

Haiti is structured by a complex caste system that stems from French colonial rule. While economic status can be either inherited or acquired, social status—in a country that is 95% black—is mainly based upon epidermal hue. The lighter the skin, the heftier the privileges. Although dark-skinned, middle-class Haitians traditionally headed the great majority of governments, the mulatto elite retained significant spheres of power and influence in every regime. Even at the height of François Duvalier's so-called *noiriste* (black-oriented) revolution, the mulatto elite kept its privileged status. Papa Doc once bragged about his daughter marrying a rich mulatto.

For those Haitian mulattos who were accustomed to these advantages, life became more complicated in the United States, where race is not solely determined by skin shade. Some Haitian mulattos found themselves grouped in the same category with the poorer, dark-skinned new immigrants. Being in large part non-professionals, some upper middle-class, light-skinned Haitians had to compete for the same manufacturing and cleaning jobs with people who were once their gardeners, cooks and maids. Haitian-born magazine editor Joel Dreyfuss alludes to this phenomenon when he calls the United States "the great equalizer."

The elite Haitian refugees found some solace in French-language Sunday church services and certain social activities where women could wear beautiful dresses and men could wear stylish suits. In a nation where Haitian Creole is the vernacular, the elite has always used French to alienate the masses. In New York, former residents of Pétionville and other wealthy Haitian neighborhoods preferred to live in Queens, Long Island or Manhattan rather than Brooklyn, where most of the new immigrants settled. These artificial and imaginary boundaries went beyond geography. Upper-class Haitians derisively referred to the newly arrived as the just come, or the "unsophisticated ones." Ironically, even among the post-1971 immigrants, many of those who had arrived in the United States by airplane felt compelled to distinguish themselves from the "boat people."

With the overthrow of Baby Doc Duvalier on February 7, 1986, Haitians in the diaspora began returning to Haiti in droves. For a brief period, thousands of Haitians poured back into the country. Some completed construction of the homes they had started building years ago; others established new businesses. But when the military—taking advantage of the democratic movement's divisions—stepped in to fill the political vacuum, these new returnees turned around and left. Once again, Haitians in the diaspora entered a state of limbo.

It is a commonplace in the Haitian community that most discussions among more than two Haitians will inevitably revolve around politics. Haitians in the diaspora are no exception to the rule. Politics in the homeland has always captured their attention. Prior to 1971, the single purpose of most Haitian political groups in the diaspora was the overthrow of the Duvalier regime. Most Haitians of this generation believed they would return to their country once this temporary obstacle disappeared.

The politically ambitious took advantage of this deep-seated desire to return that so many Haitians harbored. Some of these "candidates" raised—and many pocketed for themselves—large sums of money to plot the overthrow of Papa Doc. One such candidate, Bernard Sansaricq, a senator in the Haitian parliament during the Duvalier dictatorship, organized annual invasions of Haiti over the course of almost two decades. With two exceptions—when he sent a few subordinates to their deaths—his groups never reached Haitian shores. (A recently published document alleges that Sansaricq was a CIA operative.) Other would-be invaders only succeeded in dropping a few gas explosives on the Haitian capital. These attempts consistently failed because the opposition movement never had a strong and well-organized base in Haiti. Furthermore, in contrast to its support for Cuban exiles in Miami, the United States consistently applied the Neutrality Act to prevent Haitian exile groups from reaching Haiti.

The Haitian "boat people," although not admitted to the United States in great numbers, became the impetus for the rise of new Haitian-American political organizations; and the treatment of these refugees became a rallying cry for existing ones. This new influx, said Lionel Legros of the Haitian Information Center in Brooklyn, represented "a turning point in Haitian immigration to the United States." In contrast to the secretiveness of traditional political activity in the diaspora, the new groups began to stage public demonstrations to denounce the U.S. role in Haitian politics. Previously, Haitians had protested with their faces hidden for fear of being recognized by the hundreds of spies working in the United States for Papa Doc.

Divisions between the old and new generations of Haitian immigrants made unity within the diaspora almost impossible to achieve. Numerous political organizations—80 at last count—have sprung up in the last couple of years. "Ninety percent of these groups are composed of twenty people or fewer," says Jocelyn McCalla, executive director of the National Coalition for Haitian Refugees (NCHR). This fragmentation, he adds, makes it "hard to politically influence their representatives, whether local or national." In a "permanent ad hoc" approach, these groups come and go depending on the nature and duration of the situation at hand.

These differences were momentarily put in abeyance in April 1990, when over 85,000 Haitians and Haitian-Americans shook the Brooklyn Bridge in one of the largest marches ever organized in

New York. They came out to protest a decision by the U.S. Food and Drug Administration (FDA), to include Haitian-born immigrants among the high-risk groups prohibited from donating blood because of the HIV-virus. The specter of ostracism, job loss and stigma forced Haitians of all walks of life to come together in protest. The FDA lifted the ban a few weeks later. Many saw this important victory as the seed that would grow into a more organized unified diaspora. But the Tenth Department remains riven by divisions among different Haitian groups.

The common thread weaving all the different political groups into a single fabric has always been opposition to the Duvalier regimes and their military successors. But conflicting political and social interests have marred even this basis of unity. These conflicts are reflected in the fractious relations among the three major competing Haitian newspapers in the United States. Published mostly in French, these weekly newspapers were the primary way that the Tenth Department kept abreast of events in Haiti before the advent of daily radio programs. A mirror of the rips and tears in Haitian society, the rivalry among these weeklies often borders on ideological war.

Haïti Observateur, the voice of the conservative sector, is the oldest of the three newspapers. It was founded in 1971 in Manhattan. Raymond Joseph, its owner and editor, staunchly opposes Aristide. His virulent attacks against the president have earned him the ire of most of the Tenth Department. Indeed, many consider *Haïti Observateur* the voice of the putschists. Joseph's acidic editorials are often directed at *Haïti Progrès*, the second oldest newspaper. Founded in Brooklyn in 1983, the paper has a Marxist-Leninist political slant. An early supporter of Aristide, *Haïti Progrès* became one of his most outspoken critics, even though its editor, Ben Dupuy, was the Haitian president's ambassador at large until July 1993. The paper accuses Aristide of selling out to the international community.

Completing this three-way journalistic scrimmage is *Haïti en Marche*. Following a more moderate line, this Miami weekly, founded in 1986, is perhaps the most recognized among the three newspapers by the international community. Its editors, Marcus

Garcia and Elsie Etheart, won the 1990 Maria Moors Cabot Prize awarded annually by Columbia University for excellence in journalism. The unyielding support of *Haïti en Marche* for Aristide earned it the sobriquet "mouthpiece of the bourgeoisie" from *Haïti Progrès*.

With circulations ranging from ten to fifty thousand each, these three weeklies, which are filled with political analyses and commentaries, are considered the Haitian "think tanks." Even though *Haïti Progrès* and *Haïti en Marche* are opponents of the military regime, all three newspapers are legally distributed in Haiti. Of course, because the majority of Haitians do not read French, the language of the three publications, the papers' influence is somewhat muted.

Radio, by contrast, seems to be the optimal medium of communication among the diaspora, just as it has always been in Haiti. Wherever Haitians reside, a radio program in Haitian Creole on AM, FM or shortwave can be found. The oldest, "L'Heure haitienne," is a weekly political program on Columbia University's WKCR FM. It was founded in 1972. The latest additions in the tri-state area near New York are the sub-stations Radio Tropicale and Radyo Soley. Transmitting on special AM frequencies, these two stations do not fall under the direct control of Federal Communications Commission (FCC) regulations, and listeners must have special receivers to pick up their programs.

Because of the Haitian passion for politics, the sum of all the programs on these stations amounts to a twenty-four-hour-a-day talk show in New York. The frustration and anger at the political situation back home among radio hosts and listeners who sometimes call in translate into high-decibel shouting matches. Radio is also the foremost vehicle for political activism. Through radio announcements, thousands of Haitians can be assembled for a demonstration with only a day's notice. In the Tenth Department, radio gives a voice to the voiceless. Even the Haitian military and its supporters have managed to use this medium in the diaspora— some say for large sums of money—to spread their propaganda.

When Aristide took office in February 1991, he suggested to a visiting group of Haitian émigrés that they form a Tenth Department organization. He understood that the Tenth Department had tremendous financial and political clout. Haitians living abroad annually send over $100 million back home to families and relatives, estimates Fritz Martial, a prominent Haitian economist in New York. In 1993 the U.S. State Department publicly denounced such transfers for spoiling the already porous OAS embargo against the military regime. In addition to remittances, Haitians also dig deep to contribute to political causes. According to Cesar Dismay, Aristide's campaign treasurer, two-thirds of the $300,000 spent on the priest's 1990 presidential bid came from the diaspora. In a gesture of solidarity with the newly elected Haitian president, the Tenth Department raised nearly $600,000 on April 28, 1991, to help finance a number of development projects.

Yet the wealth of Haitian emigrants is a double-edged sword. Haitians returning home have come to be disparagingly called "diaspo" because those who never left the country resented their "developed" attitude. Many visiting Haitians were easily recognized by the "air of superiority" they exuded, the American lingo they sometimes interjected in their Creole conversation and their flashy material acquisitions. Friction arose from the perception that Haitians on the outside saw themselves as "better" than those who lived in Haiti.

Aristide helped create the Tenth Department organization in an effort to bridge the chasm that traditionally divided the diaspora from Haiti. Father Gerard Jean-Juste, a long-time activist, became its general coordinator. A liberation theologian and the first Haitian priest to be ordained in the United States, Jean-Juste defines the organization as a "gathering of the large Haitian family organically connected to the native land and united by the same ideal: to work, so that one day the sun of freedom and prosperity will shine on our beloved Haiti." His committee held a democratic general assembly on April 14, 1991. A central committee was formed to oversee regional committees representing each city of the diaspora. The Tenth Department organization was supposed to be the big tent that would house Haitians from all walks of life. The organization held numerous fundraising appeals, which raised hundreds of thousands of dollars to help the new government. In this context, it is important to remember that the United States, which has a tradition of supporting Haitian dictators, never assisted the Aristide Administration financially or otherwise.

The Tenth Department organization is not, however, without its critics. Activist Jocelyne Mayas of New York, a staunch supporter of the democratic movement, thinks it could have accomplished more. A founding member of the organization, she complains about its lack of "transparency." She acknowledges the group's efforts to hold periodic organizational elections, but says they have not been truly democratic and that "nepotism dominates the [election] process." Others feel that the Tenth Department organization has been too directly linked to the Aristide government.

The September 29, 1991 coup against Aristide caught the Tenth Department organization in the middle of consolidating and defining the roles of the many groups working under its umbrella. "We were forced to shift our focus to mobilizing the community," says Guy Victor, president of the New York chapter of the organization. Indeed, it was a daunting challenge to stretch an embryonic group to play the roles both of social unifier and of messenger to the world of the disastrous consequences of the coup. Yet the organization managed to spearhead several successful political actions. On October 11, 1991, over 60,000 people blocked downtown Manhattan for hours to protest apparent tacit U.S. support of the military coup. The Tenth Department organization also deserves credit for the turnout of between 260,000 and 300,000 Haitian-Americans who voted overwhelmingly for Bill Clinton in the 1992 U.S. presidential election.

Ironically, the coup had the salutary effect of bringing together the different factions of the Tenth Department. Haitians not previously involved in politics became activists. They discovered that the decisionmaking center affecting Haiti's future was not Port-au-Prince, but Washington, DC. Increasingly, the Haitian community made its voice heard through the telephone and the fax machine. Many Haitians routinely contacted their U.S. political representatives, the White House, the State Department and the Pentagon. During his exile after the coup, Aristide reciprocated the Tenth Department's loyalty through frequent radio addresses and numerous public appearances at community functions.

Haiti's history abounds with military coups. But, thanks to the tenacity and courage of Haitians—both dark-skinned and mulatto—in Haiti and the diaspora the latest coup could not withstand the pressure against it. While the international community, led by the United States, waffled, the Tenth Department kept the issue of President Aristide's return alive for three years. Illustrative of its influence is the fact that negotiations between Aristide and coup leader Raoul Cédras in July 1993 were moved from UN headquarters in New York City to Governors Island for fear of "disruption" by the Haitians of the Tenth Department.

After the Haitian military reneged on the Governors Island Accord, there was once again talk within the Tenth Department of armed struggle. The visceral reaction of most Haitians was a desire to wipe out the thugs who drove Haiti into the abyss. The majority of Haitians abroad, however, continued to believe that the best way to restore democracy in Haiti was to exert pressure on the international community to compel the military to abide by the July 1993 accord. A consensus on how to do this, however, never really emerged. Nonetheless, Aristide was restored to power in October 1994, and the Tenth Department remains an invaluable sociopolitical and financial asset for Haiti—for now and in the years to come.

PROGRESSIVE ACTIVISM IN THE UNITED STATES

CYNTHIA PETERS

On September 29, 1991, Haitian activist Bazelais Jean-Baptiste was on his way from New York to Haiti, having been in the United States to work on a film about the Haitian grassroots organization, the Peasant Movement of Papaye (MPP). During the stopover in Miami, he received word of the military coup that had just overthrown Aristide; no flights were landing in Port-au-Prince. Bazelais had planned on being in the United States for one week; he ended up staying for three years. Kathy McAfee, a Haiti activist and scholar whom he had met in Boston, invited him to stay with her until he figured out what to do. Thus was born a collaboration that helped spawn the Haiti Communications Project (HCP), an important conduit for information about human rights abuses in Haiti under the dictatorship. With the information flow in Haiti stifled due to extreme repression, and with international attention focused on Aristide, HCP was one of the few organizations that gave voice to the popular organizations in Haiti.

The collaboration between Jean-Baptiste and McAfee is just one example in the long and multifaceted history of U.S. activism around Haiti, which has brought together members of the Haitian diaspora and activists from the North American peace and justice movement. This chapter will offer a brief sketch of that history, with particular focus on recent years, and will highlight moments I think are particularly instructive for progressive activists.[1]

As an exile, Bazelais Jean-Baptiste became part of the long tradition of community and political organizing in the Haitian diaspora. Although the Haitian community in the diaspora is not without internal conflict, especially along the lines of class and skin color, political activity has been widespread throughout the community. This activity is manifested in strong radio programming, dynamic debates among the three weekly Haitian newpapers, which represent a full range of political perspectives, and a lively culture that includes theater, dance, folksinging and poetry.[2]

Throughout the 1970s and 1980s, when Haiti was rarely in the news and North American progressives were paying little, if any, attention to the situation there, the Haitian community in the United States—which currently numbers around one million—was taking on domestic political issues of concern to Haitians, in addition to protesting U.S. foreign policy in Haiti. In New York, for instance, Haitians fought for bilingual public education and access to social services. At the same time, they worked to reclaim and affirm their national heritage as an African people. Haitians in the United States supported the battle in Haiti to make Creole the official language. Eventually, most Haitian churches said mass in Creole and the major Haitian radio show, "L'heure haitienne," switched from broadcasting predominantly in French to entirely in Creole, a great victory for the Haitian poor.

Over and over again, the Haitian community has shown its astonishing ability to mobilize. In April 1990, in the words of radio journalist Jean Jean-Pierre, over 85,000 Haitians "shook the Brooklyn Bridge in one of the largest marches ever organized in New York."[3] The march played a key role in reversing the U.S. Food and Drug Administration's designation of Haitians as a high-risk group for HIV and therefore unable to donate blood. More importantly, however, this demonstration was the seed that would grow into a more organized, unified diaspora. In October 1991, about two weeks after the coup, over 100,000 Haitians marched from Central Brooklyn to the UN building in Manhattan. A huge rally in downtown Manhattan—the mid-point of the march—came close to shutting down Wall Street.

Many Haitian organizations in the United States are connected either formally or informally to the popular movement in Haiti, which has continued to thrive despite a long history of repression and poverty. These U.S.-based organizations have forged strong links to grassroots Haitian formations such as the liberation theology-based *Ti Legliz*, the Federation of Neighborhood Committees, the Central Workers Union and MPP. More than any other community outside Haiti, the Haitian diaspora deserves credit for maintaining grassroots opposition to the dictatorship. Their work, according to Jean-Pierre, has "sensitized American public opinion about what is going on in Haiti, kept constant pressure on the U.S. President and Congress to treat Haiti fairly, and provided resistance groups in Haiti with valuable solidarity."[4]

In the San Francisco Bay Area, Haitian activist Pierre Labossier has made it his mission to forge links among the city's small Haitian community, labor activists, churches, students and communities of color. A long-time union activist, Labossier infuses his organizing with a sharp political and economic analysis of international finance and free-trade policies. He stresses that Haitians aren't coming to the United States for jobs; rather, he argues, the jobs are going to Haiti, where they tend to represent a new form of slavery. "Haitians didn't stand for slavery [in the past]," he says, "and they won't stand for it now. And neither should we." His eloquent plea to North Americans is: "When they beat them up in Haiti, we must cry out in English." His organizing principles include constantly making the connections between oppression abroad and oppression at home, and "never turning anyone down." His dedication and commitment lead him to speak to any group, no matter how small, to reach out to everyone possible and to respond to all requests for information.

Roger Etienne, a member of a Brooklyn-based Haiti solidarity group, says, "We must continue to emphasize the fact that the United States trained and equipped the Haitian army up until the coup." Another effective Brooklyn-based organization is Haitian Women for Haitian Refugees. With only a tiny staff, the group has helped resettle many refugees freed from the Guantánamo Bay detention camp in Cuba.

This vibrant political movement among Haitians in the diaspora is made up of activists, speakers, intellectuals and priests, all of whom have helped galvanize support for democracy in Haiti and consistently put forth a strong political analysis. The Haitian immigrant community, of course, has its own set of problems: it is riven by deep divisions and antagonisms and it has had difficulty building a clear and lasting organizational structure. Nevertheless, the richness of Haitian political culture, the integration of politics, culture and social life, and the high level of political literacy make the Haitian community a model for activists looking to build a long-term movement for social change.

The struggle against internal repression and foreign military intervention in Haiti has been a long one and indeed in many ways serves as a paradigm for Northern colonialism and imperialism.[5] Nevertheless, the predominantly white middle-class peace movement in the United States has been slow to take on Haiti. During the 1970s and early 1980s, most Haiti work revolved around the refugee situation and was organized mainly by social-service and human rights organizations. In 1973, the Haitian Refugee Center began to offer legal services to Haitians seeking political asylum in the United States. The organization is now one of a number of secular and religious refugee centers in the Miami area that advocate for Haitian immigrant rights. Religious organizations such as Pax Christi were also active during the 1980s, writing reports—such as their primer on the Haitian baseball industry—and keeping the church community informed about the ongoing struggle of the Haitian poor. In 1984, the Washington Office on Haiti was founded, in part to examine the question of why so many

Haitians were fleeing their country. In 1986, when the popular movement in Haiti really took off, a small U.S. solidarity movement arose in response. Conspicuous by their absence were the many Latin America solidarity and anti-intervention activists who were busy at the time fighting U.S. involvement in El Salvador and Nicaragua.

It wasn't until Aristide came into the picture that the peace and justice movement really kicked into gear. This may be due partially to the fact that Aristide's election coincided with a tremendous loss of momentum in the Central America solidarity movement in the early 1990s, and partly because Aristide was a charismatic leader who represented a legitimate grassroots movement and put a human face on Haiti's liberation struggle. The legacy of racism in the United States and racist media images of Haitians as Voodoo-practicing, HIV-infected and prone to violence perhaps influenced the predominantly white peace movement.[6] While activists may not have consciously held racist attitudes, mainstream culture's tendency to see Haiti as a hopeless quagmire of "black-on-black" violence may have inhibited them from engaging in Haiti solidarity work. This legacy of racism may also have hindered the development of an alliance between U.S. activists and the Haitian immigrant community.

Another reason for the peace movement's late arrival to the Haiti organizing scene can perhaps be attributed to a need to identify with, and take leadership from, a semi-romanticized revolutionary body, as tended to occur with Nicaragua solidarity activists during the Sandinista revolution.[7] Indeed, the current Haitian solidarity movement runs the risk of idealizing Aristide and focusing too much on his role. While Aristide does warrant the support of activists, they must recognize that it will be impossible for him to carry out a democratic program single-handedly, given the pressure from his own still-intact military, the United States (through organizations like the Agency for International Development and the National Endowment for Democracy) and international lending institutions. The Haiti solidarity movement must recognize that grassroots democratic organizations—not political parties or individual politicians—are the force most capable of pushing for and bringing about true democracy in Haiti.

A s Haiti organizing geared up around the country after the 1991 coup, the focus was on countering the U.S. disinformation campaign about Aristide, calling for a tight embargo, criticizing the refugee policy, and consistently stressing Aristide's legitimacy. Many activists put energy into the Clinton election campaign because of his promises to enforce the embargo and immediately give temporary protected status to all Haitian refugees. Others later used Clinton's failure to follow through on his campaign pledges as part of a strategy to bring attention to the struggle in Haiti. The Quixote Center's Haiti Reborn campaign—a focal point for Haiti organizing in the United States—placed a full-page ad in the *New York Times* exhorting, "Clinton, Keep Your Promises."[8]

Although some leftists still argue that a Democratic administration is better than the alternative, others believe that it was a waste of energy and resources to work to have Clinton elected and then appeal to him for more humane policies.[9] The nationwide student campaign, "Operation Harriet Tubman," was one organizing effort that focused most of its energy on direct action. The campaign used a two-pronged strategy to try to close down the camps for HIV-infected refugees and their families at Guantánamo. On the legal front, law students from Yale's Lowenstein Human Rights Clinic litigated the issue in federal court, with help from the New York-based Center for Constitutional Rights and the San Francisco Lawyers' Committee for Civil Rights. On the activist front, students at Yale started a week-long hunger strike in solidarity with HIV-positive prisoners at Guantánamo who had vowed to fast until their demands were met. The Yale students then organized to "pass the fast" onto students at other campuses. Over several months, students from more than thirty campuses put up imitation internment camps, which they named "Camp Clinton," and participated in the fast.

Working in coalition with chapters of the Black Law Student Association, Amnesty International, the International Socialist Organization and student gay and AIDS groups, Operation Harriet Tubman played a key role in assuring that the camps were indeed later closed. Van Jones, a key organizer of the action, believes that one of the important lessons of this work is that "militancy pays." Unlike most progressives, who wanted to go easy on the new Democratic president, Jones says, the students who participated in Operation Harriet Tubman "took the opposite tack, lighting into Clinton just weeks after he took office, naming 'concentration camps' after him, and denouncing his flip-floppy cowardice at every turn."[10]

In the first months after the coup, many progressives put most of their energy into defending Aristide. Although his legitimacy was an obvious point around which to organize, and one that appealed to many Haitians and North Americans, making him the centerpiece of Haiti solidarity work was problematic. Laurie Richardson, an organizer with the Quixote Center, suggests that, by backing Aristide, progressives were pulled at times into the political center, since he was forced into agreements that clearly were not in the interest of Haitian democracy.[11] A better role for activists may have been to uphold the progressive end of the debate by pushing for those policies that Aristide could not and by refusing to compromise on the fate of the Haitian military or the terms of Aristide's return.

Haiti activists from both the diaspora and the peace and justice movement have also been divided by the question of the relative merits of U.S. intervention in Haiti. Some argue that the September 1994 U.S. intervention had the effect of "turning down the torture" against the civilian population, and therefore deserved the cautious support of progressives. Others argue that, as a general rule, "bad governments don't make good interventions" (although there can be accidental positive outcomes).[12] Activists opposed to the intervention claim that it would be naïve to trust the United States, given its history of supporting economic elites and their military allies in both Haiti and the region in general.

This debate aside, many long-term Haiti activists have come to believe that the most important thing they can do, besides try to change U.S. policy, is to reach out to and support the grassroots movements in Haiti. Aristide's hands are essentially tied, and it has fallen to the popular organizations to push for democratic reform and to contest not just the obvious repression by the military and police, but the repression that comes in the form of U.S. aid. U.S. activists need to continue to develop their knowledge and understanding of the increasingly important role that U.S.-based and international financial organizations play in determining social, economic and politicial structures in the Third World. It is these lending agencies—perhaps more than the "brutal dictator" so easy to rally against—that will be setting policy and overseeing the exploitation of Third World populations in coming years.[13]

The Quixote Center, working with Clergy and Laity Concerned, was instrumental in spurring thousands of people to action through their Haiti Solidarity Week—seven days in February of teach-ins and educational efforts that has taken place in many cities across the United States every year since 1993. The Quixote Center put together and distributed organizing manuals to activists throughout the country. These manuals were intended to educate people about the history of Haiti and the role of the U.S. government there and to offer ideas about how U.S. citizens could build solidarity with Haitian grassroots organizations.

The Lambi Fund in Washington, DC is an example of an organization dedicated to channeling financial and material resources to community-based Haitian organizations. Established in 1993, its Haiti-based advisory board works closely with a U.S.-based board of directors to directly assist the popular democratic movement in Haiti. Likewise, the MPP Education and Development Fund (MPP-EDF) was set up in the United States to undertake public education and outreach about the grassroots peasant movement in Haiti and to raise money to support its work.

Various Haiti organizing projects have received key institutional support from long-term progressive organizations such as Oxfam America, Mobilization for Survival and Grassroots International. These organizations have the resources and reach to provide important direct services. Furthermore, because they do not focus on a single issue or place, they provide continuity from one struggle to the next. Their long history and experience make them key players in new crises, as well as in the ongoing work of supporting social change.

Organized labor has also played an important role in supporting the struggle for Haitian democracy. This class-based solidarity makes salient the connection between labor rights in Haiti and in the United States. Founded in 1980 to provide an independent voice for the protection of workers' rights abroad and in the United States, the National Labor Committee (NLC) has been a key link between labor struggles in the United States and in Central America and the Caribbean. After holding a November 1992 meeting between Aristide and high-ranking union officials, the NLC—at Aristide's request—organized a labor delegation to visit Haiti and bear witness to the repression there. The trip became the basis for a lengthy report that details Haiti's role as the United States' sweatshop and names the corporations that are the most egregious offenders.[14] The report was sent to all New York labor leaders in addition to 2,000 union locals nationwide, and spawned related articles and excerpts of the report in local union newspapers. The NLC office was deluged with phone calls for more information. Two prominent exiled Haitian labor leaders also used the NLC office as a base for their organizing work, making contacts with U.S. unions and accepting invitations to speak to union members in other cities.

Many other delegations have made trips to Haiti and used their eyewitness reports to help build the Haiti solidarity movement in the United States. The New England Observers Delegation, Pax Christi, Witness for Peace, Global Exchange, the Washington Office on Haiti and Christian Peacemaker Teams have written reports and articles and participated in teach-ins—all in an effort to share what they learned about the grassroots movement in Haiti, humanize the struggle there, raise money for grassroots organizations and offer direction to U.S. activists. Although delegations do tax activists in Haiti—who must make time for interviews and tours and who are sometimes endangered by their association with

U.S. progressives—delegations will probably continue to play an important role in fortifying the U.S. soldarity movement and in making connections between U.S. and Haitian grassroots organizations. If Nicaragua offers any lesson in this regard, it is that delegations and work brigades probably *receive* more from these experiences than they *give* in return. The brigadista's real contribution is not so much coffee picked or bicycles repaired, but lessons learned and enthusiasm garnered for long-term political work at home.

The alternative media has finally gotten up to speed on Haiti as well. With rare exceptions, the issue was largely invisible in major leftist periodicals until the early 1990s. Only in the past three years have alternative media made a major effort to analyze the situation in Haiti, uncover its history and explore the role of U.S. policy. Articles and books by Z *Magazine*, the Open Magazine Pamphlet Series, Common Courage Press, Azul Editions, Monthly Review Press, South End Press, Zed, *Covert Action*, the *Nation* and the *Progressive*, among others, have provided much needed analysis and information.[15]

Conspicuously lacking in coverage of Haiti in most progressive publications, however, is any reflection on how to organize around Haiti and which issues are at stake in this struggle.[16] In fact, a major weakness in the left media in general is the lack of dialogue around strategy—what it should be, how it relates to analysis and what has been learned from previous strategies.[17] Nevertheless, the alternative press has played a key role in arming Haiti solidarity organizations with the information that activists need to develop these organizing strategies and goals. Recognizing that the mainstream media offers an extremely limited range of information and viewpoints, solidarity activists must work to build and sustain strong and vibrant alternative media to ensure access to accurate information and progressive analysis.

Haiti activism has also given rise to concerted efforts at coalition building. The Haiti National Network, formed in January 1992, is a loose network of organizations representing diverse political viewpoints. These organizations meet quarterly and share information about developments in Haiti on a weekly basis by mail and fax. Voices for Haiti, founded more recently, is attempting to build a coalition of groups with shared political principles. For example, the coalition has explicitly called for the replacement of U.S. troops in Haiti by UN forces and has strongly objected to the "deal" made by Clinton's emissaries to Haiti on September 18, 1994. Voices for Haiti's work has included sending a religious delegation to Haiti, co-sponsoring the speaking tour of community activist Alerte Belance, co-publishing a primer on Haiti with the Ecumenical Program on Central America and the Caribbean (EPICA) and coordinating teach-ins and other educational forums.

On a local level, informal coalition building is evident in many parts of the country. In the Bay Area, for example, many student and community anti-intervention, solidarity and sanctuary organizations have sprung up. These groups have been successful in building solidarity across racial, class and ethnic lines. Kiilu Nyasha, a former Black Panther, put together one of the few truly multiracial fund-raising events for Haiti in the fall of 1994. With proceeds going in part to the peasant farm union *Tèt Kole*, "Jam for Haiti" raised over $2,000 during an evening of poetry, film and music from jazz and rap artists. Various African-American churches—a potentially powerful link to Haiti, given the grassroots strength of the Haitian church community—have also sponsored a number of important events. Sister Maureen Duignan from the East Bay Sanctuary Covenant in California has been a dedicated organizer for many years, first offering sanctuary to Central Americans and now offering "accompaniment" to Haitians at risk in Haiti.

In Boston, the Association of Haitian Women (AFAB) is raising money for a women's education center in Port-au-Prince and is working to build housing for low-income Haitian women in the United States. Their work led them to help organize the Haiti Women Conference in Boston in the fall of 1994. The conference was successful in bringing together people from a wide cross-section of communities, including Haitians, Haitian Americans, African Americans, Latinos and Caribbean Americans. The conference looked at the intersection of domestic and state repression, as well as economic and development issues. It was an inspiring example of how people from different communities, backgrounds and professions can come together to share knowledge and expertise and educate themselves for their continued solidarity work.

Haiti, which boasts the first and only successful slave revolt, is an example to all of us involved in the fight for social justice. As progressives strategize on how to contest oppression both at home and abroad, and as post-Cold War globalization further links economies and political communities, the case of Haiti shows us that we must expect a long struggle. U.S. activists need to look at how they can empower their own populations to affect U.S. domestic and foreign policy. Haiti teaches us that organizing is effective when it is directed against institutions, not individuals, and when it is geared toward long-term social justice. Haiti activists have also learned that it is necessary to build alternative institutions to sustain their work and provide the needed forums for debate around strategy, analysis and vision.

22

The Significance of Haiti

PAUL FARMER

On August 28, 1994, Haitian paramilitary forces killed Jean-Marie Vincent, a forty-nine-year-old priest inspired by liberation theology. Father Vincent was best known for his efforts on behalf of the peasants of Haiti's parched Northwest; he had narrowly escaped a 1987 massacre there, and was later wounded as he shielded Aristide from a would-be assassin shortly after a mass commemorating massacre's victims.

In the North American mainstream press, many wrote of Vincent's martyrdom as the last straw, hardening resolve among those pushing for a military intervention in Haiti. The U.S. government seemed to favor this reading of events. In a mid-September speech announcing the commitment of U.S. troops to Haiti, President Bill Clinton detailed the human rights record of the Haitian army: "Cédras and his armed thugs have conducted a reign of terror, executing children, raping women, killing priests.... The message of the United States to the Haitian dictators is clear. Your time is up. Leave now, or we will force you from power."

President Clinton did not add, of course, that these thugs were *our* thugs. No mention was made in his speech of the U.S. creation and ensuing long support of the Haitian army, since this would have undermined official claims regarding the purpose of the intervention—namely, to support democracy and human rights in Haiti.

These convenient erasures have marked most official commentary on the Haitian crisis. It seems improbable that the murder of a Haitian priest should have any effect on U.S. foreign policy: the killing of progressive priests and nuns has, after all, long been a staple of Latin American politics, and has rarely discomfited Washington policymakers. For example, similar acts—including the assassination, mid-mass, of the archbishop of San Salvador, Oscar Romero, in 1981 by right-wing paramilitaries linked to the government—had no discernible effect on U.S. military aid to El Salvador.

Why, then, were U.S. troops sent to Haiti? What has been the purpose of their presence there? What has been the nature of Haitian responses—especially those registered among the poor—to these recent developments? What relevance do these developments have for those engaged in solidarity work elsewhere in Latin America? Finally, against the backdrop of numerous other interventions in Latin America—including the landing of U.S. troops in Haiti in 1915—how is this occupation unique, and in what ways is it similar to previous interventions?

In responding to the last of these questions, some mainstream pundits have impatiently noted that, in the past, the United States intervened to protect U.S. interests by propping up right-wing despots; but our doctrines have changed, this argument goes, and the deployment of U.S. troops is now a "humanitarian intervention" designed to "restore democracy" to Haiti by restoring its first popularly elected leader. Aristide's record as a hero of the poor Haitian majority has strengthened such claims. But close examination of events surrounding the intervention offers disturbing insights for those concerned with the long-term prospects for democracy in Haiti, and for progressive social movements elsewhere in the hemisphere.

U.S. troops began landing in Haiti in the third week of September 1994 with the stated goal of "restoring democracy." They entered what they termed a "permissive environment"; that is, the troops had been assured that they would not encounter hostile fire from their erstwhile partners in the Haitian army. For anyone with a modicum of knowledge about Haiti, this seemed a foregone conclusion. After all, the Haitian military had no history of engagements with armed opponents in its long existence. Its only enemies had been unarmed civilians.

These civilians wanted to see more than a walk-in. More precisely, as Haitian-American intellectual Patrick Bellegarde-Smith noted, "Most Haitians wanted the first wave of invasion to come in and obliterate the Haitian army."[1] The majority of Haitians, terrified of their own army, warmly welcomed the troops whose express intention was to rid the country of its army.

The U.S. soldiers, most of them under twenty-five, seemed a bit confused by this heroes' welcome. Their marching orders— their "Rules of Engagement," or ROEs—had changed a number of times and would continue to change. One minute, the Haitian army and police (the "thugs," "rapists," and "torturers" of Clinton's impassioned speech) were their enemies. The next, soldiers were asked to work "in close cooperation" with the Haitian armed forces. They were further ordered by the Chairman of the Joint Chiefs of Staff not to intervene in "Haitian-on-Haitian" violence, much of which involved the paramilitary Front for the Advancement and Progress of Haiti (FRAPH). The young Americans didn't like this, especially after they were asked to stand by as the Haitian military and its *attachés* began beating and killing unarmed demonstrators. "It's messing up my head," complained a twenty-year-old private. "It's wrong. And every time you have to look into the faces of the people here, the people who thought we were coming to save them from these guys, it breaks your heart."[2]

For the first time, the spectacle of Haitian troops firing on unarmed civilians, seen many times on film over the years, captured the American imagination. Millions in the United States witnessed on television the death of a young coconut vendor, as

U.S. troops, chafing, stood by. Public pressure at home, coupled with the complaints of U.S. soldiers in Haiti, led to another revision of the rules of engagement: U.S. troops would, at last, begin disarming the military and paramilitary groups.

Three months after Aristide's return, however, it was still difficult to state with confidence that any of these groups had been disarmed. The occupation's planners were either wed to the notion of maintaining the paramilitary groups as a counterweight to democracy forces—certainly, U.S. claims that "FRAPH is just a political party" lent credence to this interpretation—or were sadly misinformed about popular revulsion toward the Haitian army.

If U.S. soldiers—or, rather, their bosses—have been reluctant to dismantle the forces responsible for almost all the recent killings, why did the United States send troops to Haiti in the first place? Dismissing the dubious claims of officialdom, some have argued that the only threat serious enough to prompt military action by the United States was the prospect of thousands more poor, black refugees making their way north in rickety sailboats. Writing in the October 1994 issue of *Le Monde Diplomatique*, political scientist William LeoGrande argued that "fear of illegal immigration explains, by and large, current U.S. policies in the Caribbean."[3] Likewise, the editors of *The Progressive* observed that "Aristide's return to Haiti has become essential to America's purposes in the region because it is the only way Washington can stem the flow of Haitian refugees, which transformed Haiti from a problem into a crisis and sent the Clinton Administration into a state of near-hysteria."[4] In the same issue of *The Progressive*, Bellegarde-Smith perhaps states this position most eloquently:

> On September 15, announcing what he then expected to be an armed invasion of Haiti, Clinton buried in the middle of the speech the most important point: he talked about "the safety of our borders"—code words. He talked about the 300,000 internal exiles in the mountains of Haiti who could legitimately come to the United States because they are, indeed, political refugees— black people, mostly peasants, who qualify for political asylum. This was the key element, and I think the

American public was astute enough to recognize it: we have to protect our borders, so we have to invade Haiti, or Haitians will invade us.[5]

A second, related reason for the invasion involved the desire to restore business as usual in Haiti. As many studies of the region's economy have shown, the United States has used Haiti as chattel labor for the past two decades. By 1984, Haiti was the ninth largest assembler of U.S. goods in the world. U.S. sanctions against Haiti had been carefully formulated to go lightly on Haiti's business elite and U.S. capital in Haiti. The country's assembly industry, for instance, was exempted from the bogus embargo enacted by President George Bush in 1991 and maintained by the Clinton Administration.

The oil embargo was also largely a charade. Except for oil-rich countries, an oil blockade serves as the bite in any serious sanctions. While Jimmy Carter was dining with Cédras and company in September 1994, the news service wires were buzzing with what ought to have been a scandal. As some in Haiti had suspected, both the Bush and Clinton administrations had permitted the shipment of oil to the military and its backers. As rhetoric about the "failure of sanctions" escalated, U.S. officials loudly informed Texaco that the sale of petroleum to Haiti was illegal—but more quietly hinted that the company would not be prosecuted if it made such sales.[6] This helped to explain why, throughout the year prior to the occupation, Haitian millionaire Fritz Mevs had been busy building a huge oil-tank farm on the outskirts of Port-au-Prince. It also helped to explain why, while many in Haiti's small middle class joined Haiti's poor (who had always gone without electricity), the military and local gentry—families like the Mevs—never lacked much in the way of petroleum products.

Thus there was, in effect, no embargo against the coup supporters—at the same time that the long-standing embargo against the Haitian poor was strengthened. With the exception of a few lines in the *Miami Herald* and the *Wall Street Journal*, however, the media passed over this scoop of the summer in favor of the more compelling human interest stories that surfaced as the special forces, fresh from other areas of conflict, landed in "exotic" Haiti.

Stories about Haiti's "MRE"—morally-repugnant elite—did appear in the international press. These tepid exposés focused, however, on local actors and local factors, underscoring the ties between the Haitian elite and the Haitian military. A story in the *Financial Times* of London is a typical case in point:

> The proximity of businessmen and the military is barely disguised. When Gregory Mevs, president of the infra-structure interests of his family's multi-faceted busi-ness, fumbled to find his business card on introduction, he joked: "I have so many generals and colonels walking through my office every day, I don't need business cards."[7]

The media did not, however, discuss how these tycoons and their military protégés used U.S.-based banks and companies to grease the cogs of the 1991 coup. Nor did they examine how, for example, one member of the elite whose U.S. assets were suppos-edly frozen was able to purchase a new luxury car with cash in March 1994 in Miami.[8]

The Haitian military has always been the tool of the Haitian ruling class, which over the course of this century has turned to the United States, not Europe, for assistance and inspiration. The extent of U.S. support is only now coming to light. In *The Nation*, Allan Nairn reported that Emmanuel Constant, then working at the CIA-run National Intelligence Service (SIN), was encouraged to form FRAPH by Colonel Patrick Collins, the U.S. Defense Intelli-gence Agency *attaché* in Haiti at the time.[9]

SIN's chief activities in Haiti seem to have been political terror and drug trafficking. In its tutelage of the Haitian military, how-ever, the CIA sent U.S. citizens to teach training seminars at SIN headquarters on such topics as surveillance, interrogation and weaponry.[10] In 1991, Constant taught a course to SIN agents on liberation theology, a topic with which his U.S. mentors were obsessed. Liberation theology is disturbing to U.S. policymakers because its central ideas—such as "a preferential option for the poor"—are anathema to the rich. And U.S. policy, whether domestic or foreign, has always made an option for the rich.

So when the Mevs family calls itself "Aristide's biggest supporter," distributing 30,000 color posters of Aristide just before his return to Haiti and hosting an elegant dinner for members of the U.S. Congressional Black Caucus, one senses that the term "democracy" is extremely elastic. Any "democracy" endorsed by Washington is likely to be a version acceptable to Haiti's rich.

So when *The Financial Times* asks, "Democracy in Haiti—will the rich buy it?" one is tempted to respond, "Of course they'll buy it. They'll even pay cash for it."

If the U.S. occupation was launched, then, to prevent further immigration of Haitian refugees to the United States and restore business as usual, what do we make of the obviously widespread satisfaction with recent developments among Haitians of all classes? Many prominent Haitian intellectuals—all of whom are regarded as "pro-democracy" and thus suspect by the elite from which they sprang—have come out in support of the U.S. action. "It is an intervention desired and demanded by the mass of Haitian people," asserted Jean-Claude Bajeux, director of the Ecumenical Center for Human Rights.[11] For similar reasons, the writer René Dépestre, long exiled in Cuba and then France, endorsed the invasion in an article in *Le Monde:*

> I refuse to rigidly embrace some sort of mystical vision of past U.S. conduct. In the present situation, the landing of U.S. troops, I have good reason to believe that, for once, the interests of the United States meet those of the Haitian people, which are manifest in the person of their president, Father Jean-Bertrand Aristide.[12]

On the ground in Haiti in the autumn of 1994, popular enthusiasm for recent developments was widespread. For the poor who were the victims of most of the repression during the dictatorship, support for the U.S. landing might be likened to an endorsement of less painful methods of torture. *Any* change in the balance of power—at times, one thought even a cataclysm of nature would do—represented an improvement for the perennial victims of state power.

Shortly after Aristide's return, I interviewed a number of friends, patients and co-villagers, most of whom I'd known for many years, about their attitudes toward the U.S. occupation. In one small village in the Central Plateau, some people were downright effusive about the troops' presence, regaling me with stories about the humiliation of certain Haitian officers by U.S. soldiers. Several people said to me, "This is what we call *'ipokrit yo sezi'*," meaning "the hypocrites are shocked," or, less literally, "what goes around, comes around."

"We've been hit hard, but we're still here, as ready as ever," reported a young man who was a member of one of the local popular organizations. His analysis of current events was in many ways typical of the comments I elicited in October and November:

> The Americans would have been happy to have the coup succeed, we know that. The Bush Administration was probably involved in [the coup]. But they didn't understand Titid's [Aristide's] power. He's very small, compared to them, but much smarter. He said to resist, and we did. The military killed a lot of people, and a lot of people took to the sea. Americans didn't like that, so they saw that it would be good for them to give Titid back to us. They made him sign a bunch of bad papers, but the point is, he's back and the guys who were killing us are gone. So it's not perfect, but it's a lot better.

A new disjuncture can be noted between the comments about the U.S. occupation in *Haïti Progrès*, the left-of-center Haitian weekly most closely aligned with the popular movement, and those of my patients and friends. In its October 26, 1994 edition, the newspaper deplored the "golden exile" reserved for the second tier of Haitian army officers, who were posted as military *attachés* in embassies in Europe and Latin America. Some in the Central Plateau had a different reading of this ploy, as the words of one young woman suggest:

I think it was a great idea. People always talk about reconciliation, but it's the wealthy and the military who hate us. They hate us, they want to crush us. Nobody wants to kill another human being, but Haiti's too small for all of these people who want to crush us, crush our movement, crush our hope. They want to kill Titid, obviously—they've said so many times—so how do we get rid of them? I think sending them away to the embassies was a great idea, very smart and very much like Titid to think of such a good idea for us.

Dissent tends to come from people a level or two up from the poor themselves. Chavannes Jean-Baptiste, head of the region's most important—and much-persecuted—peasant movement, startled his peasant supporters (and irritated the U.S. troops) when, on October 16, he announced, "This is not a victory. This is not the way we should have returned. This is not the way that Titid should have returned. We shouldn't have needed a U.S. occupation to bring him back. We should have done it ourselves."[13]

According to a patient of mine, a middle-aged market woman, Jean-Baptiste's remarks elicited a sort of silence in the crowd. "We tried our best to fight back," she protested later, "but we're so small next to their big weapons." Another market woman who attended a public meeting to welcome Jean-Baptiste back to Haiti was delighted to see the peasant leader, but was nonetheless troubled by some of his remarks:

Titid is always hurting himself for our sakes. He crushes his very body to serve us. Now look at him, obliged to get on an American plane, which is not his way, you know, in order to come back to us. It's what we wanted. Chavannes [Jean-Baptiste] is a good man, but he doesn't pray for the poor as much as Titid does. He's like Titid's little brother, but he needs to listen to Titid more.

Haïti Progrès, formerly strongly pro-Aristide, praised Jean-Baptiste's lucid analysis of the U.S. occupation, but railed against his unwillingness to publicly dissociate himself from Aristide, who had clearly sold out: "How can [Jean-Baptiste] maintain an anti-occupation discourse among the peasants of Papaye and then run back to a government that collaborates fully with the occupying forces?"[14]

Back in the United States, *The Progressive* took a similar line: "U.S. Out of Haiti" stated the cover of its November issue. "Will Haitians be starved and slaughtered if the U.S. forces leave?" wrote the editors. "They're being starved and slaughtered now, with the active collaboration and connivance of the United States."[15]

There are two problems with this sort of commentary. First, it suggests that the removal of U.S. troops = "U.S. Out of Haiti." But as I have tried to show—and as the Haitian poor have long complained—there is more than one way to occupy a country. The United States may have been every bit as much "in Haiti" in the early 1980s, when the covers of progressive magazines did not call for an end to our occupation, which was then conducted by a proxy army, the CIA, and even the U.S. Agency for International Development (AID).[14] Second, while it may be true that Haitians are being "starved and slaughtered" even now, the perception in Haiti is that starvation and slaughter have significantly abated. At the close of 1994, many Haitians felt that the U.S. invasion was not the worst of all possible outcomes—which is the lot that the Haitian poor have consistently drawn.

"Of course people are relieved by the recent changes," said William Smarth, a progressive priest inspired by liberation theology, commenting on the schism between popular sentiment and the U.S. Left. "The Left in the United States doesn't really understand the historical moment. Their ideology-driven comments don't incorporate the views of the poor; such analyses rarely do."

As the euphoria that accompanied Aristide's return dies down, it would be nice to think that Haiti has gone back to square one: to February 1991, when Aristide first took office. But, of course, major changes have taken place during the past three years. The first has been the decapitation of the Haitian popular movement. Many of its key leaders were killed during the Cédras dictatorship; others have sold out, in small or in large ways. A second change has been a deepening of the enmity between Haiti's tiny elite and the rest of the population. The elite always seemed to feel only disdain for Haiti's poor majority; after the past three years, this feeling seems to be more sharply mutual.

Third, Haiti's infrastructure has continued to decline and the country's economy is in dire straits. If in 1991 the "human suffering index" could find that Haiti, alone among the hemisphere's nations, was characterized by "extreme human suffering," imagine how it would characterize the country now. The devastation wrought by Tropical Storm Gordon in November 1994—which may have cost up to 2,000 lives—is more a reflection of Haiti's fragility than of the storm's fury.

A fourth change, of course, involves Aristide himself. The author of a text entitled "Capitalism is a Mortal Sin" now meets regularly with representatives of the World Bank, the International Monetary Fund (IMF) and AID. He was once the priest of the poor; now he's the president of a beleaguered nation, run into the ground by a vicious military and business elite and by their friends abroad. Aristide finds himself most indebted to the very people and institutions he once denounced from the pulpit.

The fifth, and most important, change concerns the international neoliberal economic development plan for Haiti, which is at odds with the wishes of the Haitian electorate. In a very real sense, the World Bank, IMF, AID and U.S. State Department have their hands on the reins of state in Haiti today.[16] It is, of course, more difficult to organize opposition to this more insidious form of occupation, even though some would argue that these institutions will do far more to undermine popular democracy in Haiti than 20,000 well-armed young U.S. soldiers.

With these changes in mind, how might we assess recent developments in Haiti? What is likely to happen next? Three likely scenarios come to mind.

The best-of-all-possible-worlds scenario

Aristide is able to use his post as president to advocate for the poor majority. In this utopian scenario, there is certainly reconciliation and peace, but peace with justice. A Truth Commission documents the nature of the recent killings and massacres, families of victims are remunerated and the perpetrators are punished. Complete disarmament of the military and paramilitary forces follows. The army as an agent of repression is abolished; radical restructuring of the police force ensues. The School of the Americas at Fort Benning, Georgia, where many in the Haitian high command were trained, is closed, and the CIA shuts up shop in Haiti.

In this scenario, the Aristide government becomes strong enough to offset the ability of the IMF-World Bank-AID axis to determine Haiti's future, leaving that delicate task to the Haitian people themselves. Those in the rest of the world forge new links of "pragmatic solidarity" with the Haitian poor. Reflection on the causes of Haiti's $800 million debt to foreign lenders leads to the obvious conclusion that Haiti doesn't owe the rest of the world a penny.

Haiti takes a uniquely Haitian path toward democracy, based on the increased participation of the poor masses promised by Aristide during his 1990 presidential campaign. Aristide is allowed to serve a full presidential five-year term, discounting his period in exile, and is replaced by another strong voice for social justice.

The most likely scenario

Aristide returns, significantly constrained by his debts to Washington and international aid agencies. The most brutal killing stops; a certain calm reigns in Haiti. The army is "restructured" and remains under the influence of the United States.[17] The CIA continues to operate in Haiti (the agency has, reportedly, recently received a $5 million "emergency grant" to counter Aristide's opponents—a novel project for the agency).[18] The IMF-World Bank-AID axis pours money into the country and also sucks it out through a structural adjustment program that favors exports and the offshore assembly industry. Haiti works, with little success, at whittling down its $800 million debt. People who are genuine advocates of popular democracy are marginalized. In the event that Aristide continues to call for social justice in a meaningful way, he too is marginalized in international circles, as he was previously.

The worst-case scenario

Aristide is assassinated, either literally or morally. Haiti's profoundly anti-democratic elite continues to call the shots; and either the military and paramilitary structures of the past remain in place or new and similar come into being. The *attachés* remain armed, and the CIA continues its hijinks in Haiti, as elsewhere in Latin America. (In other words, the worst-case scenario is precisely the one that prevailed during the Cédras dictatorship.)

How can we tell which of these three scenarios is now taking shape? If the U.S. State Department were to express regret over U.S. invasions of Panama, Grenada, Guatemala and Chile, as well as the United States' murderous past policies toward El Salvador and Nicaragua, it would lend more credibility to the argument that U.S. inter-American policy has changed. In fact, however, the first two of these adventures were used by Clinton as *justifications* for his Haiti policy. And with Jesse Helms as the new chairman of the Senate Foreign Relations Committee, the chances for such change have never seemed more remote.

The scenario desired by the powerful will come to pass unless meaningful steps are taken to counter it. The rural and urban poor who constitute the vast majority of Haitians do not endorse the structural adjustment program that will now determine their fate. Those in North America who are concerned with such radical notions as democracy—that is, the right of the majority to control their own lives—should oppose this program with a pragmatic solidarity that both respects the will of the Haitian poor and is cognizant of the enormous difficulties facing a people driven to destitution.

Certainly, such efforts on the part of progressives in the United States would be dwarfed by the policies imposed by AID, the World Bank and the IMF. As the new world order takes shape, a sort of *de facto* world government has emerged with, as its treasurers, those at the helms of these so-called international "aid" agencies.

The IMF and World Bank's talk of "austerity measures" makes clear that pragmatic solidarity is not their primary concern. Austerity measures in Haiti? What could be more austere than the current lives of the Haitian poor?

Many in these U.S.-controlled financial and aid institutions share the opinion of foreign policy expert Michael Mandelbaum, who recently asserted in the *New York Times* that, in Haiti, "Prosperity will require not only indulging the rich but also frustrating the poor." Mandelbaum further informs us that "social justice may just have to wait."[19] This formula for prosperity—indulging the rich, frustrating the poor—sounds curiously familiar in Haiti, for surely it has been the standard formula for this country's long misery. Not incidentally, it has also been the formula for the misery of the poor throughout Latin America.

CONTRIBUTORS

Anne-christine d'Adesky is a print and broadcast journalist and novelist living in New York City. She is the author of *Under the Bone* (Farrar, Straus & Giroux, 1994), a political novel about Haiti.

Marx V. Aristide is a graduate student in economics at Howard University. He was formerly co-coordinator of the Quixote Center's Haiti Reborn campaign.

Barbara Briggs and Charles Kernaghan are staff members of the National Labor Committee. Their chapter is adapted from the committee's report *Haiti After the Coup: Sweatshop or Real Development?*

Greg Chamberlain has been writing about Haiti and the Caribbean for twenty-six years. He publishes *Haiti-Hebdo*, a weekly newsletter in French, and is co-author of *The Dictionary of Contemporary Politics of Central America and the Caribbean.*

Paul Farmer, author of *AIDS and Accusation* (1992) and *The Uses of Haiti* (1994), is an assistant professor at the Harvard Medical School and a fellow at Boston's Brigham and Women's Hospital. He conducts his research and medical practice in rural Haiti, where he specializes in community-based efforts to improve the health of the poor.

Michael S. Hooper (1947-1988) was a lawyer who worked on immigrant human rights issues. He was executive director of the National Coalition for Haitian Refugees from 1982 to 1988.

Kim Ives is a journalist at the weekly newspaper *Haïti Progrès*.

Jean Jean-Pierre is a musician and radio journalist. He is the host of the weekly English and Haitian Creole program "Radyo Neg Mawon" on the short-wave radio station Radio for Peace International.

Deidre McFadyen is associate editor of *NACLA Report on the Americas.*

Catherine Orenstein is a graduate student at the School of International and Public Affairs at Columbia University. She was previously NACLA's outreach coordinator.

Cynthia Peters is an editor of South End Press.

Laurie Richardson is assistant director of the Peasant Movement of Papaye Education and Development Fund, where she acts as a liaison for the movement in the United States. She was formerly co-coordinator of the Quixote Center's Haiti Reborn campaign.

J.P. Slavin was a freelance foreign correspondent based in Haiti from 1990 to 1994. He is currently at work on a book about Haiti.

Michel-Rolph Trouillot is a professor of anthropology and the director of the Institute for Global Studies in Culture, Power and History at Johns Hopkins University. He is also author of *Haiti: State Against Nation: The Origins and Legacies of Duvalierism* (Monthly Review Press, 1990).

NOTES

Notes to Chapter I

1. David Nicholls, *Haiti in Caribbean Context* (London: Macmillan, 1985), pp. 168-169.

2. Amy Wilentz, "Voodoo in Haiti Today," *Grand Street* (New York), February 1987.

3. Nicholls, *Caribbean Context,* pp. 175-182.

4. The U.S. attitude of the time was expressed by Assistant Secretary of State Alvey A. Adee in 1888 when he called Haiti "a public nuisance at our doors."

5. Robert Debs Heinl and Nancy Gordon Heinl, *Written in Blood* (Boston: Houghton Mifflin, 1978), pp. 456-459.

6. David Nicholls, *From Dessalines to Duvalier* (Cambridge: Cambridge University Press, 1979), p. 190.

7. Bernard Diederich and Al Burr, *Papa Doc* (London: Penguin, 1972), p. 97. Carlo A. Desinor, *Daniel* (Port-au-Prince, 1986), pp. 183-186.

8. *Wall Street Journal,* April 18, 1986.

9. *New York Times,* May 15, 1986; *Washington Post,* May 17, 1986; *Los Angeles Times,* March 7, 1986.

10. Greg Chamberlain, "Haitian Media Contribute to Duvalier's Fall," *Media Development* (London), No. 4 (1986).

11. Sabine Vogel, "Que Dieu Sauve Haiti!" *Geo* (Paris), December 1986.

12. *Libération* (Paris), February 14, 1986.

13. Author's interview with social democrat leader Serge Gilles, May 4, 1986.

14. *Le Monde* (Paris), April 9, 1986.

15. Author's interview, July 26, 1986.

16. *New York Times,* April 7, 1986.

17. Author's interview, February 14, 1987.

18. A few peasant uprisings over land seizures had occurred during the Duvalier years, notably in the Artibonite village of Bocozelle in March 1975, when six people were killed in a clash with the Haitian army's anti-subversion troops, the Leopards.

19. Dupuy is believed to have access to a large U.S. banking fortune through family ties.

20. *New York Times,* March 30, 1987.

21. *Haïti Progrès* (Brooklyn), January 21, 1987.

22. Author's interview, February 14, 1987.

23. Author's interview, February 14, 1987

24. Author's interview, February 19, 1987.

25. *New York Times,* November 16, 1986. Allan Ebert, "Haiti and the AIFLD," *The National Reporter* (Washington, DC), Summer 1986.

26. Author's interview, February 12, 1987.

27. Bishop François Gayot of Cap-Haïtien complained to the Bishop of Quimper, France, that one of his priests was involved in a French project—"Books for Haiti"—which shipped to Haiti several hundred thousand donated second-hand books on all subjects for general distribution. The project, headed by PUCH's deputy leader, Max Bourjolly, was communist-controlled, he charged. (Author's interview with Bourjolly, February 12, 1987.)

28. Author's interview, February 23, 1987. 29. *Liberation* August 14, 1987.

30. Author's interview, February 10, 1987.

31. Konakom press conference, Port-au-Prince, July 10, 1987.

32. Agence France Presse, August 4, 1987.

33. Author's interview, May 2, 1986.

34. Author's interview, February 19, 1987.

35. Author's interview, March 31, 1986.

36. Author's interview, February 10, 1987.

37. Author's interview, February 14, 1987.

Notes to Chapter 4

1. There are also different currents within the "democratic sector," roughly corresponding to those "democrats" more aligned with the traditional merchant bourgeoisie—such as Father Antoine Adrien, Louis Roy, Emmanuel Ambroise and Gladys Lauture—and those more aligned with U.S.-backed capital—such as Jean-Claude Roy, Serge Gilles, Jean-Jacques Honorat and Moise Senatus.

Notes to Chapter 8

1. I cite mainly the *Washington Post* and the *New York Times*, the two flagships for the opinion and analysis of U.S. officialdom and finance. However, the campaign against Aristide's human rights record appeared in the columns of all the major urban dailies, including the *Boston Globe, Miami Herald, Philadelphia Inquirer, Los Angeles Times* and *Chicago Tribune*.

2. Figures given by Jean-Jacques Honorat during an interview in October 1993. "Democracy Derailed," The 5th estate, CBC, October 26, 1993.

3. Washington Office on Haiti statement before the House Western Hemisphere Affairs Subcommittee on July 21, 1993.

4. Jean-Jacques Gilles, *Haiti en Marche* (Miami), January 1, 1992.

5. *New York Post*, October 7, 1991.

6. *The Guardian* (Manchester), January 22, 1992.

7. *Haïti Progrès*, February 26 - March 3, 1992.

8. In April 1993, the National Popular Assembly (APN), one of the leading popular organizations, proposed a "government of democratic unity," which would comprise all sectors that were anti-Macoute and were opposed to the coup, even though they may not have been party to the original Lavalas alliance. "If the traditional bourgeois sector and the petty-bourgeoisie in the Lavalas do not think that they are flirting with the putschists, then they shouldn't make demagoguery," the APN said. "They should say loudly to the people, like us, that in the government of concord, Macoutes are not included" because "the Macoutes have never been and will never be interested in democracy." The APN called Macoutism a "sickness without a cure."

9. Interview with Crowing Rooster Productions, July 23, 1992.

10. *Haïti Progrès*, December 2-8, 1992.

11. Interview conducted by the author during a trip to the Central Plateau in June 1993.

12. *Haïti Progrès*, July 7-13, 1993.

13. "The Challenges Ahead," Haiti Reborn/Quixote Center, July 9, 1993.

14. "The Challenges Ahead."

15. The Caputo quotation is from the Inter-Press Service (IPS) July 7, 1993; the Clinton quotation is from IPS, July 22, 1993.

16. Associated Press, July 3, 1993.

17. *Miami Herald*, July 3, 1993.

18. *New York Newsday*, July 4, 1993.

19. *Haïti Progrès*, July 7-13, 1993.

20. *The Globe and Mail* (Toronto), July 5, 1993.

21. *Haïti Progrès*, July 14-20, 1993.

22. *New York Daily News*, October 12, 1993.

23. Signal FM, November 9, 1993.

24. *New York Times*, November 5, 1993.

25. *New York Times*, October 31, 1993.

Notes to Chapter 11

1. *Los Angeles Times* October 27, 1993.

2. *Sacramento Bee,* October 13, 1993.

Notes to Chapter 13

1. James Ridgeway, "Family Business: Haiti's Behind-the-Scene Warriors Come out in the Open," *Village Voice*, October 26, 1992.

2. National Public Radio, November 1, 1993.

3. Michel-Rolph Trouillot, "The Odd and the Ordinary: Haïti, the Caribbean and the World," *Cimarrón, New Perspectives on the Caribbean,* Vol. 2, No. 3 (1990), pp. 3-12.

4. The most frequent warning to the U.S. Congress by Haiti specialists or policymakers—especially supporters of the authoritarian status quo—is that just policies may not be "realistic." Unfortunately, U.S. lawmakers have too often failed to ask why and how less equitable solutions would prove more effective. See U.S. House of Representatives, Committee on Foreign Affairs, *Human Rights in Haiti: Hearing before the Subcommittee on Human Rights* (1985); U.S. House

of Representatives, Committee on Foreign Affairs, *The Political Crisis in Haiti: Hearings before the Subcommittee on Western Hemispheric Affairs* (1988); U.S. House of Representatives, Committee on Foreign Affairs, *The Situation in Haiti and U.S. Policy: Hearing before the Subcommittees on Human Rights and International Organizations* (1992).

5. Michel-Rolph Trouillot, *Haiti: State Against Nation: The Origins and Legacies of Duvalierism* (New York: Monthly Review Press, 1990).

6. Michael S. Hooper, *Duvalierism since Duvalier* (New York: National Coalition for Haitian Refugees and Americas Watch, 1986), p. 10.

7. U.S. physician Jonathan Brown, who visited Haiti in the 1830s, wrote: "The country is saved from utter want and political dissolution solely through the spontaneous productiveness of its soil." Jonathan Brown, *The History and Present Condition of St. Domingo, II* (London: Frank Cass, 1971; orig. 1837.)

8. Historians regard the legislative elections of 1870 in Port-au-Prince as one of the few legitimate electoral victories of nineteenth-century Haiti. Yet, in 1870, less than a thousand Port-au-Prince residents had the right to vote.

9. See World Bank, *World Tables* (Baltimore: Johns Hopkins and World Bank, 1992) and *L'Etat du monde* (Paris: Editions La Découverte, 1993).

10. See Trouillot, *Haiti: State Against Nation*, "L'Etat prédateur," *Nicaragua Aujourd'hui,* Vol. 76-77 (1991), pp. 25-27; and "Etat et duvaliérisme," in Gérard Barthélemy and Christian A. Girault, eds., *La République haïtienne: état des lieux et perspectives* (Paris: Karthala, ADEC, 1993).

11. Haiti remains, of course, a "weak state" in academic parlance.

12. Trouillot, *Haiti: State Against Nation,* p. 103.

13. Hans Schmidt, *The U.S. Occupation of Haiti* (New Brunswick, NJ: Rutgers University Press, 1971), p. 235.

14. See Michel-Rolph Trouillot, "La lumpenisation d'une crise," *Les cahiers du vendredi* and "Etat et duvaliérisme."

15. Robert E. Maguire, "Haiti's Emerging Peasant Movement," *Cimarrón: New Perspectives on the Caribbean*, Vol. 2, No. 3 (1990), p. 28.

Notes to Chapter 14

1. UNICEF report cited in the *Miami Herald*, April 25, 1987.

2. World Bank, *Haiti, Policy Proposals for Growth*, Rpt. No. 5601-HA, June 1989, p. 11.

3. World Bank, *Proposals for Growth*, p. 4.

4. World Bank, Latin America and Caribbean Regional Office, *Memorandum on the Haitian Economy,* May 13, 1981, p. 6.

5. World Bank, *Proposals for Growth,* p. 11.

6. U.S. Agency for International Development (AID), *Haiti Action Plan,* 1985, p. 3. World Bank, *Proposals for Growth,* p. 5.

7. World Bank, *Proposals for Growth,* p. 8.

8. International Monetary Fund, *Haiti: Recent Economic Developments,* p. 49. *Le Monde Diplomatique* (Paris), August 1987.

9. Author's interview, Commission of Inquiry on Public Finance, Port-au-Prince, May 14, 1986.

10. Affidavit of Justice Minister François St. Fleur on Investigations of Public Finance, January 16, 1987.

11. Michael S. Hooper, "Haiti," in *Latin America and the Caribbean: A Contemporary Perspective* (New York: Holmes and Meier, 1985), p. 822.

12. World Bank, *Haiti: Strategy Paper,* November 1985, p. 3.

13. AID, *Country Development Strategy Assessment,* 1984.

14. AID, *Country Development Strategy Statement,* 1982, p. 89.

15. AID, *Strategy Statement,* p. 172.

16. AID, *Haiti Action Plan, 1987-88,* p. 46.

17. AID, *Haiti Action Plan,* p. 47.

18. AID, *Haiti Action Plan,* Annex 1, p. 3.

19. World Bank, *Proposals for Growth,* p. 12.

20. Author's interview with agronomist Jean-Jacques Honorat, March 1987.

21. Michael S. Hooper, *Duvalierism Since Duvalier* (New York: National Coalition for Haitian Refugees and Americas Watch, 1986).

22. World Bank, *Proposals for Growth,* p. 5.

23. World Bank, *Proposals for Growth,* p. 5.

24. Josh DeWind and David Kinley, *Aiding Migration: The Impact of International Development Assistance on Haiti* (New York: Immigration Research Program, Center for Social Sciences, Columbia University, 1986), p. 79.

25. World Bank, *Policy Proposals,* p. 74.

26. See John Cavanagh and Joy Hackel, "Multinational Subcontracting in the Caribbean Basin," *NACLA Report on the Americas,* Vol. 18, No. 3 (May/June 1984).

27. Author's interview, February 1987.

28. World Bank, *Proposals for Growth,* pp. ii and 5.

29. World Bank, *Proposals for Growth*, p. 12.

30. Author's interview with government minister, February 1987.

31. Author's interview, February 16, 1987.

32. Author's interview, February 1987.

33. *Washington Post,* February 4, 1987.

34. Author's interview with government minister, February, 1987.

35. World Bank, *Public Expenditures Review,* p. 11.

Notes to Chapter 15

1. "Haiti," *Foreign Economic Trends and their Implications for the United States,* American Embassy Port-au-Prince, U.S. Department of Commerce, International Trade Administration, April 6, 1992.

2. AID, "Haiti," *Project Paper/Export and Investment Promotion* (Project Number: 521-0186), August 8, 1986.

3. AID, "Haiti," *Project Paper/ Export and Investment Promotion.*

4. AID, *Country Development Strategy Statement: FY 1986: Haiti*, January 1984.

5. AID, "Haiti," *Project Paper/Promotion of Business and Export Project* (Amendment Number l/Project Number: 521-0186), June 29, 1991.

6. AID, *Country Development Strategy Statement.*

7. "Haiti," *Foreign Economic Trends and their Implications,* U.S. Department of Commerce.

8. *The Electrotechnical Industry in Haiti,* The Ministry of Economy, Finance, and Industry; Investment Promotion Division [Haiti], 1981 (estimated).

9. M. Catherine Maternowska, Ph.D. candidate in anthropology, Columbia University, New York. See also AID, *Concept Paper Economic Recovery Assistance II,* November 1986.

10. *Worker Rights in Export Processing Zones,* Bureau of International Labor Affairs, U.S. Department of Labor, August 1990.

11. *Worker Rights*, U.S. Department of Labor.

12. AID, *Promotion of Business and Export Project,* (Amendment Number l/Project Number: 521-0186), U.S.AID, June 29, 1991.

13. AID, "Haiti Macroeconomic Assessment," *Staff Working Papers,* February 1991.

14. AID, *Promotion of Business and Export Project.*

15. AID, "Haiti Macroeconomic Assessment."

16. AID, *Promotion of Business and Export Project,* U.S.AID.

17. AID, *Promotion of Business and Export Project,* U.S.AID.

18. "Haiti," *Foreign Economic Trends and their Implications for the United States,* U.S. Department of Commerce.

Notes to Chapter 17

1. *The Guardian* (Manchester), January 25, 1986.

2. François Duvalier reduced the term *Noirisme,* first coined by Aimé Césaire, to a combined critique of white (and mulatto) colonial domination with assertions about the originality and creativity (read superiority) of "African" ways of life.

3. *Miami Herald,* December 23, 1985.

4. Tap-taps, colorfully decorated trucks converted to haul passengers, are Haiti's most common means of transportation.

5. Author's interview with Robert Duval, president of the League of Former Political Prisoners, Port-au-Prince, May 1986.

6. Quoted in Michael S. Hooper, *Duvalierism Since Duvalier* (New York: National Coalition for Haitian Refugees and Americas Watch, October 1986) p. 19.

7. Author's interview with Colonel Williams Regala, Port-au-Prince, May 19, 1986.

8. Estimates on the number of Tontons Macoutes vary from 9,000 to 40,000.

9. Author's interview with members of the Haitian Bar Association, Port-au-Prince, July-August, 1987.

10. Author's interviews with the Center for Defense of Public Liberties, Mobile Institute for Democratic Education and League of Former Political Prisoners (human rights organizations), Port-au-Prince, July 24-August 1, 1987.

11. Press Advisory of the High Command of the Armed Forces of Haiti, Port-au-Prince, July 30, 1987.

12. Associated Press, July 25, 1987.

13. Author's interview with editor of leading Haitian daily newspaper, Port-au-Prince, February 1987.

14. Hooper, *Duvalierism,* p. 49.

15. U.S. House of Representatives, Section 203 of Foreign Assistance Act, "Promoting Democracy in Haiti," September 25, 1986.

16. "The Paths to Democracy," Remarks of the Honorable Elliott Abrams, Assistant Secretary of State for Interamerican Affairs to Washington World Affairs Council, National Press Club, Washington, D.C., June 30, 1987.

17. Author's interview with human rights groups, Port-au-Prince, July 25, 1987.

Notes to Chapter 19

1. Phone interview with authors, November 4, 1993. Because "Fritz" is underground, his real name cannot be used in this article.

2. Phone interview, November 4, 1993.

3. Phone interview, November 4, 1993.

4. *Haïti Progrès*, Vol. 5, No. 34, November 25-December 1, 1987.

5. Phone interview, November 4, 1993.

6. Interview, September 14, 1993, Port-au-Prince.

7. *Haïti Progrès*, Vol. 7, No. 49, March 7-15, 1990.

8. *Haïti Progrès*, Vol. 8, No. 30, October 24-30, 1990.

9. Radio Métropole, October 18, 1990.

10. *Haïti Progrès*, Vol. 8, No. 30, October 24-30, 1990.

11. Many FNCD parliamentarians aligned with other blocs to create gridlock by blocking key initiatives of the executive branch. They also joined the call to take a vote of no confidence against Aristide's Prime Minister René Préval in the summer of 1991, just before the coup. After the coup, FNCD parliamentarians Eddy Dupiton and Bernard Sansaricq became prominent negotiators for the coup regime.

12. Phone interview with authors, October 28, 1993.

13. As of 1503, escaped slaves, who became known as maroons, formed independent colonies of resistance on the island of Hispaniola. Bands of maroons would establish themselves in the mountains and periodically practice guerrilla warfare against white slaveholders. By the middle of the sixteenth century, runaways outnumbered Hispaniola's white male population seven to one.

14. Boukman, a maroon of Jamaican origin, led the 1791 slave revolt that culminated in Haiti's independence in 1804.

15. Interview with authors, November 15, 1993, Washington, DC.

16. "Populism, Conservatism and Civil Society in Haiti," *NED Backgrounder* (Albuquerque, NM: Inter-Hemispheric Education Resource Center, April 1992).

17. "Haiti After the Coup: Sweatshop or Real Development," The National Labor Committee Education Fund in Support of Worker and Human Rights in Central America, New York (1993), p. 17.

18. Interview with Marx Aristide, September 1993, Port-au-Prince.

19. "Key Haiti Leaders Said To Have Been In The CIA's Pay," *New York Times*, November 1, 1993. See also, "CIA Formed Haitian Unit Later Tied to Narcotics Trade," *New York Times*, November 14, 1993.

20. Interview conducted by the Haitian Information Bureau on September 8, 1993, Port-au-Prince.

Notes to Chapter 21

1. Space constraints make it impossible to offer a thorough chronology and description of Haiti activism in the United States. Nor is it possible to represent fairly all the groups and individuals that have been key to the Haiti movement. I have tried to offer a representative sampling and to paint a picture in broad brushstrokes of the work that has been done over the last decade, with particular focus on the last three to four years. My thanks to the many Haiti activists who generously told me the stories of their work and shared their organizing materials with me: Bazelais Jean-Baptiste, Beverly Bell, Patricia Berne, Gina Dorcely, Steven Forester, John Hill, Jill Ives, Marie Kennedy, Charles Kernaghan, Mel King, Pierre Labossier, Clarence Lusane, Kathy McAfee, Kiilu Nyasha, Laurie Richardson and Chris Tilly. Thanks also to the following people whose written work helped me tremendously: Michael Albert, Noam Chomsky and Paul Farmer.

2. *Haïti Progrès* offers left-wing analysis and strong criticism of Aristide; the moderately progressive *Haïti en Marche* is supportive of Aristide and less critical of U.S. intervention; and the right-wing *Haïti Observateur* is allied with the economic and military elite and is anti-Aristide.

3. Jean Jean-Pierre, "The Tenth Department," in Chapter 20 of this book.

4. Jean Jean-Pierre, "The Tenth Department," *Third Force,* Vol. 2, No. 3 (July/August 1994), pp. 26-27.

5. See Noam Chomsky's introduction to Paul Farmer, *The Uses of Haiti* (Monroe, ME: Common Courage Press, 1994).

6. For a historical example of the racist images of Haiti in the U.S. media, see "Two Wild and Busted Nephews," *Literary Digest*, May 1, 1920. For a discussion of the historical evolution of these images, see "The Progressive Interview with Patrick Bellegarde-Smith," *The Progressive*, Vol. 58, No. 11 (November 1994).

7. Although solidarity activists should seek guidance from and set up alliances with revolutionary movements abroad, they should avoid identifying completely with revolutionary parties and individuals. In the case of Nicaragua, for example, many activists staked everything on the Sandinistas and tended to romanticize the Nicaraguan revolution. These activists were slow to grapple with the Sandinistas' mistakes during the 1980s and they were unsure how to continue once the Sandinistas no longer held office. Activists were not wrong to have supported the Sandinistas. It was a grave error, however, to see the party's rise and fall as the beginning and end of support for the Nicaraguan movement toward democracy.

8. According to an interview with Laurie Richardson, November 1994. The Quixote Center was responsible for a great deal of grassroots, direct action organizing as well.

9. The September/October 1994 issue of *Mother Jones,* for example, has a cover story asking what "we" need to do to bring Clinton back for another round. The digitally manipulated photo depicts Clinton with boxing gloves on, his face bruised and swollen. The dubious implication is that he has been out there fighting the good fight against some *other* guy who does not have our interests in mind. The image suggests that Clinton is an embattled individual who would benefit by having "us" in his corner.

10. On June 8, 1993, federal judge Sterling Johnson ordered the HIV camp closed. Clinton did not appeal. Anthony "Van" Jones, "Operation Harriet Tubman," *Third Force*, Vol. 2, No. 3 (July/August 1994), pp. 24-25.

11. The Governors Island Accord is one example of an agreement that Aristide signed with which he was not in full agreement. For a detailed analysis of this process, see Kim Ives, "The Unmaking of a President," Chapter 8 of this book.

12. Steve Shalom, *Z Magazine,* June 1994.

13. Kathy McAfee, *Storm Signals, Structural Adjustment and Development Alternatives in the Caribbean* (Boston: South End Press, 1991).

14. See "Haiti After the Coup: Sweatshop or Real Development," The National Labor Committee Education Fund in Support of Worker and Human Rights in Central America, New York (1993).

15. Interestingly, *The Nation* was one of the few publications in the early part of the century to offer a progressive analysis of the U.S. invasion of Haiti. In 1921, a Haitian delegation to the United States published in *The Nation* what was probably the most substantive article available at the time on the murder, torture, false arrests, forced labor and economic deprivation under the U.S. military occupation. See "Delegation to the U.S.: Memoir on Political, Economic, and Financial...," *The Nation*, May 25, 1921, pp. 751-759. The *Nation*'s contribution to progressive analysis over the long term should remind us of the need to build lasting media organizations.

16. One exception is *Crossroads,* which put together a special issue on El Salvador solidarity work, with particular focus on the Committee in Solidarity with the People of El Salvador (CISPES). See "El Salvador ¡Presente!" *Crossroads,* No. 40 (April 1994).

17. Activists should reflect on the intensive Central America solidarity and anti-intervention work that was done during the 1980s. What lessons should be drawn from that experience? How can activists apply this knowledge to current projects? Central America activists have a wealth of experience and expertise that is useful for future solidarity work. The alternative media could play a key role in disseminating this kind of analysis and in inviting debate about organizing strategies.

Notes to Chapter 22

1. "Patrick Bellegarde-Smith" (interview), *The Progressive*, Vol. 58, No. 11 (November 1994), p. 33.

2. From material gathered by Laurie Richardson, to whom I am grateful. Other, unattributed quotations are from interviews conducted by the author in Haiti.

3. William LeoGrande, "Washington et l'écueil haïtien," *Le Monde Diplomatique*, October, 1994, p. 1.

4. "Imposing 'Democracy' in Haiti," *The Progressive*, Vol. 58, No. 11 (November 1994), p. 8.

5. "Patrick Bellegarde-Smith" (interview), *The Progressive*, p. 32.

6. Noam Chomsky, "Democracy Enhancement, II: Haiti," *Z Magazine,* Vol. 7, No. 7/8 (July/August 1994).

7. "Democracy in Haiti—will the rich buy it?" *The Financial Times* (London), October 16, 1994, p. 1.

8. "How U.S. Botched Embargo," *Miami Herald,* October 23, 1994.

9. Allan Nairn, "Behind Haiti's Paramilitaries," *The Nation*, October 24, 1994, p. 458. Also in Nairn's important report: "When I asked Constant...about the anti-Aristide coup, he said that as it was happening Colonel Collins and Donald Terry (the CIA station chief who also ran the SIN) 'were inside the [Army General] Headquarters.' But he insisted that this was 'normal': The CIA and D[efense]I[ntelligence]A[gency] were always there."

10. See, for example, Allan Nairn, "The Eagle is Landing," *The Nation*, October 3, 1994, p. 346.

11. Jean-Claude Bajeux, "An Embarrassing Presence," *The New York Review of Books*, November 3, 1994, p. 37.

12. René Dépestre, "Une parole de vérité," *Le Monde*, September 23, 1994, p. 2.

13. "Les époustouflants paradoxes de Chavannes Jean-Baptiste," *Haïti Progrès*, October 26-November 1, 1994, Vol. 12, No. 31, p. 4.

14. "Les époustouflants paradoxes de Chavannes Jean-Baptiste," *Haïti Progrès*.

15. See "Imposing 'Democracy' in Haiti," *The Progressive*, p. 8.

16. Careful review of the past policies of these agencies is only now beginning, and gives little cause for hope. Even internal reviews, such as those by the U.S. Government Accounting Office, have been scathing, while independent assessments marvel at the cynicism of many AID projects. The Washington Office on Haiti (110 Maryland Avenue NE, Washington, DC, 20002) offers important and critical documentation regarding U.S.AID projects in Haiti. See also Jane Regan, "AIDing U.S. Interests in Haiti," *CovertAction Quarterly,* No. 51 (Fall-Winter 1994-1995), pp. 7-13, 56-58.

17. The U.S. agency assigned to rebuild the Haitian police force is called ICITAP, which is an offshoot of the FBI. ICITAP is due, according to its chief Haitian planner, to stay for three years, bringing in several hundred U.S. trainers to mold a 5,000-man Haitian force" (Nairn, "The Eagle is Landing, p. 344). ICITAP was created in 1986 to help train police forces in El Salvador and Guatemala. The Haitian security forces will, then, be trained by the very U.S. agency that helped to train two of Latin America's most notorious police forces.

18. Colonel Patrick Collins, who may have helped to create FRAPH, has been recalled to Haiti by the Clinton Administration; and Allan Nairn recently reported that "Today, the CIA is beefing up its Haiti station, bringing in more operatives and recruiting new Haitian assets" ("The Eagle is Landing," p. 346).

19. See Michael Mandelbaum, "Can Aristide Be Haiti's Mandela?" *New York Times*, October 14, 1994, p. A35.

INDEX

M

Macoutes. *See* Tontons Macoutes
Magloire, Paul   128
Maitre, Elous   166
Malary, Guy, assassination of   85
malnutrition in Haiti   134
Malval, Robert   83-85, 108, 121
Manigat, Leslie   28, 35-36
march, New York anti-coup   67,
   199-200, 207
massacres   31-32, 36, 166-67, 168-
   69, 185, 196
mawonaj   188
Mayas, Jocelyne   203
Mazouka, Joseph (CDS)   156
McAfee, Kathy   205-6
McCalla, Jocelyn (National Coalition for Haitian Refugees)   199
McCandless, Robert   121
media coverage of Haiti   103-7,
   117, 214, 220-23, 226, 235n.1
   (Chapter 8). *See also* specific
   newspapers
Merceron, Franz   136
Mésidor, Jacques (Salesian Order)   27
Mesyeux, Jean-Auguste, anti-
   Aristide campaign by   180
Mevs family,   221-23
migration from Haiti. *See* diaspora
military aid, resumption of   173
military intervention   6-7, 68-69,
   73, 86, 99, 110-115, 219
   issue of   84-85, 223-26, 211
Military School   128
minimum wage   44, 53, 134-35,
   139, 190
Minoterie d'Haiti, embezzlement
   from   136
Misyon Alfa. *See* literacy campaign, Catholic
Mobilization for Survival   212-13
MPP   23, 79, 185, 187, 193, 205, 207
MPP Education and Develop-
   ment Fund (MPP-EDF)   212

mulattos   14, 197-98

N

Nairn, Allen (*Nation*)   117, 156,
   222
Namphy, Henri   23, 36, 164-65,
   167, 172
   elections   26, 29, 31-34
   labor unions   24
National Coalition for Haitian
   Refugees   104-5, 176
National Congress of Haitian
   Democratic Movements. *See*
   Konakom
National Endowment for Democ-
   racy. *See* NED
National Federation of Haitian
   Students (FENEH)   193
National Front Against Repres-
   sion   186
National Front for Concerted Ac-
   tion, election boycott by   30,
   32-33
National Government Council.
   See CNG
National Intelligence Service. *See*
   SIN
National Labor Committee, re-
   port of   190, 213
National Peasant Movement of
   the Papaye Congress   193
National Popular Assembly. *See*
   APN
National Security Volunteers
   (VSN). *See* Tontons Macoutes
National Union of Haitian Stu-
   dents (UNEH)   193
necklacing   53, 59-60, 176-77,
   180, 183-84
NED
   funding   24, 43, 67, 190, 194
   control of Haitian aid dollars   117
neighborhood committees   134, 194
Nerette, Joseph   75

publications, subsidies for cooperative 170
PUCH, opposition to 25, 168

Q

Quayle, Dan 74
Quixote Center 210-12

R

rache manyòk 33, 171, 185
racism, anti-Haitian 7, 109, 209
radio, importance of 16, 32, 57,
201, 206
Radio Haiti Inter 16-17, 20, 134
Radyo Solèy 17-20, 38, 154, 192, 201
Radio Tropicale 201
Rangel, Charles 78
Reagan 18, 172
reformist sector 182, 184-89, 191.
See also democratic sector;
Lavalas bourgeoisie
refugees 108-9, 208-10
offshore hearings 6-7, 110
US blocking exodus 5, 220-21
Regala, Williams 164, 167-68, 172
Regie du Tabac, embezzlement
and 136
remittances 135, 202
René, Claude 22
Richard, Yves (CATH) 18, 22-25
Robinson, Randall 7, 109
Romain, Franck, St. Jean Bosco
massacre and 36
Romulus, Willy 27, 72, 171
Roy, Louis 38
rural councils (CASEC) 23

S

Saint-Domingue, slavery in 122-23

Salnave, Sylvain 13
Sam, Guillaume Vilbrun 13-14
Sambour, Jean 136
San Francisco Lawyers' Commit-
tee for Civil Rights 210
Sansaricq, Bernard 199, 241n.11
School of the Americas 116
Seaga, Edward, Haitian visit by 33
section chiefs 20, 125, 128, 179,
183-84
Sheehan, John 84
Simon, Hérard (Zantray) 23
SIN, CIA funding for 191, 222
slave revolt 123
slave trade 9
Smarth, William 226
St. Jean Bosco Church 36
state industries 8, 116, 118, 142
strike, December general 32
structural adjustment 117, 227-30
student movement 193
Swing, William 154

T

tax boycott, peasant 20
tax policy 124, 130, 137, 141, 142-43
technocrat sector 42-43, 83, 112
TELECO, embezzlement from 136
Tenth Department 195, 200-202.
See also diaspora; immigrants.
Tenth Department organization
202-4
Tet Ansam massacre 168-69, 185
Tèt Kole 193, 215
Texaco, oil embargo and 221
Théodore, René 71-72, 125
Ti Legliz 17, 30, 172, 192, 207
Tontons Macoutes 15-16, 42, 59,
98, 129, 161-62, 165
Aristide 44
backlash against 19-20, 53, 177
CNG 173, 183
human rights abuses 167-69, 196
trade unions. *See* labor unions
Tropical Storm Gordon 227

The North American Congress on Latin America (NACLA)

NACLA, an independent non-profit organization founded in 1966, provides policy makers, analysts, academics, organizers, journalists and religious and community groups with information on major trends in Latin America and its relations with the United States.

For nearly 30 years, NACLA has offered resources essential to creating public awareness of U.S. policies and practices in Latin America and the Caribbean. The core of NACLA's work is its bi-monthly publication, *NACLA Report on the Americas,* which combines rigourous research and comprehensive analysis with an accessible style. With a circulation of 10,000, it is the most widely read English language publication on Latin America.

Each Report provides in-depth coverage on a single theme or topic of central concern (Haiti, Mexico, Drugs, Immigration, Women) and also offers an update section consisting of short articles on current developments. A recent redesign of the *Report* has introduced new elements such as a newsbriefs section providing updates on current events in the region from the alternative electronic press and NACLA correspondents.

NACLA Report on the Americas is essential for educators looking for informed coverage of politics and culture throughout Latin America and the Caribbean. The *Report* is an excellent resource for political science, anthropology, sociology, economic development, and history classes with a regional focus on Latin America.

Subscription Rates*

	1 Year	2 Years	3 Years
Individuals	$27	$47	$65
Institutions	$50	$85	$120

Please address correspondence to NACLA, 475 Riverside Dr., Suite 454, New York, NY 10115. Phone: 212/870-3146. (Checks are payable to "NACLA.")

*Mention this book with your subscription order, and get an extra issue free!

About South End Press

South End Press is a non-profit, collectively run book publisher with over 180 titles in print. Since our founding in 1977, we have tried to meet the needs of readers who are exploring, or are already committed to, the politics of radical social change.

Our goal is to publish books that encourage ciritical thinking and constructive action on the key political, cultural, social, economic and ecological issues shaping life in the United States and in the world. In this way, we hope to give expression to a wide diversity of democratic social movements and to provide an alternative to the products of corporate publishing.

Through the Institute for Social and Cultural Change, South End Press works with other political media projects—Z Magazine; Speak Out!, a speakers bureau; and the Publishers Support Project—to expand access to information and critical analysis. If you would like a free catalog of South End Press books or information about our membership program, which offers two free books and a 40 percent discount on all titles, please write to us at: South End Press, 116 Saint Botolph Street, Boston, MA 02115.

Other South End Press Titles of Interest

Global Village or Global Pillage: Economic Reconstruction from the Bottom Up
  by Jeremy Brecher and Tim Costello

Zapata's Revenge: Free Trade and the Farm Crisis in Mexico
  by Tom Barry with Harry Browne

Hear My Testimony: María Teresa Tula, Human Rights Activist of El Salvador
  Translated and edited by Lynn Stephen

Colonial Dilemma: Critical Perspectives on Contemporary Puerto Rico
  edited by Edwin Meléndez and Edgardo Meléndez

Year 501: The Conquest Continues
  by Noam Chomsky

Stop the Killing Train: Radical Visions for Radical Change
  by Michael Albert

Chaos or Community? Seeking Solutions, Not Scapegoats, for Bad Economics
  by Holly Sklar